IDENTITIES
AND
INTERACTIONS

IDENTITIES AND INTERACTIONS

An Examination of Human Associations in Everyday Life

REVISED EDITION

George J. McCall
and
J. L. Simmons

THE FREE PRESS
A Division of Macmillan Publishing Co., Inc.
NEW YORK

Collier Macmillan Publishers
LONDON

The Free Press
A Division of Macmillan Publishing Co., Inc.
866 Third Avenue, New York, N. Y. 10022

Collier Macmillan Canada, Ltd.

Library of Congress Catalog Card Number: 77-99093

Printed in the United States of America

printing number   **32939**

    4 5 6 7 8 9 10

JUN 1 4 1982

Library of Congress Cataloging in Publication Data

McCall, George J
  Identities and interactions.

  Includes bibliographical references and index.
    1. Social interaction.   I. Simmons, Jerry L.,
joint author.   II. Title.
HM291.M25   1978   301.1   77-99093
ISBN 0-02-920630-8
ISBN 0-02-920620-0 pbk.

CONTENTS

v

ACKNOWLEDGMENTS

This book is most heavily indebted to the thinking of the late Manford H. Kuhn, who, although he would not subscribe to all we have said here, did focus our attention on self and interaction and encouraged us most heartily to develop further our own conceptions on these topics. Some of the important specifics of our framework were developed in response to the key critical pressures of our early methodological conscience, Albert J. Reiss, Jr., though neither he nor Professor Kuhn can be held responsible for the substance of the views presented here. Our approach to theorizing owes much to Martin U. Martel, and the flavor of the book has been greatly influenced by Gordon W. Allport and George C. Homans, who taught the senior author more than they—or he—could have realized at the time.

Tamotsu Shibutani, J. E. Hulett, Jr., and Dennis W. Stampe have contributed suggestions and counsel, and endless discussion of interaction theory with Neil Friedman has provided much of the catalysis for this book.

Among our former students who have greatly sharpened our views, Michal M. McCall, Norman K. Denzin, Jack Fitzgerald, and Gerald H. Solomon stand out pre-eminently.

Finally, we wish to acknowledge the permission of the University of Chicago Press to reprint from Robert E. Park, ''Human Nature and Collective Behavior," *American Journal of Sociology*, 32 (March, 1927), 733–741; of The Free Press to reprint from *The Sociology of Georg Simmel*, copyright 1950; and of Little Blue Books to reprint Hugo von Hofmannsthal, "The Two," from *Modern German Poetry*.

George J. McCall
J. L. Simmons

IDENTITIES AND INTERACTIONS REVISITED:
Preface to the Revised Edition

This revision went to press just over a decade after publication of the original edition of *Identities and Interactions*. The years have been kind to the book. Favorable reviews have appeared, segments have been reprinted in various works, and a German-language edition has been published. The role-identity model of self in social interaction developed in that book has received modest application by scholars in several fields.

The current *Zeitgeist* of social psychology is far more favorable to the concerns and concepts of the book than was that of 1966. The striking loss of faith in the traditional positivistic, laboratory experimental, individualistic paradigm has been widely reviewed.[1] Discovery of causal laws and formal testing of theories through controlled experimentation no longer reign as the sole true aims of social psychology. Disenchantment with laboratory studies is widespread; research in natural settings is now the preferred mode.[2] Social interaction has emerged as the central focus of theorizing and research.

These massive sea changes in the concerns of social psychology are, we feel, most congenial to the concerns and style of our book. Conceptual trends over the past decade have been similarly congenial. Cognitive theories emphasizing active information-processing and symbolic representational systems have become widely accepted. Meanings, perceptions, and interpretations weigh more importantly in contemporary writings. Man is more often viewed as an active, goal-striving creature; reflection, deliberation, and choice frequently appear as important processes. The powerful influence of the individual's real-life social matrix is more often conceded, and the likelihood that situational factors typically outweigh individual factors is now widely contemplated in social psychology.[3]

The concept of *self* has enjoyed something of a renaissance over this period. Even various traditional individualistic paradigms, such as cognitive dissonance theory, have found it necessary to invoke some notion of self-concept in order to interpret discrepant results.[4] Most encouraging to us has been the sharp increase in attempts to understand and demonstrate the relevance of the self to social interaction.[5]

One of the most striking trends of the decade has been the adoption of concepts of *identity*. Not all of these concepts are closely related to our own, of course; some concern collective identity, and others concern monolithic individual identities.[6] Many scholars, however, have recognized the individual's possession of multiple identities, each somehow related to different social roles or positions. Occupational identities, gender identities, racial and ethnic identities, and age identities have been subjects of extensive research.[7] Perhaps the best of these studies have dealt with deviant identities, such as the identities of homosexual, prostitute, and delinquent.[8] Studies of deviant identities have examined closely the social psychological processes through which identities are developed, maintained, managed, and changed through social interactions.[9]

Overall, then, the tenor of contemporary social psychology is quite compatible with the concerns and concepts of this book. To review the matter more specifically, it may be most expeditious to reconsider the details of our approach chapter by chapter.

THE PROBLEM AND THE APPROACH

Analyses of social interactions are now much more abundant, but it remains the case that few if any of these analyses have sought to be as comprehensive as this attempt.[10]

Useful analytic frameworks not closely derived from symbolic interactionism have emerged for the study of face-to-face interactions. Prominent among these are ethological, psycho- and sociolinguistic, communications-theory, and systems-theory approaches.[11] These frameworks—focused on the interplay of verbal, paralinguistic, gestural, postural, and proxemic messages—have been most frequently employed by anthropologists, psychologists, and psychiatrists, and have provided substantial cross-cultural data on direct interpersonal communication and synchronization of behaviors.[12] Some of this work—especially on the vital role of eye contact—does have important roots in the general interactionist tradition of Simmel.[13]

More nearly related to symbolic interactionism but conceptually distinct are the frameworks of ethnomethodology and phenomenological sociology, which similarly focus on the negotiation or social construction of reality.[14] These frameworks, however, rely on concepts of rules rather than on the concepts of plans and purposes, and are accordingly more concerned to examine *how* it is that social reality is constructed rather than *what* reality is negotiated.

Symbolic interactionist analyses, too, have proliferated in recent years,[15] as have the special derivative theories, i.e., role theory, reference group theory, self theory, and interpersonal theory.[16] The direction of development in symbolic interactionism and in the special derivative theories has clearly been toward ameliorating precisely those difficulties, flaws, or limitations we identified in the original edition of this book. The movement in self theory toward linking of self-dynamics to social interactions has already been noted above; the movement in role theory from established social roles to negotiated roles has been most impressive. Though diminished in degree, our original dissatisfactions with these theories substantially remain. Similar observations and conclusions could be made concerning exchange theory as well.[17]

On balance, however, we judge that developments within and convergences among these various approaches bode well for the emergence of a general interactionist approach.

It seems to us that the central theoretical problem posed in this book—how and why persons allocate their interactional resources in an observed manner—is now of substantial interest to a wider range of scholars and can be related to a variety of theoretical frameworks, even beyond the field of social psychology. Moreover, we have encountered no compelling reason to alter our substantive imagery of man as "a daydreaming sort of animal who gambles his small store of 'life resources' with the empirical world in an attempt to win some measure of fulfillment of his dreams and desires."

Central issue

BOUNDARIES ON INTERACTIONS

WHO come together to do WHAT, WHEN, and WHERE? seems now to be a more feasible research question than a decade ago. Advances in methodological techniques and in theoretical conceptualization bearing on study of the four ws have contributed significantly to our knowledge of this topic.

Particularly important here has been the development of a paradigm of *social network analysis*,[18] consisting of techniques for collecting and mathematically analyzing data on the number, distribution, frequency, duration, and contents of direct and indirect contacts among persons. Especially relevant are those variants which take a single individual as the focal point of such an interpersonal network. From the perspective of this book, the graph theory techniques of analysis are perhaps of less importance than the descriptive data obtained, which have already done much to illuminate the question of WHO come together.

The study of WHAT people do together and alone has similarly been advanced through continued developments in "psychological ecology," a field-based paradigm for description, segmentation, and analysis of the "stream of behavior" in natural settings.[19] The segmentation question—i.e., how many acts, their character, relations among acts in sequences and in hierarchical organization of behaviors—has been particularly vexing but is beginning to yield.[20]

WHEN (the uses of time) has also become more susceptible to study. Technical improvements in the paradigm of time-budget studies and massive cross-cultural applications of this paradigm have substantially advanced our knowledge of how persons allocate their limited time resources.[21]

Study of the WHERE of social behavior has similarly advanced over the decade. Of particular importance has been the notable surge in micro-ecology and in environmental psychology, studying respectively the interpersonal allocation of space and the effects of places and spaces on social and psychological variables.[22] Not to be overlooked are the techniques and findings of central-place and location analysis in geography,[23] bearing on the larger-scale movements of persons in search of goods and services.

Isolated study of any one of the four WS is, of course, of limited value; conjoint analysis and multiple specifications are required to address the focal research question. Many of the paradigms reviewed in this section have indeed dealt with relations among two or more of these variables. Time-budget studies, for example, examine the allocation of a person's time among other persons, activities, and/or settings. Network analysis typically examines at least the WHO and the WHAT, and may be concerned with distribution of contacts in time and space as well.

Cultural, social, and personal boundaries on interaction opportunities have also received a good deal of recent attention in contexts other than network analysis. Perhaps the best of this work has dealt with the operation of social boundaries in public places and within cities.[24]

THE PHILOSOPHY OF CONDUCT

The fundamental concepts and principles of symbolic interaction remain, of course, unchanged.

Further explication of the idea of social reality as something that is negotiated or socially constructed has appeared, however, and may be usefully consulted.[25]

Basic philosophical investigations into the concept of self have also been resumed and warrant systematic consideration by interested scholars.[26]

Finally, the dramaturgical perspective on social life has been much more thoroughly developed over the past decade and has emerged as a quite viable and widely employed analytic framework.[27]

THE ROLE-IDENTITY MODEL

The concept of *role-identity* has attained some currency and, accordingly, some further explication.[28] Generic studies of specific types of identities (especially of deviant identities) have been noted above. Role-identities as sources of and standards for performances have received some empirical study, as has the view that *role-support* for such identities is a distinctively motivating valued commodity to be sought through interaction.[29]

The notion that the self—in its semantic rather than functional aspects—is essentially a set of such role-identities organized according to dynamic hierarchical principles has been more widely entertained.[30] The idea of a salience hierarchy of role-identities, in particular, has been further developed by both Stryker and Heiss.[31]

Social psychological mechanisms for legitimation of role-identities have been further elaborated by Secord and Backman.[32]

SOCIAL PERCEPTION AND APPRAISAL

The centrality of categorization of objects (especially persons) has been further developed not only in symbolic interactionism but also in phenomenological sociology.[33] Processes of imputation and attribution have been importantly studied over the decade, not only in psychology[34] but in sociology as well. In the latter field, imputation of deviant characteristics and identities has been emphasized, under the general rubric of labeling theory.[35]

The generic study of person perception has developed apace;[36] we have noted with special interest an increased concern within that field about the effects of interaction goals on person perception.[37]

THE DYNAMICS OF INTERACTION

The more general developments in the study of concrete interaction episodes have been mentioned above, as have advances in the study of imputation processes.

Further studies have been conducted into the details of the expressive processes of presentation of self and of altercasting.[38] Once again, some of the labeling theory work is of particular relevance to altercasting.

Occasionally, labeling theory has considered the perspectives of both parties and has thus approached the study of identity negotiation. Greater emphasis needs to be given to the interplay among labeling, self-labeling, and resistance to labeling.[39]

Strategies and tactics in the negotiation of identities and roles have been studied more explicitly.[40] The concept of role-bargaining has become more widely employed,[41] and we are hopeful that it may soon profit from the extensive general work in the social psychology of negotiation and bargaining.[42] The relevance of exchange rules in such bargaining has also been more fully explicated.[43]

The contrasts and interplay between task-focused and identity-focused interactions have been the subject of extensive consideration.[44] The phenomena of embarrassment and subsequent facework which frequently follow a sudden shift from task- to identity-focused interaction have been examined in several studies.[45]

The problem of joint or collective action in multiperson interactions has been further examined,[46] with special reference to power and coalitions.[47] Social skill and manipulativeness as factors in social interaction have also received further attention.[48]

THE CAREER OF A RELATIONSHIP

Over the decade, scholarly interest in the analysis of interpersonal relationships has increased many times over. Our own framework for analyzing the nature, initiation, development, maintenance, change, and termination of these distinctive social organizations has been substantially elaborated in subsequent works.[49]

Very similar approaches have been developed by other sociologists.[50]

Among psychologists, interest has centered heavily on the initiation and early development of relationships, under the rubric of interpersonal attraction[51] and the study of love.[52] Some psychological works, however, have taken a more comprehensive longitudinal viewpoint, emphasizing development and change in interpersonal exchange,[53] self-disclosure,[54] and the fit between selves.[55]

Problems of information control and the management of deviant identities within relationships have received considerable attention in the study of deviant behavior.[56]

THE INTERACTIVE CAREER OF THE INDIVIDUAL

The fate and significance of role-identities over the life-cycle have been rather thoroughly examined by Chad Gordon in an impressive series of works.[57]

Substantial advances have been made in our general knowledge of the life-cycle of individuals,[58] and particularly in our knowledge of primary and secondary socialization as key processes in life-cycle development.[59] Studies of the acquisition of self-and-other concepts, of role concepts, and of skill in the interaction processes are of special importance to understanding the development of role-identities.[60]

THE LOGISTICS OF IDENTITY

Scholarly developments in systems theory and operations research have displayed considerable promise for providing technical tools relevant to the study of logistics in everyday life.[61]

Since individual lives are thoroughly imbedded in a dense matrix of social organizations, social psychological studies of organizational careers and of role-bargaining are of special relevance to logistics analysis.[62]

Although in the original edition of this book we sought to be comprehensive in the range of our consideration of identities and interactions, it was never our aim to present and digest all materials relevant to such analysis. In this latest edition, similarly, we do not strive to weave into our analysis every detail of the massive accomplishments of the intervening decade. Most of the work just reviewed merely sustains—or at most extends—our original analysis, rather than altering it. In revising these chapters, then, we have changed little of the text, but have striven to note in some detail those assertions which have been significantly sustained and/or extended through the collective works of a decade. This book presents, after all, a perspective—a framework and an agenda for social psychology. In issuing this revised edition, we reassert the relevance and value of that perspective in light of the decade's documentation of these qualities.

Accordingly, the chapter most substantially revised in this edition is:

EPILOGUE: A RESEARCH PERSPECTIVE

As noted earlier, social psychology has undergone marked changes in the aims, spirit, and criteria of its general research enterprise. Moreover, during the past ten years, a good many relevant but quite divergent approaches to the empirical study of identities and interactions have been employed. In the revised epilogue, we review these changes and developments and reconsider how identities and interactions might now be studied.

NOTES

[1]Perhaps the most thorough review is Lloyd H. Strickland, Frances E. Aboud, and Kenneth J. Gergen, editors, *Social Psychology in Transition,* New York: Plenum Press, 1976. See also Nigel Armistead, editor, *Reconstructing Social Psychology*, Baltimore: Penguin Books, 1974; Alan C. Elms, "The Crisis of Confidence in Social Psychology," *The American Psychologist,* 1975, 30:967–976; Elms, *Social Psychology and Social Relevance*, Boston: Little, Brown, 1972; M.

Brewster Smith, *Humanizing Social Psychology*, San Francisco: Jossey-Bass, 1974; and Joachim Israel and Henri Tajfel, editors, *The Context of Social Psychology: A Critical Assessment*, New York: Academic Press, 1972.

² Leonard Bickman and Thomas Henchy, editors, *Beyond the Laboratory: Field Research in Social Psychology*, New York: McGraw-Hill, 1972; Paul G. Swingle, editor, *Social Psychology in Natural Settings*, Chicago: Aldine, 1973; and Edwin P. Willems and Harold L. Rausch, editors, *Naturalistic Viewpoints in Psychological Research*, New York: Holt, Rinehart & Winston, 1969.

³The references in footnote 1 recount these conceptual changes as well. See also Sheldon Stryker, "Developments in 'Two Social Psychologies': Toward an Appreciation of Mutual Relevance," *Sociometry*, 1977, 40: 145–160.

⁴E.g., Dana Bramel, "Dissonance, Expectation, and the Self," in Robert P. Abelson *et al.*, editors, *Theories of Cognitive Consistency*, Chicago: Rand McNally, 1968, pp. 355–365; Daryl J. Bem, "Self-perception: An Alternative Interpretation of Cognitive Dissonance Phenomena," *Psychological Review*, 1967, 74:183–200; and Elliot Aronson, "Dissonance Theory: Progress and Problems," in Abelson *et al., op. cit.*, pp. 5–27.

⁵E.g., Kenneth J. Gergen, *The Concept of Self*, New York: Holt, Rinehart & Winston, 1971; and Chad Gordon and Gergen, editors, *The Self in Social Interaction* (Volume 1), New York: Wiley, 1968.

⁶Ronald C. Benge, *Communication and Identity*, London: Clive Bingley, 1972, is a representative work on the concept of collective identity. A useful instance of the monolithic sense of individual identity is Orrin E. Klapp, *Collective Search for Identity*, New York: Holt, Rinehart & Winston, 1969.

⁷Virginia L. Oleson and Elvi W. Whittaker, *The Silent Dialogue: A Study in the Social Psychology of Professional Socialization*, San Francisco: Jossey-Bass, 1968; Betty Yorburg, *Sexual Identity: Sex Roles and Social Change*, New York: Wiley, 1974; George DeVos and Lola Romanucci, editors, *Ethnic Identity*, Palo Alto, Calif.: Mayfield, 1975; Stuart T. Hauser, *Black and White Identity Formation*, New York: Wiley, 1971; Janet G. Hunt, "Race and Identity," unpublished Ph.D. dissertation, Indiana University, 1973; and Elizabeth Mutran, "The Meaning of Old-Age Role/Identity and Its Social Determinants," unpublished Ph.D. dissertation, Indiana University, 1977.

⁸Sue K. Hammersmith and Martin S. Weinberg, "Homosexual Identity: Commitment, Adjustment, and Significant Others," *Sociometry*, 1973, 36:56–79; Norman R. Jackman, Richard O'Toole, and Gilbert Geis, "The Self-Image of the Prostitute," *The Sociological Quarterly*, 1963, 4:150–161; and Michael Schwartz and Sheldon Stryker, *Deviance, Selves and Others*, Washington, D.C.: American Sociological Association, 1971.

⁹John Lofland, *Deviance and Identity*, Englewood Cliffs, N.J.: Prentice-Hall, 1969; J. L. Simmons, *Deviants*, Berkeley: Glendessary Press, 1969; David Matza, *Becoming Deviant*, Englewood Cliffs, N.J.: Prentice-Hall, 1969; Earl Rubington and Martin S. Weinberg, editors, *Deviance: The Interactionist Perspective*, New York, Macmillan, 1968; Kenneth Plummer, *Sexual Stigma: An Interactionist Account*, London: Routledge & Kegan Paul, 1975; Barry M. Dank, "Coming Out in the Gay World," *Psychiatry*, 1971, 34:180–197; Carol A. B. Warren, *Identity and Community in the Gay World*, New York: Wiley, 1974; James H.

Bryan, "Apprenticeships in Prostitution," *Social Problems*, 1965, 12:287–296; Nanette J. Davis, "The Prostitute: Developing a Deviant Identity," in James M. Henslin, editor, *Studies in the Sociology of Sex*, New York: Appleton-Century-Crofts, 1971, pp. 297–322; Earl Rubington, "Drug Addiction as a Deviant Career," *International Journal of the Addictions*, 1960, 2:3–20; and Harvey W. Feldman, "Ideological Supports to Becoming and Remaining a Heroin Addict," *Journal of Health and Social Behavior*, 1968, 9:131–139.

[10]Among the more comprehensive of these works are Michael Argyle, *Social Interaction*, New York: Atherton Press, 1969; and Muzafer Sherif, *Social Interaction*, Chicago: Aldine, 1967.

[11]Adam Kendon, Richard M. Harris, and Mary Ritchie Key, editors, *Organization of Behavior in Face-to-Face Interaction*, The Hague: Mouton, 1975; N. G. Blurton-Jones, editor, *Ethological Studies of Child Behaviour*, London: Cambridge University Press, 1972; Aaron Siegman and Benjamin Pope, editors, *Studies in Dyadic Communication*, Elmsford, N.Y.: Pergamon, 1972; Albert E. Scheflen, *The Stream and Structure of Communicational Behavior* (rev. ed.), Bloomington: Indiana University Press, 1973; Mario von Cranach and Ian Vine, editors, *Social Communication and Movement: Studies of Interaction and Expression in Man and Chimpanzee*, New York: Academic Press, 1973; John Laver and Sandy Hutcheson, editors, *Communication in Face to Face Interaction*, Baltimore: Penguin Books, 1972; Starkey Duncan, Jr., and Donald W. Fiske, *Face-to-Face Interaction*, Hillsdale, N.J.: Lawrence Erlbaum Associates, 1977; and Gerald R. Miller, editor, *Explorations in Interpersonal Communication*, Beverly Hills, Calif.: Sage Publications, 1976.

[12]Mark L. Knapp, *Nonverbal Communication in Human Interaction*, New York: Holt, Rinehart & Winston, 1972; Albert E. Scheflen, *Body Language and the Social Order*, Englewood Cliffs, N.J.: Prentice-Hall, 1972; Robert Sommer, *Personal Space*, Englewood Cliffs, N.J.: Prentice-Hall, 1969; and O. Michael Watson, *Proxemic Behavior: A Cross-Cultural Study*, The Hague: Mouton, 1970.

[13]Adam Kendon, "Some Functions of Gaze Direction in Social Interaction," *Acta Psychologica*, 1967, 26:1–47; Ralph V. Exline, "Visual Interaction: The Glances of Power and Preference," *Nebraska Symposium on Motivation*, 1971, pp. 163–206; Michael Argyle and Mark Cook, *Gaze and Mutual Gaze*, Cambridge: Cambridge University Press, 1976; and Georg Simmel, "Sociology of the Senses: Visual Interaction," in Robert E. Park and Ernest W. Burgess, *Introduction to the Science of Society*, Chicago: University of Chicago Press, 1921, pp. 356–361.

[14]Harold Garfinkel, *Studies in Ethnomethodology*, Englewood Cliffs, N.J.: Prentice-Hall, 1967; Aaron V. Cicourel, *Cognitive Sociology*, Baltimore: Penguin Books, 1973; David Sudnow, editor, *Studies in Social Interaction*, New York: Free Press, 1972; Peter L. Berger and Thomas Luckman, *The Social Construction of Reality*, Garden City, N.Y.: Doubleday, 1966; George Psathas, editor, *Phenomenological Sociology*, New York: Wiley, 1973; and Paul Filmer *et al.*, *New Directions in Sociological Theory*, Cambridge: MIT Press, 1973.

[15]E.g., Rom Harré and Paul F. Secord, *The Explanation of Social Behavior*, Oxford: Blackwell, 1972; Erving Goffman, *Interaction Ritual*, Garden City,

N.Y.: Doubleday, 1967; Goffman, *Strategic Interaction*, Philadelphia: University of Pennsylvania Press, 1969; Goffman, *Relations in Public*, New York: Basic Books, 1971; Goffman, *Frame Analysis*, Cambridge: Harvard University Press, 1974; Sheldon Stryker, "Fundamental Principles of Social Interaction," in Neil J. Smelser, editor, *Sociology* (2nd ed.), New York: Wiley, 1973; and George J. McCall, "Social Roles and Interaction," in *Society Today*, Del Mar, Calif.: CRM Books, 1971, pp. 118–129.

[16]Michael Banton, *Roles: An Introduction to the Study of Social Relations*, New York: Basic Books, 1965; J. W. Jackson, editor, *Role*, London: Cambridge University Press, 1971; Ralph H. Turner, "Role: Sociological Aspects," in David L. Sills, editor, *International Encyclopedia of the Social Sciences*, New York: Macmillan, 1968, 13:552–557; Herbert H. Hyman and E. Singer, editors, *Readings in Reference Group Theory and Research*, New York: Free Press, 1968; Raymond L. Schmitt, *The Reference Other Orientation: An Extension of the Reference Group Concept*, Carbondale: Southern Illinois University Press, 1972; and Robert C. Carson, *Interaction Concepts of Personality*, Chicago: Aldine, 1969. See also footnote 5.

[17]E.g., Richard M. Emerson, "Exchange Theory: A Psychological Basis for Social Exchange" and "Exchange Theory: Exchange Relations and Exchange Networks," in Joseph Berger, Bo Anderson, and Morris Zelditch, editors, *Sociological Theories in Progress* (Volume II), Boston: Houghton Mifflin, 1972, pp. 38–87; Emerson, "Social Exchange Theory," *Annual Review of Sociology*, 1976, 2:335–362; J. K. Chadwick-Jones, *Social Exchange Theory*, New York: Academic Press, 1976; and James S. Coleman, "Systems of Social Exchange," *Journal of Mathematical Sociology*, 1972, 2:145–163.

[18]E.g., J. Clyde Mitchell, editor, *Social Networks in Urban Situations*, Manchester: Manchester University Press, 1969; Jeremy Boissevain and J. Clyde Mitchell, editors, *Network Analysis: Studies in Human Interaction*, The Hague: Mouton, 1973; Boissevain, *Friends of Friends: Networks, Manipulators and Coalitions*, Oxford: Blackwell, 1974; and Norman E. Whitten, Jr., and Alvin W. Wolfe, "Network Analysis," in John J. Honigmann, editor, *The Handbook of Social and Cultural Anthropology*, Chicago: Rand McNally, 1973, pp. 717–746.

[19]E.g., Roger G. Barker, editor, *The Stream of Behavior*, New York: Appleton-Century-Crofts, 1963; Barker, *Ecological Psychology*, Stanford, Calif.: Stanford University Press, 1968; and R. E. Herron and Brian Sutton-Smith, editors, *Child's Play*, New York: Wiley, 1971.

[20]W. S. Condon and W. Ogston, "A Segmentation of Behavior," *Journal of Psychiatric Research*, 1967, 5:221–235; Darren Newtson and Gretchen Enquist, "The Perceptual Organization of Ongoing Behavior," *Journal of Experiemental Social Psychology*, 1976, 12:451–463; and Alvin I. Goldman, *A Theory of Action*, Englewood Cliffs, N.J.: Prentice-Hall, 1970.

[21]Alexander Szalai, editor, *The Use of Time*, The Hague: Mouton, 1973; and F. Stuart Chapin, Jr., *Human Activity Patterns in the City: Things People Do in Time and in Space*, New York: Wiley, 1974.

[22]E.g., Sommer, *op. cit.*; Irwin Altman, editor, *The Environment and Human Behavior*, Monterey, Calif.: Brooks-Cole, 1975; and Albert Mehrabian, *Public Places and Private Spaces*, New York: Basic Books, 1976

[23]Raymond E. Murphy, *The American City: An Urban Geography,* New York: McGraw-Hill, 1966, pp. 51–97; and Peter Haggett, *Locational Analysis in Human Geography*, New York: St. Martin's Press, 1966.

[24]Lyn Lofland, *A World of Strangers*, New York: Basic Books, 1973; Gerald D. Suttles, *The Social Order of the Slum*, Chicago: University of Chicago Press, 1968; Goffman, *Relations in Public, op. cit.*; and David A. Karp, Gregory P. Stone, and William C. Yoels, *Being Urban: A Social Psychological View of City Life*, Lexington, Mass.: D. C. Heath, 1977.

[25]Berger and Luckman, *op. cit.*; Harvey A. Farberman and Erich Goode, editors, *Social Reality*, Englewood Cliffs, N.J.: Prentice-Hall, 1973; and Stanford M. Lyman and Marvin B. Scott, *The Drama of Social Reality*, New York: Oxford University Press, 1975.

[26]E.g,, Theodore Mischel, editor, *The Self: Psychological and Philosophical Issues*, Oxford: Blackwell, 1977; and Amelie O. Rorty, editor, *The Identities of Persons*, Berkley: University of California Press, 1976.

[27]Dennis Brissett and Charles Edgley, editors, *Life as Theater*, Chicago: Aldine, 1974; Elizabeth Burns, *Theatricality: A Study of Convention in the Theatre and in Social Life*, New York: Harper Torchbooks, 1972; Lyman and Scott, *op. cit.*; and Harré and Secord, *op. cit.*

[28]George J. McCall, "The Social Looking-Glass: A Sociological Perspective on Self-Development" in Mischel, *op. cit.*, pp. 274–287; Chad Gordon, "Systematic Senses of Self," *Sociological Inquiry*, 1968, 38:161–178; Peter Burke and Judy C. Tully, "The Measurement of Role/Identity," *Social Forces*, 1977, 55:881–897.

[29]Carl W. Backman and Paul F. Secord, "The Self and Role Selection," in Gordon and Gergen, editors, *The Self in Social Interaction, op. cit.*, pp. 289–296; Phillip W. Blumstein, "An Experiment in Identity Bargaining," unpublished Ph.D. dissertation, Vanderbilt University, 1970; and Blumstein, "Identity Bargaining and Self-Conception," *Social Forces,* 1975, 53:476–485.

[30]Such ideas are critically reviewed in Arthur Brittan, *Meanings and Situations*, London: Routledge & Kegan Paul, 1973, Chapter 9. Cf. the rejoinder in George J. McCall, "Communication and Negotiated Identity," *Communication*, 1976, 2:173–184.

[31]Sheldon Stryker, "Identity Salience and Role Performance," *Journal of Marriage and the Family*, 1968, 30:558–564; and Jerold Heiss, *Family Roles and Interaction*, Chicago: Rand McNally, 1968.

[32]Backman and Secord, *op. cit.*

[33]See footnote 14. Also, Henri Tajfel *et al.,* "Social Categorization and Intergroup Behaviour," *European Journal of Social Psychology*, 1971, 1:149–175.

[34]Kelly G. Shaver, *An Introduction to Attribution Processes,* Cambridge: Winthrop, 1975; E. E. Jones *et al.*, editors, *Attribution: Perceiving the Causes of Behavior*, Morristown, N.J.: General Learning Press, 1971; Ralph H. Turner and Norma Shosid, "Ambiguity and Interchangeability in Role Attribution: The Effects of Alter's Response," *American Sociological Review*, 1976, 41:993–1006; and Jean M. Guiot, "Attribution and Identity Construction," *American Sociological Review*, 1977, 42:692–704.

[35]Howard S. Becker, *Outsiders*, New York: Free Press, 1963; Edwin C. Schur, *Labeling Deviant Behavior*, New York: Harper & Row, 1971; and Edwin C. Lemert, *Social Pathology*, New York: McGraw-Hill, 1951.

[36]Gustav Ichheiser, *Appearances and Realities: Misunderstanding in Human Relations*, San Francisco: Jossey-Bass, 1970; Albert H. Hastorf, David J. Schneider, and Judith Polefka, *Person Perception*, Reading, Mass.: Addison-Wesley, 1970; Peter B. Warr and Christopher Knapper, *The Perception of People and Events*, New York: Wiley, 1968; Henry Clay Smith, *Sensitivity to People*, New York: McGraw-Hill, 1966; Theodore Mischel, editor, *Understanding Other Persons*, Oxford: Blackwell, 1974; and Leonard W. Doob, *Pathways to People*, New Haven: Yale University Press, 1975.

[37]E.g., Argyle, *Social Interaction, op. cit.*, Chapter 4, "Perception of the Other During Interaction."

[38]See, e.g., Part I In Rom Harré, editor, *Life Sentences: Aspects of the Social Role of Language*, New York: Wiley, 1976. Also, Eugene A. Weinstein and Lawrence S. Beckhouse, "Audience and Personality Factors in Presentation of Self," *The Sociological Quarterly*, 1969, 10:527–537; and David J. Schneider, "Tactical Self-Presentation after Success and Failure," *Journal of Personality and Social Psychology*, 1969, 13:262–268.

[39]Mordechai Rotenburg, "Self-Labelling: A Missing Link in the 'Societal Reaction' Theory of Deviation," *Sociological Review*, 1974, 22:335–356; Joseph W. Rogers and M. D. Buffalo, "Fighting Back: Nine Modes of Adaptation to a Deviant Label," *Social Problems*, 1974, 22:101–118; and R. C. Prus, "Resisting Designations: An Extension of Attribution Theory into a Negotiated Context," *Sociological Inquiry*, 1975, 45:3–14.

[40]Goffman, *Strategic Interaction, op. cit.*; Eugene A. Weinstein, "Toward a Theory of Interpersonal Tactics," in Carl W. Backman and Paul F. Secord, editors, *Problems in Social Psychology*, New York: McGraw-Hill, 1966, pp. 394–398; Blumstein, *op. cit.*; Blumstein "Audience, Machiavellianism, and Tactics of Identity Bargaining," *The Sociological Quarterly*, 1973, 36:346–365; and John P. Hewitt and Randall Stokes, "Disclaimers," *American Sociological Review*, 1975, 40:1–11.

[41]Paul F. Secord and Carl W. Backman, *Social Psychology* (2nd ed., New York: McGraw-Hill, 1974, pp. 401–457.

[42]Over three thousand studies are reviewed in Jeffrey Z. Rubin and Bert R. Brown, *The Social Psychology of Bargaining and Negotiation*, New York: Academic Press, 1975.

[43]Emerson, "Social Exchange Theory," *op. cit.*

[44]Ralph H. Turner, "The Self-Conception in Social Interaction," in Gordon and Gergen, editors, *The Self in Social Interaction, op. cit.*, pp. 93–106; Turner, *Family Interaction, op. cit.,*; G. J. McCall, "Communication and Negotiated Identity," *op. cit.*; and Shelley Duvall and Robert A. Wicklund, *A Theory of Objective Self-Awareness*, New York: Academic Press, 1972

[45]Erving Goffman, "Embarrassment and Social Organization," *American Journal of Sociology*, 1956, 62:264–274; Edward Gross and Gregory P. Stone, "Embarrassment and the Analysis of Role Requirements," *American Journal of Sociology*, 1964, 70:1–15; Andre Modigliani, "Embarrassment and Embarrass-

ability," *Sociometry*, 1968, 31:313–326; Bert R. Brown, "The Effects of Need to Maintain Face on Interpersonal Bargaining," *Journal of Experimental Social Psychology*, 1968, 4:107–122; Brown, "Face-Saving Following Experimentally Induced Embarrassment," *Journal of Experimental Social Psychology*, 1970, 6:225–271; W. Peter Archibald and Ronald L. Cohen, "Self-Presentation, Embarrassment, and Facework as a Function of Self-Evaluation, Conditions of Self-Presentation, and Feedback from Others," *Journal of Personality and Social Psychology*, 1971, 20:287–297; Goffman, *Relations in Public, op. cit.*; Marvin B. Scott and Stanford W. Lyman, "Accounts," *American Sociological Review*, 1968, 33:46–62; Phillip W. Blumstein *et al.*, "The Honoring of Accounts," *American Sociological Review*, 1974, 39:551–566; and Nancy M. Shields, "On Being Believable: Impression Formation in a Credibility Detracting Context," unpublished Ph.D. dissertation, Southern Illinois University at Carbondale, 1977.

[46]Mancur Olson, Jr., *The Logic of Collective Action*, Cambridge: Harvard University Press, 1965; James Coleman, *The Mathematics of Collective Action*, Chicago: Aldine, 1973; and Randall Stokes and John P. Hewitt, "Aligning Actions," *American Sociological Review*, 1976, 41:838–849.

[47]Theodore Caplow, *Two Against One: Coalitions in Triads*, Englewood Cliffs, N.J.: Prentice-Hall, 1968.

[48]Michael Argyle, *The Psychology of Interpersonal Behaviour*, London: Methuen, 1967; and Blumstein, "Audience, Machiavellianism, and Tactics of Identity Bargaining," *op. cit.*

[49]George J. McCall, Michal M. McCall, Norman K. Denzin, Gerald D. Suttles, and Suzanne B. Kurth, *Social Relationships*, Chicago: Aldine, 1970; and G. J. McCall, "A Symbolic Interactionist Approach to Attraction," in Ted L. Huston, editor, *Foundations of Interpersonal Attraction*, New York: Academic Press, 1974, pp. 217–231.

[50]Turner, *Family Interaction, op. cit.*; Murray S. Davis, *Intimate Relations*, New York: Free Press, 1973; Thomas J. Scheff, "On the Concepts of Identity and Social Relationship," in Tamotsu Shibutani, editor, *Human Nature and Collective Behavior*, Englewood Cliffs, N.J.: Prentice-Hall, 1970, pp. 193–207; and Goffman, *Relations in Public, op. cit.*

[51]See, e.g., the compendia by Ted L. Huston, editor, *Foundations of Interpersonal Attraction*, New York: Academic Press, 1974, and by Bernard I. Murstein, editor, *Theories of Attraction and Love*, New York: Springer Publications, 1971. Also, Ellen Berscheid and Elaine H. Walster, *Interpersonal Attraction*, Reading, Mass.: Addison-Wesley, 1969; and Donn Byrne, *The Attraction Paradigm*, New York: Academic Press, 1971.

[52]Zick Rubin, *Liking and Loving: An Invitation to Social Psychology*, New York: Holt, Rinehart & Winston, 1973; and George Levinger and J. D. Snoek, *Attraction in Relationship: A New Look at Interpersonal Attraction*, New York: General Learning Press, 1972.

[53]L. Rowell Huesmann and George Levinger, "Incremental Exchange Theory: A Formal Model for Progression in Dyadic Social Interaction," in Leonard Berkowitz and Elaine Walster, editors, *Advances in Experimental Social Psychology* (Volume IX), New York: Academic Press, 1976, pp. 191–229.

[54]Irwin Altman and Dalmas A. Taylor, *Social Penetration: The Development of Interpersonal Relationships*, New York: Holt, Rinehart & Winston, 1973; and Miller, *op. cit.*

[55]Steven W. Duck, *Personal Relationships and Personal Constructs: A Study of Friendship Formation*, New York: Wiley, 1973.

[56]Barney Glaser and Anselm Strauss, "Awareness Contexts and Social Interaction," *American Sociological Review*, 1964, 29:669–679; Paul Ekman and Wallace V. Friesen, "Nonverbal Leakage and Clues to Deception," *Psychiatry*, 1969, 32:88–106; Goffman, *Relations in Public, op. cit.*; Edwin M. Lemert, "Role Enactment, Self, and Identity in the Systematic Check Forger," in Lemert, *Human Deviance, Social Problems, and Social Control*, Englewood Cliffs, N.J.: Prentice-Hall, 1967, pp. 119–134; and Richard J. Bord, "The Impact of Imputed Deviant Identities in Structuring Evaluations and Reactions," *Sociometry*, 1976, 39:108–116. See also the references in footnote 9.

[57]Chad Gordon, "Development of Evaluated Role-Identities," *Annual Review of Sociology*, 1976, 2:405–433; Gordon, "Role and Value Development Across the Life Cycle," in Jackson, editor, *Role, op. cit.*, pp. 65–105; Gordon, Charles M. Gaitz, and Judith Scott, "Self-Evaluations of Competence and Worth in Adulthood," in Silvano Arieti, editor, *American Handbook of Psychiatry* (2nd ed.), New York: Basic Books, 1975, pp. 212–229; and Gordon and Gaitz, "Leisure and Lives: Personal Expressivity Across the Life Span," in Robert Binstock and Ethel Shanas, editors, *Handbook of Aging and the Social Sciences*, New York: Van Nostrand-Reinhold, 1976, pp. 310–341.

[58]Paul B. Baltes and K. Warner Schaie, editors, *Life-Span Developmental Psychology: Personality and Socialization*, New York: Academic Press, 1973; Rose Laub Coser, editor, *Life Cycle and Achievement in America*, New York: Harper Torchbooks, 1969; and Theodore Lidz, *The Person: His and Her Development through the Life Cycle*, New York: Basic Books, 1968.

[59]David Goslin, editor, *Handbook of Socialization Theory and Research*, New York: Russell Sage Foundation, 1969; and John A. Clausen, editor, *Socialization and Society*, Boston: Little, Brown, 1969.

[60]Paul F. Secord and Barbara Hollands Peevers, "The Development and Attribution of Person Concepts," in Mischel, editor, *Understanding Other Persons, op. cit.*, pp. 117–142; W. J. Livesley and D. J. Bromley, *Person Perception in Childhood and Adolescence*, New York: Wiley, 1973; Secord and Backman, *Social Psychology, op. cit.*, pp. 477–487 ("Role Learning: Content and Process"); and Dorothy Flapan, *Children's Understanding of Social Interaction*, New York: Teachers College Press, 1968.

[61]E.g., Murray A. Geisler, editor, *Logistics*, New York: American Elsevier Publishing Co., 1975.

[62]Barney Glaser, editor, *Organizational Careers: A Sourcebook for Theory*, Chicago, Aldine, 1968; John Van Maanen, editor, *Organizational Careers: Some New Perspectives*, New York: Wiley, 1977; Erving Goffman, "The Underlife of a Public Institution: A Study of Ways of Making Out in a Mental Hospital," in Goffman, *Asylums*, Garden City, N.Y.: Doubleday, 1961, pp. 171–320; and Suzanne B. Kurth, "Friendship and Friendly Relations," in McCall *et al.*, *Social Relationships, op. cit.*, pp. 136–170.

IDENTITIES
AND
INTERACTIONS

Chapter 1

THE PROBLEM
AND THE
APPROACH

Interacting with other people is a sometimes perilous, often boring, always effortful venture. Seldom thoroughly satisfying, such interaction nevertheless remains the constant lot and recurring hope of individuals everywhere. Nothing occurs in the social world except through the struggle and more or less mutual influence of individuals, which social scientists have colorlessly termed "interaction."

All socialized human beings are thoroughly steeped in interaction experiences. Indeed, "adequate" performance in interaction situations is the acid test of eligibility for the status of full-fledged humanness; the misfit, the handicapped, and the psychologically disturbed are defined by the degree to which they impede "normal" human interactions.

Yet our very familiarity with human interactions misleads us into thinking that we understand this most fundamental human activity and leads us into mistaking the thick undergrowth of habit and local custom for genuine knowledge of what goes on in interaction.

It is difficult for man to develop deep insights into social interactions, just as it would be difficult for a fish to discover water, for he is so used to them that he takes them more or less for granted. Only the occasional individual—poet, prophet, or psychotic, but more often merely an astute social psychologist—has partially succeeded in unfettering himself from these preconceptions and has called into question what others were taking for granted.

With no pretension to charisma or revealed knowledge, this book too tries to develop such an unfettered, questioning framework for the consideration of human interaction and of the self-conceptions or "identities" that nurture and are nurtured by them. Its focus is on the seemingly simple question of WHO comes together to engage in WHAT social acts WHEN and WHERE, a question that conceals within itself innumerable and unexpected complexities. The substantive imagery of the book is of man as a day-dreaming sort of animal who gambles his small store of "life resources" with the empirical world in an attempt to win some measure of fulfillment of his dreams and desires. To explain the manner in which he allocates his "life capital" among his various speculative social enterprises—that is, to explain WHO does WHAT, WHEN, and WHERE, socially speaking—we shall pursue at great length the more theoretical questions, HOW do people interact and WHY?

How and why do people associate differentially with one another? What is the "division of labor" (in the very broadest sense of the term) in a given population, and why does it take that form? How and why are types of people and activities characteristically segregated, spatially and temporally?

Unlike the sociological approaches to these questions, this book does not attempt to answer them at a societal or "social system" level. Rather, it seeks to approach them from the perspective of the individual in society who is plugging along in an attempt to live the good life as he sees it. The theoretical framework developed in this book—and it is as yet scarcely more than a framework—necessarily retains a certain flavor of ordinary life, which we feel need not represent a serious obstacle to scientific strivings.

And in fact we hope to avoid being forced to take sides in the dispute between the scientific and humanistic approaches to many-sided man. The humanist too often accuses the scientist of defiling the human essence by attempting to capture it with a set of statistics; the behavioral scientist often suspects that the humanist merely mouths sentimentalities. Then, too, the humanist of the new generation often gives lip service to the value of a more objective approach to man but, in the body of his work, goes his merry way, extrapolating an entire world view from his scattered personal experiences, his prejudices, and his predilections. The "broad minded" social scientist now also gives a nod to the contributions of the humanities, by beginning his otherwise pedantic chapters with quotations from John Donne or the diary of Mary Baker Eddy.

We believe that both traditions have won a good deal of insight into the human condition, and for the most part we shall try to approach our scientific labors with our scrutiny fixed on the concerns of individual human beings striving to wend their way through the web of social relationships and institutions. Our primary concession to the strain between these approaches is the confinement of research operations and data concerns to the epilogue, which may accordingly be omitted by those disinclined toward methodological considerations. It is our hope, however, that the scientific relevance of the major (theoretical) portion of the text is not thereby impaired.

This issue of scientism *vs.* humanism brings in its train a number of somewhat related issues concerning our conception of man and his nature, and perhaps these issues can be disposed of here in summary fashion.

The most important is the dualism persistent in Western thought between matter and mind, beast and spirit. We shall be making much of the fact that man exhibits both aspects; indeed, it remains the central problem of social science, as well as of philosophy, to explain this wondrous and perplexing fact. We do not presume to have solved this problem, but we do emphasize its centrality by speaking of man as dwelling in two quite distinct "worlds," the physicalistic world of animals and the idealistic world of mind and culture. From the outset we wish to allay the possibility that some readers may mistakenly take us to be asserting the literal ontological existence of two separate realms of mind and matter. This assertion represents neither our intent nor our metaphysical stance. Our frequent talk of "man's two worlds" embodies merely a rhetorical figure to sharpen the reader's awareness of certain contrasting but only analytically separable features of man's condition and the relations among them. This point should become somewhat clearer in the succeeding chapters.

A related issue on which we should clarify any possible misunderstanding is the tension between the view of man as primarily a conscious and rational thinker and the opposing view of his basic mental functioning as largely unconscious or at least nonrational. Our position on this question is that most of the cognitive processes we shall attribute to men occur at all levels of consciousness. At times these processes display surprising degrees of rationality, but rationality must not be confused with deliberation or a high degree of self-awareness. For much of men's behavior evinces a great deal of system and strategic effectiveness, often apparently without the intervention of deliberate or conscious calculation. Therefore many of the complex decisions with which we credit man in this book should not be interpreted as necessarily the results of deliberate reasoning.

Along these lines, we must also raise the issue of possible ethnocentrism in our approach. In the history of the social sciences, subsequent advances have shown again and again that formulations put forth to explain "societies" or "human behavior" generally have been but special cases that mostly illuminate nineteenth-century English mercantile institutions or the behavior of middle-class educated Americans during the first half of the present century. Our _aim_ is to live up to the more universal implications of our title and of the titles of our chapters by analyzing the fundamental and generic processes involved in identities and interactions, which hold for all human beings in all times and places. But our examples will, of necessity, be drawn disproportionately from contemporary American life, as we have experience of no other. Accordingly, our work will no doubt reflect some of the biases inherent in this perspective. As far as possible, however, we have tried always to remember that there are also other cultures and other times.

Many books, reflecting divergent schools of thought, have been written on human interactions. The largest number of these books has stemmed from the orientation usually called "symbolic inter-actionism." From the early writings of William James down to the present day, there has accumulated an impressive body of literature on the interrelations among self, role, and interaction, as these concepts illuminate the complexities and profundities of ordinary human lives.

As this line of social thought has evolved, through the works of James, Baldwin, Cooley, Mead, Dewey, Thomas, Park, Goffman, and numerous other writers,[1] it has broadened to become a perspective in the social sciences rather than merely a school of thought in sociological social psychology. As noted by Kuhn, this approach is represented in psychiatry by Sullivan and his students, in cultural anthropology by Benedict and Linton, in psychology by

[1]Among the landmarks of this developing line of thought are William James, *Principles of Psychology* (2 vols.), New York: Holt, 1890; James Mark Baldwin, *Social and Ethical Interpretations in Mental Development*, New York: Macmillan, 1897; Charles Horton Cooley, *Human Nature and the Social Order*, New York: Scribner's, 1902; Cooley, *Social Organization*, New York: Scribner's, 1909; George Herbert Mead, *Mind, Self, and Society*, Chicago: University of Chicago Press, 1934; John Dewey, *Experience and Nature*, Chicago: Open Court, 1925; W. I. Thomas and Florian Znaniecki, *The Polish Peasant in Europe and America* (5 vols.), Chicago: University of Chicago Press, 1918-1920; Robert E. Park, *Society*, New York: Free Press, 1955, *passim;* Park, *Race and Culture*, New York: Free Press, 1950, *passim;* Ellsworth Faris, *The Nature of Human Nature*, New York: McGraw-Hill, 1937; Erving Goffman, *The Presentation of Self in Everyday Life*, Garden City, N.Y.: Doubleday Anchor, 1957; and Anselm Strauss, *Mirrors and Masks*, New York: Free Press, 1959.

Recent developments have been surveyed in Manford H. Kuhn, "Major Trends in Symbolic Interaction Theory in the Past Twenty-Five Years," *Sociological Quarterly*, 1964, 5: 61–84; in Arnold M. Rose, editor, *Human Behavior and Social Processes*, Boston: Houghton Mifflin, 1962; and in Jerome G. Manis and Bernard Meltzer, editors, *Symbolic Interaction: A Reader in Social Psychology* (2nd ed.), Boston: Allyn & Bacon, 1972. Recent statements include Herbert Blumer, *Symbolic Interactionism: Perspective and Method*, Englewood Cliffs, N.J.: Prentice-Hall, 1969; and John P. Hewitt, *Self and Society: A Symbolic Interactionist Social Psychology*, Boston: Allyn & Bacon, 1976. Some leading textbooks exemplifying this point of view include Alfred R. Lindesmith, Anselm L. Strauss, and Norman K. Denzin, *Social Psychology* (4th ed.), New York: Holt, 1974; Tamotsu Shibutani, *Society and Personality*, Englewood Cliffs, N.J.: Prentice-Hall, 1961; and Gregory P. Stone and Harvey Farberman, editors, *Social Psychology Through Symbolic Interaction*, Waltham, Mass.: Ginn-Blaisdell, 1970.

See Preface, footnote 15, for recent applications of this viewpoint to the analysis of social interaction.

Bruner and the person-perception school among many others, and to a lesser but unmistakable degree by the ego psychologists.[2] The symbolic-interactionist orientation has become an intrinsic part of American sociology; it is reflected in every major sociology text and is employed extensively by Parsons, Merton, and other major theorists not usually associated with this school of thought.

In fact, many of these theorists are quite unacquainted with the central line of development of symbolic-interactionist writings in sociological social psychology. Rather, their connection with the school is through elaboration of concepts widely diffused from the major interaction writings, concepts like role, self, and the social anchorage of self-evaluation. Separate schools of thought have grown up about these derivative concepts, typically without reference to their origins. Chief among these derived schools are those of role theory, self theory, reference-group theory, and interpersonal theory. All have contributed much that we can make use of, but none characterizes our own approach. It may perhaps be helpful, therefore, to specify our divergences from each of these approaches.

Although the concept of social role occupies an important place in our framework, our approach is certainly not that of role theory. To theorists like Parsons, Merton, and Gross, a role is a set of expectations held toward the occupant of a particular social status or position in a social system.[3] Role-performance then consists of conforming behaviorally to those expectations, with the goal of attaining positive sanctions from those holding the expectations or of avoiding their negative sanctions. In our opinion, this sort of mechanistic conformity to a role script is observed only in unusual circumstances, as in fairly tightly structured organizations in which roles in this sense are formally defined. Even then the utility of this model is highly limited: Although the professor and the groundskeeper both occupy roles in the same formal organization,

---

[2]Kuhn, *op. cit.*

[3]Talcott Parsons, *The Social System,* New York: Free Press, 1951; Robert K. Merton, *Social Theory and Social Structure* (rev. ed.), New York: Free Press, 1957, especially Chapter 9; and Neal Gross, Ward S. Mason, and Alexander W. McEachern, *Explorations in Role Analysis,* New York: Wiley, 1958.

the professor would be at a loss to specify the role relationship between them in terms of specific expectations, rights, and duties. We submit that no script exists for this role relationship, as indeed for the great majority of relationships, and therefore that the individuals involved must somehow *improvise* their roles within very broad limits. To the role theorist, the archetypal role is that seen in ritual or classic drama, in which every line and every gesture of each actor is rigidly specified in the sacred script. In our view, the archetypal role is more nearly that seen in improvised theater, such as provided by the Second City troupe, which performs extemporaneously within only the broad outlines of the sketches and of the characters assumed. This view of role has been discussed most fully by Turner, although the discussion by Goode is also pertinent.[4]

We also have our differences with the related *reference-group theory*, which has tended to emphasize the importance of abstract social categories and of aspired but unfamiliar formal associations in providing standards by means of which the person can orient his strivings.[5] In our opinion, this emphasis is an unwarranted exaggeration of the importance of abstract social anchorages, neglecting the more pervasive influence of concrete relationships and social groups in shaping frames of reference. Furthermore, these theorists typically omit the most important "reference point" of all, the reflective self of the individual in question. More fruitful are the recent reworkings of the reference-group concept in the work of Shibutani, Turner, Strauss, Kuhn, and Schmitt.[6]

[4]Ralph H. Turner, "Role: Sociological Aspects," in David L. Sills, editor, *International Encyclopedia of the Social Sciences,* New York: Macmillan, 1968, 13: 552–557; Turner, "Role-Taking: Process Versus Conformity," in Rose, *op. cit.*, pp. 20–40; William J. Goode, "A Theory of Role Strain," *American Sociological Review,* 1960, 25: 483–496; and J. W. Jackson, editor, *Role,* London: Cambridge University Press, 1971.

[5]Herbert H. Hyman and E. Singer, editors, *Readings in Reference Group Theory and Research,* New York: Free Press, 1968.

[6]Shibutani, "Reference Groups as Perspectives," *American Journal of Sociology,* 1955, 60: 562–569; Turner, "Role-Taking, Role Standpoint, and Reference-Group Behavior," *American Journal of Sociology,* 1956, 61: 316–328; Strauss, *op. cit.*, pp. 56–57; Kuhn, "The Reference Group Reconsidered," *Sociological Quarterly,* 1964, 5: 5–21; and Raymond L. Schmitt, *The Reference Other Orientation: An Extension of the Reference Group Concept,* Carbondale: Southern Illinois University Press, 1972.

The errors of mechanistic role and reference-group theories have been totally avoided by the *interpersonal school* of psychiatric thought, which has restored primary emphasis to the emergent relationships between unique personalities in interaction.[7] These theorists, however, too often focus exclusively on the dyad in isolation from its social matrix of institutions and interested third parties, and thus they fail to take into account external social forces working upon the dyad.

Perhaps the most important of the special theories for our purposes is *self theory*, although we must also voice our differences with the self theorists. All too often, these theorists treat the self as the "end-all" and "be-all" of social psychological inquiry. The effect of various social variables upon the self, or even of the self upon the self, delimits their sphere of interest.[8] It is our view that the importance of the self lies not in its reflexive churnings and seethings but in its directive influence on human behavior. That is, we do not wish to treat the self as our dependent variable of concern but as a most important variable intervening between the antecedent events of the social world and the consequent actions of the individual. Our position on this point is further buttressed by the unhappy fact that subtle dynamics of a postulated self are most difficult to observe empirically, whereas social actions lend themselves fairly readily to empirical observation.[9]

[7]H. S. Sullivan, *The Collected Works of Harry Stack Sullivan* (2 vols.), New York: Norton, 1964; Patrick Mullahy, editor, *A Study of Interpersonal Relations,* New York: Hermitage, 1949; and Robert C. Carson, *Interaction Concepts of Personality,* Chicago: Aldine, 1969.

[8]Ruth Wylie, *The Self Concept: A Review of Methodological Considerations and Measuring Instruments* (rev. ed.), Lincoln: University of Nebraska Press, 1974.

[9]The frustrations of research on the self are codified in the first chapters of Wylie, *op. cit.* Nonetheless, a certain amount of progress has been achieved in recent years. See, for example, Chad Gordon, "Self-Conceptions Methodologies," *Journal of Nervous and Mental Diseases,* 1969, 148: 328–364; Kenneth J. Gergen, *The Concept of Self,* New York: Holt, 1970; and Theodore Mischel, editor, *The Self: Psychological and Philosophical Issues,* Oxford: Blackwell, 1977. Especially promising are those studies relating the dynamics of self to the dynamics of social interaction, e.g., Gordon and Gergen, editors, *The Self in Social Interaction* (Volume I), New York: Wiley, 1968.

Perhaps intermediate between the extreme social mechanism of role and reference-group theory and the emphasis on unique persons and relationships in interpersonal and self theory is the currently fashionable *exchange theory* of interaction.[10] In this view, relationships are negotiated through "economic" bargaining and exchange of social valuables and are therefore emergent. Yet much of this bargaining is viewed as taking place within social groups and reflecting social position; the effects of external social forces are thus recognized, while the concept of relationships *emerging* through the interaction of individuals, rather than being completely imposed upon them, is retained. On the other hand, exchange theory deals almost entirely with enduring relationships, rather than with the actual conduct of persons in face-to-face confrontations. Furthermore, this approach typically fails to specify what is actually valued by these bargainers and why, treating these important questions as "givens."

Thus, none of these theories quite meets our needs in this book. It is our feeling, however, that these and other theories developed

[10]After an auspicious beginning in the works of Georg Simmel ("Exchange," in Donald N. Levine, editor, *Georg Simmel on Individuality and Social Forms,* Chicago: University of Chicago Press, 1971, pp. 43–69) and of Willard Waller (*The Family,* New York: Holt, 1938, Chapter 10), exchange theory lay dormant until revived by George C. Homans, "Human Behavior as Exchange," *American Journal of Sociology,* 1958, 63: 597–606. This seminal paper has given rise to a spate of books and articles elaborating and testing the propositions of exchange theories. Among these works are Homans, *Social Behavior* (rev. ed.), New York: Harcourt, 1974; John W. Thibaut and Harold H. Kelley, *The Social Psychology of Groups,* New York: Wiley, 1959; Peter M. Blau, *Exchange and Power in Social Life,* New York: Wiley, 1964; Eugene A. Weinstein and Paul Deutschberger, "Tasks, Bargains, and Identities in Social Interaction," *Social Forces,* 1964, 42: 451–456; Richard M. Emerson, "Exchange Theory," in Joseph Berger *et al.,* editors, *Sociological Theories in Progress* (Volume II), Boston: Houghton Mifflin, 1972, pp. 38–87; Emerson, "Social Exchange Theory," *Annual Review of Sociology,* 1976, 2:335–362; J. K. Chadwick-Jones, *Social Exchange Theory,* New York: Academic Press, 1976; and James S. Coleman, "Systems of Social Exchange," *Journal of Mathematical Sociology,* 1972, 2:145–163.

Because we have framed our problem largely in terms of explaining a person's *allocation* of his limited interactional resources, "economic" notions are necessarily somewhat prominent in portions of this book. We have therefore drawn upon these exchange theorists, although we recognize from institutional economics that exchange itself is not the sole process even in economic life proper. We do by behavioral scientists remain quite useful for explaining the particular *aspect* of interaction and the human condition that is the special subject matter of each. In their pure forms, of course, these theories are not entirely compatible in the assumptions they make about mankind, but each does help to explain a different aspect of the total picture. The rich diversity of these theories serves to underline the very lushness of human interaction, a multiplex process containing within itself an astonishing variety of component strands.[11] When one of the special theories seems to us particularly helpful in following one of these strands, we shall seize upon it. And just as the special, derived theories do not accurately represent our approach, the central line of *symbolic* interactionism itself provides us directly with little more than a set of broad, guiding outlines. In short, we are striving here for a simply *interactionist* approach, unadorned with adjectives or hyphens, in the general mode established by Georg Simmel and Robert E. Park.[12] Hoping not to slide into a haphazard eclecticism, we shall try to listen respectfully to the various specialized theories whenever we feel their answers to the HOW and the WHY of people's behavior can aid

---

not wish to emphasize the "economic" aspect of interaction but only to recognize it and to give it its due place; indeed, we wish rather to emphasize the political, rhetorical, dramaturgical, and symbolic modes of social influence that are less commonly recognized today. It is central to our point of view that man is a creature of ideas and illusions, as well as of values and calculations. The importance of this fact was not lost upon Adam Smith, but it has received much less recognition in the work of his modern descendants.

[11]This amazing richness of interaction is nowhere more clearly exemplified than in Robert E. Pittenger, Charles F. Hockett, and John J. Danehy, *The First Five Minutes: A Sample of Microscopic Interview Analysis*, Ithaca, N.Y.: Paul Martineau, 1960. This unique endeavor analyzes a good many of the strands, or levels, of interaction involved in the first five minutes of the initial interview between a psychiatrist and a particular patient. One index of this complexity is that the analysis of these five minutes filled a 264-page volume.

For a wider sampling of the diversity of theories of social interaction, see Preface, footnotes 11–13.

[12]Georg Simmel, *The Sociology of Georg Simmel* (trans. Kurt H. Wolff), New York: Free Press, 1950; Park, *Society;* and Park, *Race and Culture*. See also their selections in Park and Ernest W. Burgess, *Introduction to the Science of Sociology* (2nd. ed.), Chicago: University of Chicago Press, 1924, Chapter 6 ("Social Interaction").

us in understanding WHO come together to engage in WHAT social acts WHEN and WHERE.

We have chosen to focus upon these four ws as our "dependent" or "effect variables," the phenomena to be explained in this book, for two principal reasons: (1) Empirically, they are fairly clear-cut, yet (2) they are also of human importance to ordinary individuals.

All scientific theories must specify a set of effects or variables that are to be explained in terms of other, antecedent variables. In our view, the inner dynamics of some postulated but unlocalizable psyche system—however important they may be to the human condition—are simply too metaphorical and insubstantial to serve as *effect* variables to be explained scientifically. Methodologically, we believe it strategically more sound to focus on a set of dependent variables that are relatively unequivocal and easily measured, admitting the less determinate variables of personality into theory only in the role of independent or intervening variables.[13]

Our dependent variables, the four ws, are also *humanly* important, for they comprise the very fabric of daily living. Life, as far as man is a social being, consists in coming together with others in order to do things. In fact, a person's whole life history can be viewed as nothing more than a long series of interpersonal encounters, liberally garnished with expectations and remembrances, as most biographies attest. We feel it is scarcely accidental that the working journalist, charged with portraying, with human interest, the changing contours of developing history, has likewise formalized the questions Who? What? When? Where? Why? and How? as his orienting framework.[14]

[13]If the problem of scientific explanation is posed statistically as one of accounting for the variance in data pertaining to dependent variables through the introduction of independent variables, the grounds for this strategy are clear. Extraneous variance due to errors of measurement can be compensated for much more easily in the case of independent than of dependent variables, for example, through the use of partial correlation and analysis of covariance techniques.

[14]Similar questions also underlie the dramatistic framework of Kenneth Burke, which has influenced several recent interactionist works. Burke's central questions include: Agent? Act? Scene? Agency? and Purpose? See, for example,

Accordingly, our aim in this book is somewhat unusual. The book does not offer a comprehensive treatise on the sprawling field of social psychology or a new personality theory of some kind. Neither is it an attempt to synthesize in some fashion the diverse theories already mentioned. It is rather an attempt to illuminate systematically what is known—along with a great deal that is as yet only suspected—about the fine-grained processes of human face-to-face interaction. We have tried to pull together in this book perhaps the widest range of questions concerning interaction yet posed in a single volume and to frame some systematically inter-related answers to many of them. The overarching concern that serves to unify these questions is our concern to explain the manner in which men allocate their limited life capital among the bewildering variety of social enterprises potentially open to them. The four ws thus constitute our touchstones for the many questions of interaction but not primarily in terms of simply describing the observed permutations of these variables. Although we shall talk most often of WHO, WHAT, WHEN, and WHERE, of sheer *descriptive* variables, we shall be primarily concerned with the HOW and the WHY of social behavior: how and why a given person distributes his interactional resources as he does.

In our account of why people do things, it will, of course, be necessary to explore what goes on *inside* people as well as between them. That is, although we have not previously stressed the point (save in the title of this volume), a very great deal of the book has to do with mind, self, and problems of identity. We shall, in fact, put forward a somewhat novel view of the self and its struggles with its social environs. This *role-identity model* of the self, as we call it, is the chief locus of our tentative answers to the HOW and, especially, to the WHY of social interaction. As we raise an extensive series of questions and problems concerning human interaction in the chapters to follow, we shall attempt to confront each from the vantage point of this model. Nonetheless, we remain interested in these inner dynamics of people *only as they affect our*

---

his *A Grammar of Motives,* Englewood Cliffs, N.J.: Prentice-Hall, 1945. The family resemblance of our approach to that of Burke is, however, but shallow and coincidental, though perhaps felicitous.

empirical dependent variables—WHO come together to engage in WHAT social acts WHEN and WHERE? We are centrally concerned in this book with the subtle intertwinings of the social careers of individuals, and all our considerable talk about their self-dynamics is principally a means to this end, not an end in itself.

Before we can take up the complexities of identities or the interaction drama, however, we must set the stage by examining our dependent variables more closely in the next chapter, for the inner constraints of these variables set the boundaries within which human beings may pursue their interactive careers.

~ recognize limitations + clearly state problems
— outline opponents + mediate btwn them
— draws from both sci + humanistic
   approaches

Chapter 2

BOUNDARIES
ON
INTERACTIONS

From the perspectives of world history and anthropology, the sheer variety of things that people do with, to, for, against, and in spite of one another constitutes perhaps the most impressive fact about human life, aside from its very existence. To demonstrate their affection they kiss, rub noses, pluck worms and lice from one another, or commingle their bloodstreams. The mere presence of others motivates people to sing, tell dirty jokes, or sit in painful silence. They prove themselves worthy by earning degrees, fattening themselves up, tracing their descents, going into epileptic trances, or running twenty miles with mouthfuls of water. They carry out ritual ceremonies to legitimate sexual intimacies, to narcotize their prey, to celebrate the mechanics of the solar system, and to negotiate with a bewildering variety of gods. They seal themselves away from others before doing such private things as going to the bathroom, eating food, or having their names spoken. They dream, work, and strive for the day when they can move into their own homes, see visions, eat their enemies in ritual feasts, or perpetrate their own deaths.

If we limit ourselves to considering only one particular society during a single period of its history, this incredible mélange of "social actions" shrinks a good deal. But even from this narrowed perspective, the diversity of life styles (or subcultures) remains quite vast. When we focus our attention still more narrowly upon a single individual, we find that, although his life pattern still includes a diversity of activities, this range is but a minute fraction of the total range of human activities.

Too often, the provincialism of our own world view and the fundamental human tendency to formulate generalizations that accentuate the average and the typical lead us to minimize our sense of the range of this diversity. If this unawareness is true with respect to abstract types of human activities, how much more true it is with regard to the diversity of concrete interactional encounters.

If, in imagination, we were to take all the conceivable alternative persons, acts, times, and places (the four ws) and then combine them in all possible ways, the universe of conceivable concrete interactions would be so vast and multitudinous that it would overwhelm the human mind.

Yet a very large proportion of the conceivable possibilities generated in this manner would of course be *empirically* impossible under any circumstances, and a great many others could only occur under very special circumstances. That is, perhaps the bulk of the imagined combinations of these four components resulting from this mechanical combinative procedure would be utterly fantastic (like Gandhi and Julius Caesar wrestling on the moon in 1776) and could be ruled out at once. Nevertheless, an incredible number of these fourfold combinations might indeed occur (or have occurred), even though the empirical probability of most would be negligible. The intriguing fact remains, however, that of these improbable combinations a certain proportion become actualized, constituting the events of daily life and of history.

Our task in this volume, as mentioned in Chapter 1, is to explain, for a specified set of persons, which of these innumerable combinations are most likely to be empirically actualized. That is, for the given person(s), we wish to explain WHO come together to engage in WHAT social acts WHEN and WHERE.

This task is simplified by the fact that, as noted, the vast majority of even the relevant conceivable combinations can immediately be ruled out as impossible or entirely improbable. This tremendous curtailment of conceivable interactions results, broadly speaking, from certain attributes of the physical world and from certain characteristics of men and the societies they build and inhabit. These factors set limits, or boundaries, on the freedom of each of the components—the WHO, WHAT, WHEN, and WHERE—to vary in the empirical world. Or, to look at it from the point of view of the individual, these factors place overwhelming restrictions (boundaries) upon the manner in which the individual may distribute his life resources among associates, activities, times, and locales.

In this chapter, we shall examine the nature of these constraining factors and the manner in which they impinge on the individual. These constraints serve to define the broad bounds within which persons must enact their lives. It will remain to the theoretical schema set forth in the remainder of the book to explain which of the many alternative interactions within these bounds will in fact be actualized.

The constraining factors of which we have been speaking can be divided into two principal varieties: the extrinsic and the intrinsic. By *extrinsic* constraints we mean those that stem from "accidental" characteristics (in the Aristotelian sense) of men and their social orders. These cultural, social, and personal constraints upon the individual's identities and interactions will be discussed in later sections of this chapter.

INTRINSIC CONSTRAINTS

The class of *intrinsic* constraints upon conceivable interactions includes those that are inherent in the logical and "ecological" structure of man's world. Chief among them are the limitations stemming from the fact that the four components, the four ws, are not independent of one another, logically and "ecologically" speaking. Each influences and curtails the others. That is, if one focuses upon a specific value of one of the components—for example, the component WHEN and the year A.D. 1060 in particular—one sets empirical limits on the values of other components. Empirically, one is then restricted to the total possible combinations of persons alive in 1060, of activities known to the population alive in 1060, and of those places to which people were able to travel at that time. These elements represent enormous constraints on the total range of variation in the separate components. The constraints would differ in specifics but not in nature if we had chosen the year 1000 B.C. or A.D. 2584.

No matter which component one specifies, constraints of this same sort are thereby placed on all the others. And if one simultaneously specifies two (or three) components, the range of empirically possible variation in the other(s) is constrained to a much *greater* degree than if only one is so specified. In this section, we examine the constraining effects of the others on each of the four components in turn, as well as some of the effects of multiple specification.

The WHO

Consider first the bare question: WHO does an individual interact with? There are now over four billion people on earth, but for any given individual the factor of distance alone is sufficient to eliminate almost the entire human population from interacting with that individual. Human mobility is today remarkable and ever increasing, but the costs of transportation, the press of subsistence activities, and the rush of time prevent even the most footloose cosmopolitan from personally interacting with more than a paltry few thousand people during his entire lifetime. And an "interaction-partner" map would show that even these few thousand are highly clustered geographically.[1] Most persons' associates are drawn almost exclusively from the populations of the little communities within which they live out their entire lives.

Where one is located, geographically speaking, thus greatly limits whom one interacts with. In the overwhelming number of cases one must select interaction partners from among those at hand. As Thibaut and Kelly have pointed out,[2] the costs incurred

[1] Jeremy Boissevain and J. Clyde Mitchell, editors, *Network Analysis: Studies in Human Interaction*, The Hague: Mouton, 1973.

[2] John W. Thibaut and Harold H. Kelley, *The Social Psychology of Groups*, New York: Wiley, 1959, pp. 39–42.

in interacting with someone at any considerable distance makes all but the most rewarding interactions unprofitable. We choose, then, not the best of all possible interaction partners, but the best of the *available* interaction partners: a simple point but one that has many ramifications, as we shall see in later chapters.

The WHERE is of course not the only factor that imposes constraints upon WHO. When WHAT is brought into the picture, the range of alternative possible WHOS is cut perhaps more drastically than by any other factor. If we focus upon a *particular* role activity that the individual needs or desires to perform, the range of alternative WHOS shrinks to those who are available, willing, and competent as role partners.

Simple ascribed characteristics will prevent millions of WHOS from being able to participate in particular WHATS. Age, for example, sets great limits upon interactions—coitus is rare with infants and the aged, as are warfare, motherhood, and major league baseball. Sex, too, is a great limiter, for men give birth as rarely as women are acclaimed All-American tackles. Native language poses almost insurmountable barriers to interactions between countless persons of different linguistic stocks, as communication is usually a prerequisite for human interaction of any involved variety.

Much of the variation in WHO thus turns out to be determined by WHAT. And, as a large proportion of human activities depend upon a plurality of actors, the variation in who interacts with whom is further reduced by the necessity for matching the necessary roles and counterroles.

WHEN also impinges upon WHO. For activities involving more than one person, there must be a matching in terms of WHEN, just as a matching in terms of WHERE and of WHAT are needed. People who at one time were real possibilities as alters for a given individual may not be so at a later time, simply because they have become involved elsewhere or their interests have shifted.

Probably the most important limitation that time imposes upon who interacts with whom is the fact that interaction with a given individual automatically precludes interaction, during the same time period, with a host of other individuals. At its most primitive level, this point is one of the major factors in the economy and logistics of identities and interactions, and its implications are far-reaching, as we shall see in later chapters.

The WHAT

WHAT is the component of human behavior that receives the most attention from social scientists. The range of alternative acts is, as we have seen, almost infinite, but again there are many factors that impose restrictions upon this variation.

Even without considering the other components, there is one characteristic of most human activities that imposes boundaries on this component: the fact that most human acts are not isolated events but are intrinsic parts of *sequences* of necessary, sufficient, and contributing conditions—sequences of other acts. The probability of particular acts occurring is, therefore, not the simple calculus of single or joint independent events, but the far more complicated calculus of conditional probabilities and stochastic chains. We shall see that many cultural patterns and social arrangements have precisely the function of facilitating and impeding various clusters of WHATS under certain conditions.

We have seen that WHAT is one of the major constraints upon WHO, and it should not be surprising that the converse is also true; WHO is one of the factors that most limit WHAT. WHAT an individual will do is heavily contingent upon who is at hand, both in the positive sense of necessary role partners and in the negative sense that the presence of certain others will prevent many otherwise quite likely activities from occurring.

Not every pairing of two individuals will yield the necessary skills and willingnesses to produce a dance interaction, a knife fight, a kiss, or a consideration of the merits of Sanskrit poetry. And even when the circumstances do not preclude or mitigate against such activities, one or more of the actors may be bent upon other role performances—other WHATS.

WHAT occurs is just as much a function of WHERE as of WHO. WHERE partly determines WHAT, not only in the gross sense of different culture areas as the anthropologists have delineated them, but also, and perhaps more pervasively, in the micro-ecological sense in which certain towns, certain neighborhoods, certain buildings, and certain rooms are functionally specialized.[3]

Many activities require the availability of equipment, in the broadest sense, and these activities will be confined to areas where the equipment is. Swimming, for example, requires a certain minimal volume of water, skiing entails a snow-packed gradient, preparing a meal usually requires some means of heating food. Human beings are not so passive that they will always confine their activities to only those that have been designated for particular locales; we must often "make do" with the locations at hand. "Keep Out" and "Off Limits" signs have always challenged the adventurous, and the inventiveness of lovers in finding a place to be lovers in is legendary. But most types of human acts, in the majority of their enactments, are performed in those WHERES that have been deemed appropriate and have been equipped accordingly. Where one is located thus limits what one does by facilitating certain activities and precluding others.

WHEN is also a major determinant of what activities occur. Especially in our age of rapid technological change, we can hardly escape the extent to which WHAT is contingent upon WHEN. It is only during our own lifetimes that certain acts have become possible, such as swimming through space in zero-gravity, buying frozen foods, and watching television. And conversely, certain acts are no longer possible, such as catching dinosaurs or making love to Queen Victoria. History is thus one of the great determinants of what activities occur. And, in fact, if all the details and nuances of any particular act are specified, it becomes historically unique.

What activities occur is a function of the WHEN of personal history, as well as of world history. Each season in life has its graces and its shortcomings in terms of the activities that are possible and

---

[3]Robert Sommer, *Personal Space*, Englewood Cliffs, N.J.: Prentice-Hall, 1969; Roger G. Barker, *Ecological Psychology*, Stanford, Calif.: Stanford University Press, 1968; and Irwin Altman, editor, *The Environment and Human Behavior*, Monterey, Calif.: Brooks-Cole, 1975.

impossible within its span. The specification of activities within each of the life phases is the result of complex interrelationships between biological and social factors, as we shall see in Chapter 8.

Most human activities are similarly associated with distinctive temporal cycles, so that they are ordinarily performed only by day or by night, on certain days of the week, during certain seasons of the year, or on specific dates like the Fourth of July. The calendar thus exerts considerable influence on the WHAT of interactions. In December one does not opt for baseball, and there is no Christmas caroling in July.

The WHERE

We have already hinted that the major constraint upon WHERE is based on the fact that different locales have come to be designated for and often expressly designed to facilitate particular kinds of activity (WHATS). Locales are thus limited to certain activities, just as certain activities are limited to certain locales. Beyond this functional specialization of areas, Erving Goffman has shown how geographical milieux are divided into "frontstage" and "backstage" regions, where characteristically different activities are carried out.[4]

The variations in WHERE is also curtailed by WHO. Many locales and many areas within locales are differentially accessible to different classes of people. Knowledge of locales is one source of constraint, but there are others, most notably differential access to areas in terms of race, sex, and social class.

The major constraint of WHEN upon the range of WHERES stems from the physical laws of the movement of bodies. Because we are subject to the laws of motion, even in this day of swift transportation, we must choose not the best of all possible locales but the best among the locales that can be reached with reasonable amounts of time and effort.

---

[4]Erving Goffman, *The Presentation of Self in Everyday Life*, Garden City, N.Y.: Doubleday Anchor, 1959, *passim*, especially pp. 106–141.

The WHEN

Perhaps the most important thing to be noted about the component WHEN is that it is a "scarce resource." Man's life span is relatively long and ever increasing, but, as a legion of poets has pointed out, it is also only a brief candle in comparison to the larger sweep of time. This limitation is one of the ties that bind us inexorably to the constraints of physics and biology.[5]

The WHEN of interaction is important in its own right, furthermore, as witnessed by the increasing importance of calendar and clock in today's industrializing societies. Accordingly, some social scientists have begun to emphasize the profound effect of temporal cycles—the seasons, the school year, holiday periods, and especially the day-night cycle—on the web of human behavior.[6] Certain places and people are accessible, and certain activities are possible, only at particular points in these cycles. Given knowledge of the WHO, the WHAT, or the WHERE, the range of possible WHENS is therefore considerably reduced. The same is true, of course, when dealing with longer spans of time in the context of historical configurations.

Multiple Specifications

We have seen that specifying the value of any one of the four components enables us to narrow the range of possible values of any of the other components. This effect is considerably more pronounced, the larger the number of components that are simultaneously specified, for the WHO and WHAT are distributed in space and time in highly distinctive patterns. If we can specify, for example, that a given person (a) had a haircut (b) yesterday (c) in Flatville, we can narrow the class of possible participants in this in-

---

[5]For studies of how persons allocate this scarce resource, see Alexander Szalai, editor, *The Use of Time,* The Hague: Mouton, 1973; and F. Stuart Chapin, Jr., *Human Activity Patterns in the City: Things People Do in Time and in Space,* New York: Wiley, 1974.

[6]See the excellent summary of this work in Wilbert E. Moore, *Man, Time and Society,* New York: Wiley, 1963. Also, George A. Theodorson, editor, *Studies in Human Ecology,* New York: Harper, 1961, *passim.*

teraction to our given person and those few people who were barbering in Flatville at that time—a finite and very small range indeed.

Each of the four ws is relevant to any concrete interaction, of course, and all four are involved, at least indirectly, in virtually all the scientific questions about identities and interactions that we shall explore in this book. We shall most often be asking about WHO or about WHAT, given some partial specification of two, or sometimes three, of the other components. At one point or another, however, we shall be concerned with almost every one of the possible twofold and threefold specifications.

With this multiple specification of components, one is able to eliminate the greater proportion of the possibilities in the unspecified component(s), owing to nothing more than the intrinsic interdependence of the four ws as we have sketched them. These possibilities can be still further limited, however, by taking into account extrinsic factors such as cultural, social, and personal barriers.

CULTURAL BOUNDARIES

The cultural patterns that we learn during socialization further restrict the content of identities and interactions. In the very process of providing rules and opportunities for winning prestige, getting food, and making love, the culture declares other criteria of worthiness, other food sources, and other love-making techniques out of bounds.

> The cultural pattern of any civilization makes use of a certain segment of the great arc of potential human purposes and motivations. . . . The great arc along which all the possible human behaviors are distributed is far too immense and too full of contradictions for any one culture to utilize even any considerable portion of it.[7]

If we represent by the letters *A* through *Z* all the items that might possibly serve as bases for establishing and ranking man-

[7]Ruth Benedict, *Patterns of Culture*, Boston: Houghton Mifflin, 1934, p. 237.

hood, that might provide sound nourishment, or that might be used as sexual outlets, we find that each particular society employs only a few and does not even regard many of the others as possible alternatives. For example, American nutrition books do not usually point out the quite high nutritional value of seaweed and lizard, nor do friends invite us to join them at the neighborhood restaurant for a bowl of fried worms. Variation within a society is not from A to Z but from A to E or even from A_1 to A_3.

Cultures are, of course, not all that simple or homogeneous. As Kluckhohn has pointed out, the best conceptual models of cultures can only state correctly the central tendencies of ranges of variation.[8] When we speak of the dominant patterns or themes in a particular society, we are employing distilled abstractions that may describe the public culture of ideals more than they describe what most members actually do.

Within every culture there are *preferred* WHOS, WHATS, WHENS, and WHERES, which are held up as models to be emulated. Beyond these models, there is a larger range of more or less *accepted* components that are accorded neither praise nor blame and that constitute the path usually followed by the majority of members. Shading off from these components are the interactions regarded as "deviant" and more or less actively *disapproved* by most members under most circumstances. And even beyond these deviant interactions, there are alternatives that are *unthinkable* to the members of that culture under ordinary, and most extraordinary, circumstances.

Even "simple" preliterate cultures thus turn out, upon closer inspection, to be far from monolithic. And when we turn to more "complex" societies, like modern industrial ones, our discussion is further complicated by the fact that there is usually a good deal of subcultural variation within each, by region, by ethnic background, by religious affiliation, by occupation, and so forth. In some ways these subcultures can be treated as miniature cultures in themselves, but in other important ways they cannot. For one

[8]Clyde Kluckhohn, "The Study of Culture," Chapter 5 in Daniel Lerner and Harold D. Lasswell, editors, *The Policy Sciences,* Stanford, Calif.: Stanford University Press, 1951.

thing, they are not so well insulated from one another as full-fledged cultures tend to be. For another, they are only "partial cultures" derived from larger total cultures and dependent upon the latter in a great many ways.

Surveys and public-opinion polls demonstrate that there is much difference of opinion, at least on many topics, in modern societies. These findings tend to refute the notion that culture is an overwhelming determinant of the content of identities and interactions and suggest that the force of cultural tradition is to some extent attenuated in such societies. That is, the values of our major variables cannot be very accurately explained or predicted from knowledge of an individual's nationality.

Yet even when internal differentiation and subcultural divergences are taken into account, we can see that the individual is recognizably and irrevocably a member of his society. The effects of socialization into his particular culture are so deep and long-lasting that he will never escape them. The *émigré* continues to think and swear in his native tongue, the Jewish apostate cannot cultivate a taste for pork, the Greenwich Village homosexual drives on the right-hand side of the street and takes Bayer aspirin, and the language of even a beatnik poet is unmistakably English.

What membership in a given culture does, then, is to limit the range of alternative WHOS, WHATS, WHENS, and WHERES. Individuals are free to develop many alternative styles of life within the broad purview of these cultural boundaries, but the boundaries can be transcended only partially and with difficulty.

SOCIAL BOUNDARIES

Each individual has a position or, more accurately, a number of positions in the social structure of his society. The importance of these positions is demonstrated by the fact that, aside from the characteristics of the individual who holds them, the positions themselves have vast influence upon whom he is likely to interact with, in what ways, when, and where.

For example, few college students have any rank-and-file dock workers among their acquaintances, few middle-aged laborers are well traveled in management circles, and most Protestants are not very conversant with the Jewish life style. As a more stark example, simply being a Negro in America entails an average loss of more than a hundred thousand dollars in total earnings and about seven years of life, in comparison with the white population.

Our set of positions makes up the sphere or "world" within which we move and live and from which most of us stray only seldom and temporarily. This world that each of us inhabits is, of course, only a segment or province of the total social structure. Whereas being an American places only very wide limits upon the individual, being (for example) a Connecticut exurbanite who works in advertising or a Mexican-American garage mechanic in Texas determines to a much greater extent the content of the individual's self-conceptions and the contours of his interactions with others.

An important feature of social boundaries is that they face in two directions: Not only do they prevent us and those very much like us from moving out of our social spheres to interaction possibilities beyond, but they also prevent many categories of dissimilar people from entering the sphere we inhabit.[9] Consequently, by virtue of our positions in the social structure, we are thrown together willy-nilly with just those persons who are similarly situated. However they may feel toward one another on individual grounds, men stranded together on a raft—or on a college faculty—are nevertheless going to interact with one another. In fact, it may be more accurate to say that we come to like some of those with whom we are thrown together than to say simply that we interact with those we like.[10]

Such more or less ascribed statuses as sex, age, race, and region of origin, as well as the more or less "achieved" statuses like occupational position, residence area, religion, and so forth, thus throw us together with a similarly positioned subgroup from which

[9]E.g., Gerald D. Suttles, *The Social Order of the Slum*, Chicago: University of Chicago Press, 1968.

[10]George C. Homans, *The Human Group*, New York: Harcourt, 1950, pp. 110–113.

we usually draw our friends, acquaintances, spouses, and even our personal enemies. Viewed through time with an eye toward social mobility, this subgroup might be said to be composed of fellow travelers, and, even in a society characterized by high mobility rates, most individuals do not wander far from the "channels" their overall positions engender.

We must make several qualifications to this discussion, or our characterization of the social boundaries will be too simply mechanistic. In the first place, most boundaries are differentially permeable, depending on which side one is coming from. For example, upper-class people can make sexual forays into lower-class territories far more easily than lower-class people can invade their territories. Adults can impinge upon children to greater degrees than children can invade the adult world. Whenever there is a power differential, the more favored group generally has more freedom to cross barriers than has the less favored, although its penetration tends to be superficial.

Second, people often do not regard social boundaries as constraints but are thankful that they exist, for, in many cases, we do not care to have anything to do with certain people, at least in connection with certain acts. That is, in many cases, people think of social barriers as means of keeping others out and never even consider the fact that they themselves are thereby kept in.

Finally, it should be noted that there is a certain amount of self-recruitment into social positions and, thereby, into the confines established by the social boundaries that surround such positions. The channel that runs within such barriers is thus often part of the "life package" we aspire to and strive for. This point probably holds true primarily for the more favorable positions and perhaps not at all for the least privileged ones. But it must be remembered that such channels are not simply ranked on a vertical scale of favorability; each social stratum is composed of many different but relatively equal positions, and many of the social "worlds" cut across large segments of the stratification system.

As we have hinted, social boundaries affect not only WHO we are likely to interact with; they also constrain WHAT we can do. Position in the stratification system, for example, exerts considerable influence on one's life chances and privileges.[11] Lower-class children are unlikely to become violin virtuosos, fly their own private planes, or journey up the Amazon in search of rare ornithological specimens. The sword cuts both ways, however, for certain activities open to the humblest citizen, like a lonely walk on a star-filled night, are denied to the President of the United States.

The demands of such more differentiated positions as jobs and family roles actually prescribe in rough outline many of the activities we must engage in. Conversely, the demands of these positions often prevent us from doing other things that we, as individuals, might desire to do, if for no other reason than that these demands consume most of our time and energies. Furthermore, there is a range of activities that are regarded as "unbecoming" to each position in the social structure. Social opinion on whether particular activities are acceptable or unacceptable is, in the majority of cases, not free-floating judgment but is related to the social positions of the individuals involved.

Social structural factors similarly affect the WHEN and WHERE of interactions. For example, occupational positions force some people into night work or extensive travel, and these people find that much of the ordinary social world is thereby denied them, simply because they are on completely different schedules or are too much on the move to establish social connections outside their occupational communities, the members of which all share the same constraints. These people—railroaders, entertainers, newspapermen —are thus forced to create their own worlds of valued outlets.[12]

Put simply, many of the things one can and cannot do are strictly determined by one's positions in the social structure alone, and the *probability* of doing still other things is also greatly affected. Although several of the most important social structural boundaries (for example, age, sex, race, and class origin) have some con-

[11]See the summary table in Leonard Broom and Philip Selznick, *Sociology* (6th ed.), New York: Harper, 1977, pp. 170–171, for a representative set of findings.

[12]See, for example, W. Fred Cottrell, "Of Time and the Railroader," *American Sociological Review*, 1939, 4: 190–198; and Howard S. Becker, *Outsiders*, New York: Free Press, 1963, pp. 79–119.

nection with biological attributes, they nevertheless must be considered social structural in that societal definitions largely determine what it means to be a woman or a youth or a Negro. The acid test for the existence and influence of social structural boundaries is, What do we know about the individual merely by knowing his positions—without reference to any of his personal characteristics? In most cases, we know a great deal, as we have seen. Again, however, these positions only affect the *range of alternative* WHOS, WHATS, WHENS, and WHERES and leave much still to be explained.

Position in the social structure also influences the amount, kinds, and variety of interactions a person has. Research on social contacts has shown that occupation is the primary determinant in this respect, although social status, marital status, and residence are also important factors.[13] These findings underline the importance of institutional ties in human interaction: the difficulty of meeting anyone without them or of maintaining many kinds of relationships without their support. During some phases of the life cycle, these institutional ties—those of family, school, work, or church, for example—may constitute virtually the entire opportunity structure for many people. The very young, the prisoner, the mental patient are all virtually dependent upon such institutional ties for what limited interaction they may share.

These ties derive much of their importance from the operation of still another set of boundaries upon interaction possibilities, the societal codes that restrict the initiation of interaction with persons one might simply chance to encounter. These codes, partially explored by Erving Goffman,[14] rigidly specify the kinds and degrees of permissible interaction among strangers of this sort, as well as the circumstances under which interaction can be initiated (for example, formal introduction).

From these considerations, it should be abundantly clear that the social order of a society imposes quite stringent bounds upon

[13]Albert J. Reiss, Jr., "Rural-Urban and Status Differences in Interpersonal Contacts," *American Journal of Sociology*, 1959, 65: 182–195.

[14]Goffman, *Behavior in Public Places*, New York: Free Press, 1963; Goffman, *Relations in Public*, New York: Basic Books, 1971; and Lyn Lofland, *A World of Strangers*, New York: Basic Books, 1973.

the interaction possibilities within its culture. One further set of boundaries must be superimposed upon those of the society and the culture: those stemming from the natures of the persons themselves.

PERSONAL BOUNDARIES

The statement that "all men are created equal" is, of course, a legal and moral ideal, rather than a valid description of the population of any society. A walk through the streets will show that people differ markedly in body build, physical appearance, coordination, and agility. Observation of any group of children at play will demonstrate that people differ tremendously in "basic personality structure," intelligence, creativity, and mode of handling interpersonal situations. Examination of any attitude survey or set of interviews will show that people vary almost endlessly in their life histories and configurations of beliefs and values. Even at the organic level, physiologists have discovered a wide range of variations in sensory acuity, location of nerve endings, hormone functionings, and blood chemistry, all of which may directly and indirectly affect self-conceptions and interactions with others.[15]

Many of the fundamental factors that shape the WHOS, WHATS, WHENS, and WHERES of an individual's interactions come into play before he is even born. The first set of these factors includes those that determine which two people are involved in his conception. Because mating is virtually never random, the social forces that determine who becomes pregnant by whom largely determine the individual's biologically inherited characteristics.

But aside from biological inheritance, much of the individual's life is determined by the social positions of his mother and father and the social relationship between them. That is, many facts of an individual's life course are determined by the family into which he is born. In societies with caste systems or with clearly developed and segregated classes, an individual's subsequent life may be determined to an extent that Western man, with his high valuation of freedom and individuality, finds quite disturbing.

[15]Anne Anastasi, *Differential Psychology,* New York: Macmillan, 1958; and Roger J. Williams, *Biochemical Individuality,* New York: Wiley, 1956.

Beyond the biological inheritance from parents and the, at first passive, sharing of their social positions, the fledgling individual falls heir to the influence of prenatal factors and to the internal character of the family he joins.

The effects of the prenatal phase are still largely unknown, but the first glimmerings of evidence suggest that, while the infant is still nestled within the body of its mother, many different life possibilities are heightened, impeded, and entirely ruled out. Such far-reaching characteristics as sex and "race" have already been fixed at conception, and to some extent level of native mental ability, bodily characteristics, and basic character predispositions are cast between conception and birth, at least for many individuals.[16] Not inexorably, of course, for all these attributes, even sex and race, are subject to the possibility of some modification. But in most cases such modifications are spectacular exceptions, which find their way into the newspapers rather than into most people's lives.

At the time of birth, then, many things have already been resolved for the individual; the count of his resources and the broad outlines of his opportunity structure have already been settled to some extent. It is difficult for a good Lutheran who likes roast beef and slim blondes to believe that, except for an "accident" of birthplace, he would have been a good Mohammedan who liked slightly rotted camel and obese brunettes, but it is nonetheless true.

The infant tumbles into a ready-made world, and he is molded by it to a far greater extent than he molds it. A selected and modified portion of the total dominant cultural pattern (or dominant subcultural pattern in the case of complex societies) continues to echo throughout the course of his life. Which part of the total culture he is taught depends largely upon the positions in that culture occupied by his parents.

There are two factors, however, that tend to prevent the infant from becoming completely a product of his culture. In the first place, his family, which usually has the major share in socializing him into his culture, is often far from a passive agent or mere

[16]Ashley Montagu, *Prenatal Influences*, Springfield, Ill.: Thomas, 1962.

"gatekeeper" in this process. The family selects, adapts, modifies, and interprets those aspects of the culture or subculture it is aware of and concerned with. Bottle-fed babies, for example, are not necessarily all presented with similar feeding experiences, for the manner in which the bottle is administered to a baby—lovingly, perfunctorally, or even spitefully—is as much a part of his experience as is the mere fact of bottle-feeding itself. Beyond this level, each family develops a somewhat unique elaboration of the overarching cultural patterns, which further colors the fledgling individual's world view and opportunity structure. In this sense, every family is a tiny subculture in itself, which develops its own norms, traditions, and group life in addition and sometimes in partial opposition to the cultural patterns.

The second factor that prevents complete or automatic inculcation of the culture is that the fledgling person, even from birth, is not an altogether passive recipient of the socialization attempts of his elders—of the messages sent him. Innate response predispositions and the individual variations in them are still largely uncharted, but anyone who has nurtured infants knows that differences in predisposition to act and react do exist and are almost impossible to obliterate.[17]

The importance of all such individual differences is that the opportunity structures are, in effect, different for different people. These personal differences thus engender different boundaries to interaction possibilities. Having a body that does not easily assimilate fat molecules, a facial structure that is out of style, or excellent coordination may have tremendous and life-long influence upon identities and interactions.

HISTORICAL PERSPECTIVE[18]

A comparison of contemporary world conditions with those of earlier historical periods suggests that one of the major historical

---

[17]Arnold H. Buss and Robert Plomin, *A Temperament Theory of Personality*, New York: Wiley, 1975.

[18]The following remarks are drawn extensively from William McNeill, *The Rise of the West*, Chicago: University of Chicago Press, 1963.

trends is the progressive attenuation of the boundaries we have discussed in this chapter, giving rise to widened opportunities. Scientific advances and mass production and mass consumption, stemming from the Industrial Revolution, have led to continuing increases in the ease of mobility and have made such increased mobility possible for an increasing proportion of the population. The proliferation of alternative opportunities has given more individuals more freedom to choose spouses, careers, places of residence, leisure activities, and goods. Rapid social change and the conditions of urbanism seem to have resulted in greater self-determination in the societal positions one achieves. And the fading of provincialism and traditionalism, along with the proliferation of subcultural variations, has given the individual more alternatives (and ambiguities) in role models and values.

From all evidence it appears that these boundaries to interactions have been much more stringent throughout the previous epochs of human history than they are in most current societies. One's choices were often few and highly circumscribed in major life decisions and in smaller daily activities. But we must be wary of overestimating the constraint of such parameters in former ages and of underestimating their operation in the most mobile of modern societies.

The history of almost every culture is replete with examples of physical and social mobility of individuals and of whole groups. Travel throughout the length and breadth of the Eurasian ecumene, for example, was not uncommon through many centuries of the past two millennia. The circulation of elites and other groups has been fairly common, and a fair proportion of such historical figures as Confucius, Genghis Khan, and Harmhab has risen from obscurity or even slavery. And the Viking penetrations of the North American continent, the coasts of Africa, and the Asian steppes were perhaps greater voyages than our own recent journeys to the moon in all respects except technical requirements and the mere count of miles. Such examples were exceptions perhaps to the highly bounded existences of most people in former times, but they were not infrequent exceptions.

Over the span of a few years, most cultures—even modern ones—present images of stability and integration, but from the only slightly longer perspective of a generation the sense of order is replaced by a sense that change is the common fact of human life. Because historical analyses and anthropological reports usually describe central tendencies and, almost of necessity, underplay the degrees of variation, we tend to exaggerate the monolithic natures of other times and other cultures. This exaggeration may lead us to assume that others have been far more bound by the chains of tradition and the sacred cows of their cultures than they actually were. And the almost inevitable ethnocentrism of one's historical perspective tends to engender in each population the sense that its society is riding the crest of historical development, a bias not confined to laymen.[19] But, as Raymond Aron and others have pointed out, such conclusions are interpretations imposed upon history rather than generalizations of the facts of history.[20] It may well be that boundaries were less formidable obstacles to building a meaningful and enjoyable life in Gupta India or the Neolithic farming communities than they are in contemporary America.

The comparison of the current historical period with previous ones would suggest that boundaries have changed more in their nature than in their extent. As the sheer physical constraints of time and distance have faded somewhat, equally constraining social factors like knowledge, differential association, and subcultural standards have come into greater play, not because their force has increased, but simply because the force of physical factors has lessened. These social factors have, of course, always existed throughout history, just as ecological factors are still very much present and in force today. But the relative influence of the two sets of factors seems to have shifted.

In summary, there has probably been a net increase in the breadth of most people's opportunity structures. There has certainly been a great lessening of physical constraints, although the

---

[19] As a recent notable example, Parsons takes a position that strongly implies that contemporary America is the best of all empirical worlds in Talcott Parsons, "Evolutionary Universals in Society," *American Sociological Review,* 1964, 29: 339–357.

[20] Raymond Aron, "Evidence and Inference in History" in Lerner, editor, *Evidence and Inference,* New York: Free Press, 1958, pp. 19–48.

continuing strength and somewhat similar effects of social constraints have meant that the total lessening of the boundaries has not been so great.

Nor are those boundaries likely to disappear in any conceivable future epoch or society. The extent of physical mobility will almost certainly continue to increase, and a larger and larger proportion of the total human population will probably be involved in it. The time and the resources available to individuals will also probably continue to increase. But these trends may mean only that knowledge, familiarity, value consensus and need complementarity, social barriers, and force of personal habit will come to have ever-larger shares of influence. Most individuals will continue primarily to inhabit neighborhoods, not Chicago or London or New York, and so forth. Most people will continue to accumulate their life experiences within the confines of a few overlapping subcultures, rather than those of America, Lebanon, or the world community. Most travelers abroad will probably continue to travel within a highly circumscribed circuit of accommodations expressly tailored to make them feel "at home," and the bulk of their interactions will continue to be with fellow travelers.

And if we reach the other planets and establish colonies there, Coca-Cola (or vodka) will no doubt be among the first imports.

BOUNDARIES AND
THE HUMAN ACTOR

As stated previously, our task in this book is to develop a theoretical framework in terms of which we can explain, for a given person or persons, WHO come together to engage in WHAT social acts WHEN and WHERE. So far in this chapter we have examined certain general factors that serve to simplify this task somewhat by ruling out vast numbers of conceivable interaction alternatives that are empirically impossible or entirely improbable. The interaction alternatives remaining are proportionally very few, but in terms of absolute numbers they are very numerous indeed. These alternatives constitute the very "social universe," the *interaction-op-*

Cloward + Ohlin

portunity structure, [21] for the person(s) in question; we have so far delimited only the field over which our theory must operate. How will the individual(s) distribute his life resources among these remaining alternatives?

This question is of a different order, requiring a different order of variable to frame an adequate answer. We must consider characteristics of the individual: his *knowledge* of the interaction-opportunity structure, the life resources at his disposal, and, most important, his desires, ambitions, and fears. None of these factors is a constant characteristic of the individual, but in fact all change continually as he picks his way through the jungle of interaction alternatives. They do not change randomly, however, and we shall attempt to depict these changes and their effects on the individual's interaction choices by means of the role-identity model of his self-organization.

As we shift now to the point of view of the human actor, some qualifications must be made to our discussion of the various boundaries on interaction possibilities. [22]

First of all, we have seen that most of the boundaries we have discussed are not absolute or impenetrable. Because in most cases the boundaries *impede* rather than totally prevent the individual from "crossing" them, the largest proportion of conceivable interactions is rendered highly improbable rather than impossible. As he contemplates his lot, the individual will, in many circumstances, correctly judge that he could overcome the barriers against any particular interaction. He could deliberately seek to *change* his social positions, to internalize a new culture, or to overcome a personal deficiency of some sort. And indeed, he may in fact do just that, thereby confirming the need for a social psychological, as well as a purely sociological, approach to the problem of the four ws. Much more often, however, he will conclude that the

[21]The concept of opportunity structure has been applied most extensively to the area of delinquency and deviance; see Richard W. Cloward and Lloyd E. Ohlin, *Delinquency and Opportunity,* New York: Free Press, 1960.

[22]*Cf.* Geoffrey Hutton, "Assertions, Barriers and Objects: A Conceptual Scheme for the Personal Implications of Environmental Texture," *Journal for the Theory of Social Behavior,* 1972, 2: 83–98.

effort that such an attempt to change would entail and the uncertainties of commensurate reward would make the cost of the attempt prohibitive. And in making this judgment, the individual gives mute testimony to the fact that the boundaries do exist.

Second, it should be noted that these limitations upon the logically conceivable alternatives may constitute no problem at all from the subjective point of view of the individual, for the reason that he is most preoccupied with making his way among the *perceived opportunities* at hand. Often he is not even aware that his alternatives have been so limited, and consequently he feels no deprivation. In fact, he usually defines his lot positively, in terms of the opportunities it *provides*, rather than negatively, in terms of the opportunities it precludes.

This fact points up the importance of knowing not only the individual's objective situation but also the range of alternatives he is aware of. If he becomes aware of a wider range of possibilities while the boundaries continue to restrain him from realizing them, his knowledge may create discontent and restlessness: the phenomenon of "relative deprivation."[23]

Even if he is not thus made aware, however, and remains concerned primarily with those alternatives he perceives, the individual may nonetheless feel a vague dissatisfaction with the way things are, simply because his ability to manipulate symbols enables him to imagine a course of affairs more pleasing and satisfying. If these points are granted, it follows that a sense of deprivation is always at least a potential reaction when one contemplates his lot and that we live in the margin between our existence and our daydreams.

[23]Perhaps the most extensive discussion of relative deprivation within the context of reference groups remains Robert K. Merton, *Social Theory and Social Structure* (rev. ed.), New York: Free Press, 1957, pp. 225–387. For a more provocative discussion, see Peter Blau, *Exchange and Power in Social Life,* New York: Wiley, 1964, especially Chapter 6 ("Expectations") pp. 147–167.

Chapter 3

THE PHILOSOPHY
OF
CONDUCT

Our statements so far about the phenomena with which we are basically concerned—the WHO, WHAT, WHEN, and WHERE of human interaction—may strike the reader as too mechanistic to warrant our claim of descent from the fathers of symbolic interactionism. That school of thought is famous for its use of somewhat "idealistic" concepts (philosophically speaking) like human nature, the looking-glass self, significant symbols, empathy, and the theorem that "if men define situations as real, they are real in their consequences."

It is our intent to make use of these well-known and idealistic concepts in attempting to explain empirical patterns of the rather mechanistic dependent variables with which we are concerned. We feel no particular discomfort in having thus divided our allegiances between the diverse philosophies of mechanism and idealism, for it is precisely this divided allegiance that highlights our underlying imagery of man's nature, his predicament, and his fate.

We believe that perhaps the most important thing about man's situation is that he lives simultaneously in two very different "worlds." In the first place, man is a mammal, of quite ordinary properties, and is subject to all the blind determinisms of his anatomy, chemistry, and physiology—the heritage of eons of mammalian selection and evolution. He must ingest nutrient substances and evacuate waste products; he must sleep; he must maintain a specified range of body temperature and blood pressure. Like every other animal, he is subject to the ups and downs of his hormones and neurohumors—he is subject to all the animal lusts and fears that are concomitants of mammalian machinery.

Yet, at the same time, man lives in a symbolic universe not unlike Plato's realm of ideals. There man is a conscious, self-conscious, reasoning being—a creature of ideas, evaluations, and volition. His actions are the result not of blind causal forces but of his own considered and willed choices. Consequently, he is a creature of responsibility, pride, and dignity, which in turn implies that he is also a creature of guilt, shame, and humiliation.

In fact, man finds this very situation of having to live simultaneously in two such disparate "worlds" most embarrassing in itself. Therefore he struggles mightily to free himself from the fate of his fellow animals, to live solely in the world of ideas. He finds it most inconvenient that his noblest actions need be interrupted to satisfy such elemental animal urges as evacuation. He finds it rather embarrasing that he can discover no other way to reproduce himself than by the grotesque posturing of copulation. He finds it terrifying that his existence in the world of ideas is unconditionally dependent upon his continued existence and functioning in the animal world. The prospect of decline, death, and decay is a most cruel one to a being who aspires to live in a timeless world of ideals.

The strategy that man has typically adopted to deal with this embarrassing animal existence is to ignore it as far as possible, to blind himself to the facts until they force themselves upon him at irregular intervals. We all try to restrict our attention to those aspects of our lives that are consonant with our view of ourselves as gentlemen and ladies who regulate their conduct in accordance with the very highest moral, legal, and spiritual codes, not as animals. We pursue one another in the manners prescribed by these codes, scoring points—hopefully enough to make it into heaven as well as to succeed on earth. Pursuing one another in these moral and social games, we scarcely notice (except in rare moments of jaundiced reflection) that the conventional goals of these games turn out to involve the very animal directions we had hoped to escape—alimentary engorgement, genital friction, mild toxic delirium, and all the rest.

But, *as* men, social theorists must take man as man is. Our task must be to grapple with the fact of man's double existence, to try to describe and explain the peculiar relationship between his two "worlds." As men, we can hardly hope to escape man's proclivity to emphasize the degree to which he lives in the world of ideals; if we exaggerate this degree, it is because we too are subject to all the frailties and blindnesses of our peculiar species.

Still, we should try to remember the considerable extent to which man's actions are the results of forces other than conscious, reasoned choices based on ideal considerations. Despite all a person's thinking and pondering, he is constantly doing things of which he is only partially aware and doing them for reasons still more obscure to him. These kinds of action he is always having to legitimate after the fact, having to interpret in some fashion to make them consonant with the various ideal codes and prescriptions that have dominion over him. At all costs, as we shall see, he must preserve his picture of himself as an ideal being. Among these costs are those of selective attention and inattention, of rationalization and projection, of ambivalence, alienation, and mistrust, of conscience and guilt.

Man is, then, a brooding animal, concerned about his past actions and looking forward to the future with mingled hopes and fears. Anxiety and ambivalence are for him a way of life. Acting always on inadequate and biased information, man makes his crucial life choices and allocates his very limited resources. His most vital choices must, perforce, be made almost completely in the dark. He must choose today, knowing but little of the alternatives or the consequences of his choice. This discomfiting fact lies at the base of tragedy and of comedy. Man does his best to grapple with this truth and spends an amazing amount of time constructing alternative lives from which to choose at any point, although his subjective sense of freedom to choose among them is often unrealistic and illusory.

Although man is an introspective creature, he is not solitary. It would be easier for him, as an ideal being, if he were. For it is perhaps not so hard to legitimate our actions to ourselves, from our own egocentric perspectives, but our fellows remain harsh judges. They are not so easily taken in by our alibis, our yarns and tall tales. They shake us out of our reveries and demand that we convince them that we are indeed what we claim to be, that things are indeed as we seem to think they are. If we are to maintain our shaky hold on our ideals, we are forced to become rhetoricians—experts in forensic disputation. We must persuade others, *as well as ourselves,* that things are indeed as we construe them.

Reality, then, in this distinctively human world, is not a hard, immutable thing but is fragile and adjudicated—a thing to be debated, compromised, and legislated.[1] Those who most succeed in this world are those who are most persuasive and effective in having their interpretations ratified as true reality. Those who do not are relegated to the fringes of the human world, are executed as heretics or traitors, ridiculed as crackpots, or locked up as lunatics. The vast majority of us occupies the middle ground on most issues of social reality, climbing aboard the bandwagons of the leading "parties," voting for the incumbents, so to speak. Consequently, for we who are passively oriented, reality seems given, in the nature of things. It is only when confronted with inescapable conflict that most of us come to question the accepted order of things. In other times, we fail to see all the little interstices of arbitrariness and ambiguity that could be seized upon to legislate reality *in our own favor.*[2]

It is precisely this flexibility of the ideal realm that makes man—for all his animal weakness, ignorance, self-pity, ambivalence, and arbitrariness—a heroic figure fit to play the leading role in the drama of human life. Like the gods, he creates and shatters whole worlds. He decrees new spiritual codes of the highest order, creates out of nothingness and chaos new orders of men. Out of lusts he creates passions and noble strivings; out of discomforts he

[1]We are speaking now, it must be emphasized, of symbolic, *social* reality only; in no way are we adopting any sort of skeptical or solipsistic view of metaphysical reality. The precise nature of our claims concerning the distinctive social reality is considerably elaborated on pp. 48–50, which discussion should help to clarify the respective roles of such adjudication and reality-testing. See also Peter L. Berger and Thomas Luckman, *The Social Construction of Reality,* Garden City, N.Y.: Doubleday, 1966; Stanford M. Lyman and Marvin B. Scott, *The Drama of Social Reality,* New York: Oxford University Press, 1975; and Harvey A. Farberman and Erich Goode, editors, *Social Reality,* Englewood Cliffs, N.J.: Prentice-Hall, 1973. The references cited in the Preface, footnote 14, might also be consulted.

[2]Berger and Luckman, *op. cit.*

creates agonies and degradations. Out of animal existence on earth he creates both heaven and hell and strives to lift himself bodily, by his bootstraps, out of the "hell" of animal existence into the "heaven" of his ideal realm.

> The lower animals have neither words nor symbols; nothing, for them, has what we may describe as meaning. The lower animals have, in the words of Durkheim, no "collective representations." They do not organize processions and carry banners; they sing, and sometimes, we are told, even dance, but they do not celebrate; they acquire habits which are sometimes transmitted as a kind of social tradition, but they have no customs, and for them nothing is either sacred or lawful. Above all, the animals are natural and naive, and not concerned, as human beings are, about their reputations and their conduct.[3]

As Walt Whitman put it, in his poem, "Song of Myself,"

> They do not sweat and whine about their condition;
> They do not lie awake at night and weep for their sins;
> They do not make me sick discussing their duty to God;
> Not one is dissatisfied—not one is demented with the mania
>   of owning things;
> Not one kneels to another, nor to his kind that lived
>   thousands of years ago;
> Not one is responsible, or industrious over the whole earth.[4]

Whitman, of course, is *praising* animals for being so "placid and self-contained" and fain would go live with them, whereas

[3]Robert E. Park, "Human Nature and Collective Behavior," *American Journal of Sociology,* 1927, 32: 737. These remarks apply to the overwhelming majority of the animal kingdom. In recent years, however, a very few of the highest species, like wolves, apes, and dolphins, have been found to possess rudimentary selves and communicative signs that border on being true symbols. See, for example, A. Irving Hallowell, "Behavioral Evolution and the Emergence of the Self," in Sol Tax, editor, *Evolution After Darwin,* Chicago: University of Chicago Press, 1960, pp. 309–371; Edward O. Wilson, *Sociobiology,* Cambridge: Harvard University Press, 1975; William Etkin, editor, *Social Behavior and Organization Among Vertebrates,* Chicago: University of Chicago Press, 1964; Donald R. Griffin, *The Question of Animal Awareness,* New York: Rockefeller University Press, 1976; Thomas A. Sebeok, editor, *Animal Communication,* Bloomington: Indiana University Press, 1968; and Eugene Linden, *Apes, Men, and Language,* New York: Dutton, 1974.

[4]Walt Whitman, "Song of Myself," Section 32, lines 2–8, *Leaves of Grass,* Philadelphia: McKay, 1900.

the sociologist Park (in the preceding selection) is trying to emphasize that it is *just* the symbolic ability of human beings that leads them to agonize over their reputations and their souls that is also the basis for the mode of social organization that has set man so far above the animals in the evolutionary scheme. Symbols, language, and the role-taking ability that these imply transform man's behaviors into an entirely different level of behavior, which we regard as the special *province* of social psychology, that is, *conduct*.

> One consequence of the fact that man is (a symbolic), political animal is that human behavior is fundamentally neither reflexive, instinctive, nor even habitudinal merely, but conventional and rational, that is to say governed by rules, codes, and institutions; controlled by fashion, etiquette, and public opinion. Thus man turns out to be a sophisticated animal, keenly conscious of himself, knowing good and evil, calculating and casuistic, concerned at once about his reputation and his soul. Behavior of this sort is what we ordinarily call conduct, when that word is given an ethical connotation. *Conduct is that form of behavior we expect in man when he is conscious of the comment that other men are making, or are likely to make, upon his actions.* Conduct, in short, is behavior that is sophisticated.[5]
>
> In human society every act of every individual tends to become a gesture, since what one does is always an indication of what one intends to do. The consequence is that the individual in society lives a more or less public existence, in which all his acts are anticipated, checked, inhibited, or modified by the gestures and the intentions of his fellows. It is in this social conflict, in which every individual lives more or less in the mind of every other individual, that human nature and the individual may acquire their most characteristic and human traits.[6]

In these terms, our enterprise in this volume is twofold: (1) to elaborate a theory of human conduct (the role-identity model mentioned earlier) and (2) to explain the WHO, WHAT, WHEN, and

---

[5]Park, "Human Nature, Attitudes, and Mores," in Kimball Young, editor, *Social Attitudes,* New York: Holt, 1931, p. 36. Italics added.

[6]Park, "Human Nature and Collective Behavior," *op. cit.,* p. 738. For an analysis of these distinctive features of human conduct in terms of identity negotiation, see Michael Oakshott, *On Human Conduct,* Oxford: Clarendon, 1975.

WHERE of social interaction in terms of this characteristic "social conflict" in which all a person's acts are "anticipated, checked, inhibited, or modified by the gestures and intentions of his fellows."

SOME PRELIMINARY CONCEPTS

To do so, however, will require some brief discussion of certain key concepts upon which we can begin to build our theory in the following chapters. These include (1) the concept of interaction itself, (2) the intertwined concepts of social act and social object, (3) the concept of the self, and (4) the dramaturgical perspective.

Interaction

For most students, one of the greatest obstacles to achieving a thorough grasp of social psychological theories is learning to think in terms of interaction, a concept that seems foreign to ordinary ways of thinking. Perhaps the best way to approach this troublesome idea is to consider why it has this reputation.

One of the prime aims of science is to explain and control phenomena of the empirical world. The best means we have of attaining this goal is the discovery of *causal laws*. Ideally, scientists would like to discover a single, reasonably small set of causal laws that would allow us to explain and control everything we are interested in.

What is a causal law? Let us begin with an example or two. If we are interested in explaining and controlling certain characteristics of electric currents, we are happy to discover that, if an electromotive force is applied to the ends of any piece of metal (of constant resistance), an electric current will be generated in that piece of metal proportional to the magnitude of that electromotive force (Ohm's Law).

Or if we are interested in the characteristics of moving bodies, like a billiard ball, we are delighted to learn that, if a force is suddenly applied to it, the ball will move in exactly the manner described by one of Newton's laws: If force is applied to a body, it produces a change in the momentum of that body directly proportional to that force.

In general, we should like to discover more such laws which take the form: Every event of a certain class C produces an event of the class E. Note the characteristics of the connection imputed between events of this sort: (1) uniqueness of connection, (2) invariability of connection, (3) productivity, and—most important to our present concerns—(4) a one-sided dependence of the effect upon the cause.

One does not have to be in science very long to discover that this type of law is the exception rather than the rule. There are many kinds of scientific, deterministic law other than causal laws.

For instance, to name a few, there are laws of (1) quantitative self-determination, (2) mechanical determination, (3) structural determination, (4) statistical determination, (5) teleological determination, and (6) interaction. It is not our interest here to explain each of these types of law and their roles in science, for this book is not a treatise on the philosophy of science. Nevertheless, we must make clear what *interaction* is and how it differs from the classical notions of causality.[7]

To begin, let us take a familiar physical example, the law of gravity. We have all learned that the earth attracts the moon, and those of us who have seen tides on the ocean may know that the moon also exerts attraction on the earth. Each physical body generates a gravitational field in relation to every other body in the universe, affecting the momentum of each of those bodies. Newton's law of universal attraction says that

$$F = G\,\frac{m_1 m_2}{r^2}$$

that the force of attraction between two bodies equals some constant times the ratio of the product of the masses of those bodies to the square of the distance between them.

[7]For an excellent discussion of the various types of determinism, see Mario Bunge, *Causality*, New York: Meridian, 1963, especially pp. 18–21, 148–164, on which much of the present discussion of interaction is based.

Is the mass of body 1 the cause of the acceleration of body 2, or is the mass of body 2 the cause of the acceleration of body 1? The question is clearly absurd, for Newton's law says that there is only *one* force and that it is a joint function of *both* bodies. Attraction is a reciprocal or mutual kind of influence. There is not a one-sided dependence of effect upon cause but a two-sided dependence—an *inter*dependence—between two events. From one side of this dependence, event *A* is cause and event *B* effect, but, from the other side of the dependence, event *B* is cause and event *A* effect.

Whenever a relationship of deterministic influence between two events cannot be resolved into a simple function of one but instead must be treated as a *joint* function, as a mutual or reciprocal influence, we have a case of interaction.[8]

One can see, then, why in physics causal laws are preferred to interaction laws and why causal laws are easier to grasp. We have a long cultural heritage concerning causation, making it seem more intuitive to us than does interaction.

Similarly in human affairs we have a long cultural tradition that predisposes us to think in terms of causation rather than of interaction. Our systems of morals, ethics, and law, from the times of the Jews, Greeks, and Romans, have been predicated on a sort of simple, causal type of psychology. Western culture has viewed man as an individual, self-determining psyche, which (for good or evil) causes the body in which it resides to carry out certain actions. Each person, as an independent agent, must therefore be respon-

---

[8]For those readers with backgrounds in statistics, interaction may be profitably viewed in the same way that the term is used in experimental design. Interaction is said to have taken place if two (or more) independent variables produce results that cannot be ascribed simply to the effects of either of them *or* to the effects of their simple additive coaction. See, for example, the discussion in Hubert M. Blalock, Jr., *Social Statistics,* New York: McGraw-Hill, 1960, pp. 256–257. The topic receives more important treatment in Blalock, "Theory Building and the Statistical Concept of Interaction," *American Sociological Review,* 1965, 30: 374–380. Also of some interest is Guy E. Swanson, "On Explanations of Social Interaction," *Sociometry,* 1965, 28: 101–123, to be compared with the classic definitions of interaction in Chapter 6 of Park and Ernest W. Burgess, *Introduction to the Science of Sociology* (2nd. ed.), Chicago: University of Chicago Press, 1924.

sible for the actions of the body he controls. From our earliest years, this picture has been drummed into our heads until it is second nature to us. But, just as a simple causal picture of physical reality does not begin to cover the facts, this simple causal picture of man does not cover the facts. Other types of determinism are operating in the social world, one of the most important of which is interaction.

What are some examples of social interaction? A conversation, a knife fight, a chess game, love-making. None of these things can be done by one. It takes two to tango, just as it takes two bodies to produce gravitational attraction or two electrons to produce electrostatic repulsion. None of these things can be viewed simply as a result of two independent units simultaneously unwinding their self-determined lines of action. The action of one unit is dependent upon the action of the other, *and vice versa.* One person shoving pieces over a chessboard plus another person shoving pieces a chessboard does not constitute a chess game. Unless the shoves of one person are made in a specific fashion, dependent upon the actions of the other, and vice versa, there is only piece-shoving, not chess. There must be mutual influence, not mere additive concatenation.

Surely the most beautiful statement of these notions is contained in a little sonnet by the great German poet Hugo von Hofmannsthal:

The Two

Her hand a goblet bore for him—
Her chin and mouth curved like its rim—
So gentle and so sure her tread,
No drop was from the goblet shed.
So gentle and so firm his hand:
A tameless steed allured his daring
And with a gesture swift, uncaring
He forced its trembling form to stand.

But when at last from her pale hand
He was to take the cup of gold,
Too heavy for them both it was:
For they so trembled like the grass,

That neither hand the other found
And on the ground the dark wine rolled.[9]

Hofmannsthal is trying to show that each of the two people is, as an independent agent, characteristically sure, confident, and controlled in his actions but that, when their respective lines of action *cross*, a reciprocal influence is set up that modifies these characteristics in an unexpected manner—unexpected, at least, from the classic causal view of man. He is arguing, poetically, that we must be prepared to see interaction in the social world.

It must be emphasized that not all interaction is debilitating, as it is in the present case. Often quite the opposite is true. It has been shown, for example, that mutually satisfying sociable interaction can produce significant increments even in levels of athletic performance.[10] Of course, Hofmannsthal suggests nothing about how or why this kind of mutual influence takes place, upsetting as it does our ordinary notions of human action.

It is precisely this latter sort of question that we shall try to answer in this book.

Social Acts and Social Objects

The next ideas we must assimilate are those contained in George Herbert Mead's theory of acts and objects.

According to Mead, any act of any animal consists of three components, or stages:

(1) There are in the animal *impulses* (incipient acts) seeking enactment;

(2) the animal then encounters *stimuli* favoring one or another of these incipient acts;

(3) there follows, then, a *response* to these stimuli in terms of the favored impulse.[11]

[9]Hugo von Hofmannsthal, "Die Bieden," trans. Ludwig Lewisohn, *Modern German Poetry, Little Blue Book No. 775,* Gerard, Kansas: Haldeman-Julius Publications. Reprinted in Mark Van Doren, editor, *An Anthology of World Poetry* (rev. ed.), New York: Halcyon House, 1939, p. 926.

[10]William F. Whyte, *Street Corner Society* (rev. ed.), Chicago: University of Chicago Press, 1955, pp. 14–25, 318–320, 327–328.

[11]George Herbert Mead, *The Philosophy of the Act,* Chicago: University of Chicago Press, 1938, p. 65, *passim*.

Acts, in this view, are present in latent form in the animal and are *released,* not "stimulated," by configurations of stimuli that the animal *seeks out* in order to fulfill these impulses, or incipient acts. The animal is thus not a passive robot merely reacting to the environment of stimuli but an active agent seeking to *act upon* that environment—Mead would say, to *create* the objects of his environment.[12]

The reader should not allow himself to become confused by this claim about the animal creating his environment. Mead was perfectly aware that *things*—the bundles of stimuli the animal encounters—exist prior to and independent of the animal. Mead was simply drawing a distinction between such "things" and what he called *objects*, which exist only in relation to acts. In brief, "things" are converted to "objects" through acts.

Perhaps the best way to wrestle with this point is by example. What is the object of a given act? Let us take eating. The object of the act of eating is *nutrition.* Therefore, if one is hungry (has an impulse to eat), he seeks out stimuli that will release the act of eating. If, in this seeking, he comes across a tomato, he picks it up, puts it in his mouth, chews it, and swallows it. The object of this act is nutrition.

But if he has a different impulse—if he is angry at someone nearby—and he comes across that same tomato, he may suddenly snatch it up and throw it at his tormentor. And what is the object of that act? Expression of his anger.

Really to grasp Mead's concept of objects, we have to play on his *double-entendre*. Let us take our tomato, which is simply a red, leathery, firmly soft, juicy spheroid with a mildly pungent smell and a slightly acid taste. This same bundle of stimuli, this one "thing," releases two very different acts (eating and throwing) with two very different objects (nutrition and expression of anger). Now, this tomato *serves* as both of these objects of acts. It is nutrition when eaten, and it is an expression of anger when hurled at someone. A thing thus *becomes* an object, through the completion of an act. The tomato is not nutrition until it is eaten, nor is it an expression of anger until it is thrown.

[12]Mead, "The Mechanism of Social Consciousness," *Journal of Philosophy,* 1912, 9: 401–406.

Thus, in Mead's theory, "things" are made to serve as various "objects" (in an enriched sense of that word), objects of acts— that is, the *consummations* of those acts.[13]

But this usage is somewhat confusing as long as we confine our- selves to what we ordinarily think of as *physical* objects. The strength of Mead's notion is more apparent when we consider *social objects,* which are the objects of *social acts* (acts involving the coordinated activity of a plurality of persons).[14] Let us consider one admittedly bizarre act. A rather young man, in a park in the Bronx, is standing quietly but very alertly in the afternoon sun. Suddenly he tenses and scurries a few tentative steps to his right, still rather frozen, his gaze locked on a man only a few feet away. This other man makes a sudden movement with his right arm, and the first fellow breaks into sudden flight. Twenty or thirty yards away, still another fellow starts to run to cut him off, and the first man falls flat on his face, skidding and bouncing roughly along the ground for several feet as a result of his great momentum.

What object has this act created? What was the object of the act? Male readers, at least, may have recognized this common so- cial object for what it is, a "stolen base." It has no physical struc- ture but is simply a social object, a symbolic structure generated by a cooperative social act. A stolen base cannot be touched, smelled, or tasted, but it does exist, through the joint efforts of human actors. No one person can create a stolen base all by himself. It takes at least eleven men, laboring together under a common rule, to do so.

Such social objects are insubstantial, but they are extremely abundant and important. Most of the things we officially strive for—marriage, academic degrees, occupational positions, grades —do not exist in nature but are created jointly by the persons in- volved. Perhaps the reader has never pondered the metaphysical status of these social objects, but it is sobering to do so, and it raises profound theoretical questions as to why we should be so ex- clusively oriented to such "insubstantial" objects. We shall have many occasions to return to these concepts and this question.

[13]Mead, *The Philosophy of the Present,* Chicago: Open Court, 1932, pp. 190 *ff.*
[14]*Ibid.,* pp. 180, 185.

The Social Self[15]

The third concept we shall need in our preliminary armamentarium is the concept of the self. For this idea, we again turn to Mead's influential formulations, in his theory of mind and self.

The key concept in Mead's theory of mind is the *gesture*, which is originally the first element of some act but comes eventually to serve as a *sign* of the whole act.[16] If we see a television cowboy's hand stiffen near his holster, that is a sign that pretty soon he is going to go for his gun and "drill" the outlaw in the black hat. Why is this gesture a sign of that act? Because it is the first component of that act and presages the rest of it. When we see that first component, we need not wait to see the rest of it—in fact, a gunslinger had better not. He knows what is coming, and he had better go for his own gun. This first component of the act, then, has become a gesture.

The meaning of a gesture is the response of the audience *to* that gesture. This response in turn serves as a gesture to the original actor, and his response to it serves as a further gesture, and so on, ad infinitum, in a "conversation of gestures."[17]

If a gesture elicits the same response from the actor and his audience, it is said to be a "significant gesture," or a *symbol*.[18] Vocal gestures, as opposed, for instance, to facial gestures, are especially important in this connection, for one hears his own voice in the same fashion as his audience does, so that he is more nearly able to respond to his vocal gestures in the same way the audience does. By means of these vocal symbols, one can in fact carry on a conversation with himself, first uttering something and then responding (like an audience) to what he has said, and this response is in turn a meaningful gesture to which he himself responds, and so forth.

[15]*Cf.* Kenneth J. Gergen, *The Concept of Self*, New York: Holt, 1971; and Theodore Mischel, editor, *The Self: Psychological and Philosophical Issues*, Oxford: Blackwell, 1977.

[16]Mead, *Mind, Self, and Society*, Chicago: University of Chicago Press, 1934, pp. 76 *ff.*

[17]*Ibid.*, p. 43.

[18]*Ibid.*, pp. 45–46.

In fact, the initial phases of uttering these vocal gestures come themselves to serve as signs *of* those gestures, so that a solitary conversation of vocal gestures can take place *internally,* without anything actually being uttered aloud. This kind of internal conversation is of the utmost importance to intelligent behavior, for it makes possible elaborate vicarious trial-and-error activity. Mead claimed that intelligence arises when an act is blocked and ways must be found to circumvent the block. Instead of physically trying out impulses that come to mind in this effort, the intelligent creature can react to his own verbal formulations of these impulses, and, because the symbols call out the same responses in him that they would call out in an audience of his fellows, he has a social check on his immediate impulses. And this inner social check is, of course, the basis of *conduct*, and it leads us directly to Mead's idea of self.

The individual achieves selfhood at that point at which he first begins to act toward *himself* in more or less the same fashion in which he acts toward other people. When he does so, he is said to be "taking the role of the other toward himself."[19] It is important not to become confused by this phrase. The individual, John Doe, *is* still himself, and others act with respect *to* him. But when he too begins to act toward John Doe in some similar fashion, he can be said to be serving *in the role of* an other, an alter. This concept is all that is meant by that harried phrase, "taking the role of the other toward oneself." It is nothing more than responding to oneself, quite as other people might respond to one. It is still he who is doing this responding, even though he is also the object *toward* which he is responding.

This reflexiveness is what William James meant when he wrote that the self as subject and the self as object—the "I" and the "me"—are not distinct entities but merely analytically separable aspects of the same thing.[20]

Mead used the terms "I" and "me" in a similar but importantly different sense. Both James and Mead took over Kant's defini-

[19]Mead, *Philosophy of the Present*, p. 189.
[20]William James, *Psychology: The Briefer Course*, New York: Harper Torchbooks, 1961, p. 43.

tion of the "I" as the essentially unknowable active agent of the personality—that which *does* the thinking, the knowing, the planning, the acting.

But, whereas James meant by the "me" all those aspects of the personality that the "I" knows and cares about, Mead meant something rather different. By the "me," Mead meant all those *perspectives* on oneself that the individual has learned from others—the *attitudes* that the "I" assumes toward his own person when he is taking the role of the other toward himself.[21]

If the "I" and the "me" constitute the totality of the self, this self is best seen in what Mead called the "inner forum," the silent internal conversation that is continually going on inside the human organism. But the reader should avoid the fallacy of thinking of this conversation as a simple dialogue between something called the "I" and something called the "me." Many people have tried to think of the internal conversation as going something like this: The person, as "I," says something; then, assuming the role of other toward himself, the person responds to what the "I" has said; then the "I" in turn responds; and so forth. This conception is too simple, although on occasion it does seem to work this way.

More generally, the person does *not* act out, successively, the parts of a model dialogue. The human mind is not so simple and monolithic. Ordinarily, one's mind is reacting to what one is saying or thinking *as one is saying or thinking it.* One does not wait until he has said something to see just what it is that he was going to say. One monitors oneself *throughout* the process and from a multiplicity of perspectives and contexts. And it is this organization of multiple perspectives and contexts for reaction that is the "me," in Mead's terms. The "me" is best thought of, not as the antagonist in a dialogue with the "I," but as an *audience*, all the people in a *multiperson discussion* who are temporarily silent while the "I" holds the floor. But though they are politely silent, they are evaluating and criticizing all the while that the "I" is talking. Each has a somewhat different reaction, corresponding to his unique perspective, and, when the "I" has finished and relin-

[21]Mead, *Mind, Self, and Society,* pp. 173–177, 192–199, 209–213, 272–280.

quished the floor, so to speak, every member of this metaphorical audience strives to inform him of his own personal reaction to what was said. It is not accidental that Mead chose the metaphor of "inner *forum.*" And, of course, if any of the "audience" objects really strongly to what the "I" is saying or doing, he may not restrain himself until the "I" has completed his act but may instead rudely interject his reactions and disrupt or suspend the ongoing action.

But of course metaphors are merely crutches, and we must not allow ourselves to hypostatize this picture of the self as inner forum. We recognize that there is not really any formal gathering of little men—learned homunculi—convened inside the head. *The "me" is merely the organized cognitive frames of reference in terms of which the mind appraises and evaluates and monitors the ongoing thought and action of its own person, the "I."* And if this statement sounds much duller than Mead's metaphor, we must nevertheless avoid underestimating the profound importance of this continual self-appraisal, which is carried on in terms of standards internalized from significant others and individually elaborated. As Mead and others have suggested, this process is the basis for that intelligent, controlled, socialized behavior of which we are so proud, the singular accomplishment of the human animal.[22]

> One thing that distinguishes man from the lower animals is the fact that he has a conception of himself, and once he has defined his role he strives to live up to it. He not only acts, but he dresses the part, assumes quite spontaneously all the manners and attitudes that he conceives as proper to it. Often enough it happens that he is not fitted to the role which he chooses to play. In any case, it is an effort for any of us to maintain the attitudes which we assume; all the

[22]See, e.g., George J. McCall, "The Social Looking-Glass: A Sociological Perspective on Self-Development," in Mischel, *op. cit.,* pp. 274–287. Processes of self-knowledge, self-control, and self-intervention are most thoroughly analyzed in the Mischel volume as a whole. See also Amelie O. Rorty, editor, *The Identities of Persons,* Berkeley: University of California Press, 1976; and G. J. McCall, "The Self: Conceptual Requirements from the Interactionist Perspective," paper presented at annual meeting, American Sociological Association, Chicago, 1977.

more difficult when the world refuses to take us at our own estimates of ourselves. Being actors, we are consciously or unconsciously seeking recognition, and failure to win it is, at the very least, a depressing, often a heartbreaking, experience. This is one of the reasons why we all eventually conform to the accepted models and conceive ourselves in some one or other of the conventional patterns.

The consequence of this, however, is that we inevitably lead a dual existence. We have a private and a public life. In seeking to live up to the role which we have assumed, and which society has imposed upon us, we find ourselves in a constant conflict with ourselves. Instead of acting simply and naturally, as a child, responding to each natural impulse as it arises, we seek to conform to accepted models, and conceive ourselves in some one of the conventional and socially accepted patterns. In our efforts to conform, we restrain our immediate and spontaneous impulses, and act, not as we are impelled to act, but rather as seems appropriate and proper to the occasion.

Under these circumstances our manners, our polite speeches and gestures, our conventional and proper behavior, assume the character of a mask.[23] . . . (It is probably no mere historical accident . . . that the word "person," originally meant a mask).[24] . . . In a sense, and in so far as this mask represents the conception which we have formed of ourselves, the role we are striving to live up to, this mask is our "truer self," the self we should like to be. So, at any rate, our mask becomes at last an integral part of our personality; becomes second nature. We come into the world as individuals, achieve character, and become persons.[25]

The Dramaturgical Perspective on Life

These concluding remarks on the self by Park suggest that there is more than a little of the theatrical in ordinary human conduct. Indeed, this idea has been a prevalent theme in symbolic interac-

[23]Park, "Human Nature and Collective Behavior," pp. 738–739.

[24]*Ibid.*, p. 738.

[25]*Ibid.*, p. 739. Cf. Helen Harris Perlmann, *Persona: Social Role and Personality*, Chicago: University of Chicago Press, 1968.

tionism from Mead's early writings on role down to the elaborate "dramaturgical" frameworks of Goffman, Burke, and others.[26] We too shall make heuristic use of a good many of these similarities of the theater to life.

The key concepts here are character, role, and audience. The first two are very closely intertwined and must be carefully differentiated. In the fullest sense, a *character* is a person with a distinctive organization of such personal characteristics as appearance, mannerisms, habits, traits, motives, and social statuses. A *role*, on the other hand, is the characteristic and plausible line of action truly expressive of the personality of that character.[27] If the actor's performance (all those of his actions that can be construed as relevant to the role) is congruent with that role, the audience attributes to him the corresponding character. The audience is taken in by the act and is absorbed in the emergent dramatic reality. If, however, the actor's performance is *not* congruent with that role, is incongruous, the audience regards him as "out of character."

Of course, the success or failure of a performance is not entirely in the hands of the actor himself. The props and supporting cast can often make or break an actor's performance, whatever his own ability. In an important sense, then, the success of an actor's performance depends on whether or not each entire *scene* of the play is well staged, "comes off" dramatically.

Even the audience is a factor in the actor's success. No matter

---

[26]Erving Goffman, *The Presentation of Self in Everyday Life*, Garden City, N.Y.: Doubleday Anchor, 1959; Kenneth Burke, *The Grammar of Motives*, Englewood Cliffs, N.J.: Prentice-Hall, 1945; Hugh Dalziel Duncan, *Communication and the Social Order*, New York: Bedminster, 1962; Dennis Brissett and Charles Edgley, editors, *Life as Theater*, Chicago: Aldine, 1974; Elizabeth Burns, *Theatricality: A Study of Convention in the Theatre and in Social Life*, New York: Harper Torchbooks, 1972; Lyman and Scott, *op. cit.*; Rom Harré and Paul F. Secord, *The Explanation of Social Behavior*, Oxford: Blackwell, 1972; and Simmel, "The Dramatic Actor and Reality," in K. Peter Etzkorn, editor, *Georg Simmel: The Conflict in Modern Culture and Other Essays*, New York: Teachers College Press, 1968, pp. 91–97.

[27]Note that "role" in this sense must not be confused with the notion of role as an element of social structure. The distinction between these two usages is sharply drawn on pp. 64–65.

how brilliant the script, characters and their roles are always largely implicit; much of the art in acting and directing lies in making out the nascent anatomy of characters and roles as they are suggested in the meager lines and stage directions. Audiences, as well as actors, differ widely in their ability to see plausible characters and roles in what are merely parts, in their ability to clothe these parts with dramatic reality. The same performance may strike one audience as overdrawn and entirely unconvincing, yet it may impress a more naive audience as nightmarishly gripping.

All this is theater, yet it serves to illuminate much of human conduct. If each of us has a part to play in the larger human drama, in terms of the positions we occupy in the web of societal institutions, we must first conceive the role implicit in that part and perform in a manner expressive of that role if we are at last, in Park's terms, ''to achieve character and become persons.'' We shall have occasion later to consider props, supporting casts, scenes, and audiences in ordinary human conduct. Before leaving our consideration of the dramaturgical perspective, however, let us make use of it briefly to take another look at the structure of the social self.

In this perspective, what we have been referring to as the ''I,'' the active agent of the personality, can be thought of as the *performer* or actor. And, as we have already hinted, what we call the ''me'' can profitably be thought of as a very important internal *audience* of that performer. We want now merely to add that, if an actor is successful, he is never seen by his audience as an actor but as the character he strives to represent. Accordingly, then, we want to distinguish yet a third component of self, the self as *character*.

These components, of course, are not distinct entities or homunculi within the person but are merely *aspects* of the person that can be distinguished for analytic purposes:

(1) the self qua performer;
(2) the self qua audience to that performer; and
(3) the self qua character.[28]

[28]Goffman, *op. cit.*, pp. 80–81, 253–255.

SOME BASIC PRINCIPLES

Let us conclude this prefatory review by setting out, very baldly, some important propositions about parts of man's behavior that underlie one key interactive process, the process of *symbolic* interaction. There are, of course, many other processes simultaneously involved in any concrete interaction (processes of exchange, task performance, social control, and so forth), but in most instances these additional processes take place within the arena carved out by symbolic interaction. Therefore, we take time here to consider this important process.

1. *Man is a planning animal.* Man is a thinker, a planner, a schemer. He continuously constructs plans of action (what Mead called "impulses") out of bits and pieces of plans left lying around by his culture, fitting them together in endless permutations of the larger patterns and motifs that the culture presents as models. This ubiquitous planning is carried on at all levels of awareness, not always verbally but always conceptually.

2. *Things take on meaning in relation to plans.* The meaning of a "thing" (as a bundle of stimuli, in Mead's sense) can be taken as its implications for these plans of action we are always constructing. Its meaning can be thought of as the answer to the question, "Where does it fit into the unfolding scheme of events?" If a plan of action is visualized in the form of a flow chart, things may be regarded as the nodes or choice points, which always require that choices be made between alternative courses of action: "Where do we go from here?" It can be seen from this description that the same "thing" can present different meanings, in this sense, relative to different plans of action. An ordinary beer bottle, for instance, means two very different things, depending on whether one is contemplating a cool drink or barroom violence. But insofar as we have all absorbed the same plans of action from the culture, the thing can yet have consensual meaning, in our sense. A beer bottle, after all, is still a beer bottle, whatever our momentary proclivities may be.

3. *We act toward things in terms of their meaning for our plan of action.* Or, better stated, the execution of our plan of action is

contingent upon the meaning *for that plan* of every "thing" we encounter. If we bend down to pick up a stick and that stick turns out to be a dead snake—or vice versa—the chances are that that plan of action will be suspended and superseded by some other plan.

4. *Therefore, we must identify every "thing" we encounter and discover its meaning.* We have always to be identifying (categorizing, naming) the "things" we encounter and interpreting (construing, reconstructing) them to determine their meanings for our plans of action. "No longer in a merely physical universe, man lives in a symbolic universe . . . Instead of dealing with the things themselves man is in a sense constantly conversing with himself. . . . 'What disturbs and alarms man,' said Epictetus, 'are not the things, but his opinions and fancies about the things.' "[29] Until we have made out the identity and meaning of a thing *vis-à-vis* our plans, we have no bearings; we cannot proceed.

5. *For social plans of action, these meanings must be consensual.* If a plan of action involves more than one person and we encounter a "thing" whose meaning for this plan of action is unclear—not consensual among those involved—the meaning must be hammered out by collective effort in the rhetoric of interaction. As the consummation of a social act, the resulting attributed meaning is a "social object." It is this process of arriving at a meaning for a problematic "thing," of structuring an unstructured situation, that lies at the core of that fascinating subject we call "collective behavior." This meaning will seldom be clear and identical in the minds of all concerned, yet it will still be consensual, in the pragmatic sense that the understanding will at least be sufficiently common to permit the apparent mutual adjustment of lines of action, whether in cooperation or conflict.

6. *The basic "thing" to be identified in any situation is the person himself.* For each actor there is one key "thing" whose identity and meaning must be consensually established before all else—namely, himself. "Who am I in this situation? What implications do I have for the plans of action, both active and latent, of

---

[29]Ernst Cassirer, *An Essay on Man,* New Haven: Yale University Press, 1944, p. 25.

myself and of the others?'' The answers to these questions, if *consensually* arrived at as already described, constitute what we have called the *character* of that person. Self qua character, then, is not alone a personal thing but also a *social object*.

In these terms, the study of symbolic interaction is the study of how social acts generate social objects—especially that important class of social objects we call ''selves'' (as characters). It is largely an attempt to account for the dynamics of this process of arriving at social consensus on the identities and meanings of all the warm bodies on the scene, after which the various plans of action of the performers can ripple more or less smoothly together into a stream of behavior. This process of achieving consensus is conceived of as an interaction, as we have so laboriously defined that term.

This process of symbolic interaction will be prominent in the remainder of the book as we progressively complicate this simple picture of interaction by invoking other social processes in our attempt to predict and explain the WHO, WHAT, WHEN, and WHERE of human behavior. Symbolic interaction is important, not because it takes place on the plane of symbols and ideals, but precisely because it is this process that *links* man's two worlds, the world of physical ''things'' and the world of symbolic ''objects.'' It is this process that transposes behavior into conduct, thus setting the stage for still other social processes that assume the possession of selves and that, in turn, have considerable effect on our dependent variables. Let us, then, elaborate in the next chapter our view of selves and their relation to interaction.

Chapter 4

THE
ROLE-IDENTITY
MODEL

We have proposed that perhaps the most distinctive fact about man as a species is that he lives simultaneously in two very different worlds. On one hand, he is a quite ordinary mammal in an animalistic, physicalistic world where there are cold winds, empty bellies, offensive odors, the terror of darkness, and hostile animals of every kind. Man defecates, and his skin wrinkles, and he is as like as not to die of cancer.

But man is also a dreamer, an idealizing creature. As Santayana put it: "Man is certainly an animal that, when he lives at all, lives for ideals. Something must be found to occupy his imagination, to raise pleasure and pain into love and hatred, and change the prosaic alternative between comfort and discomfort into the tragic one between happiness and sorrow."[1] He is a brooding, introspective, sensitive, intensely self-conscious beast.

He is, to repeat, a dreamer. And each of us men dreams centrally about himself—both by day and by night.[2] Each is always *in* his

[1]George Santayana, *Winds of Doctrine* and *Platonism and the Spiritual Life,* New York: Harper Torchbook, 1957, p. 6.

[2]See, for a sample of 10,000 cases, Calvin S. Hall, "What People Dream About," *Scientific American,* 1951, 184 (May): 60–63; and Hall, *The Meaning of Dreams,* New York: Harper, 1953. Also see Edwin Diamond, *The Science of Dreams,* Garden City, N.Y.: Doubleday, 1962; Jerome L. Singer, *Daydreaming,*

own dreams and in fact can always be more easily identified in them than can anyone else. This fact is not merely incidental, for, in the peculiarly elusive reality of the dream world, the identities of the chimerical players are extremely hard to establish. We have all experienced this phenomenon in trying to recount our dreams in the morning. Characters whom, at the time, we seemed to recognize quite definitely turn into ghosts when we try to remember the dreams in our waking moments. Or, on analysis, a character in our dream turns out to be a strange composite of several people we know.

These problems of identification are by no means limited to dreams, although they no doubt attain their zenith of difficulty in that fantastic realm. We have argued, in Chapter 3, that identification of persons and of other "things" is the key to symbolic interaction; once things are identified and their meanings for us established, we can proceed with our individual strivings, but not before. Accordingly, we must consider more closely what is involved in this process of identifying things.

Identification, in the generic sense, consists of placing things in terms of systematically related categories.[3] One relevant set of related categories for identifying certain persons, for example, is the system of military ranks: private, corporal, sergeant, lieutenant, captain, major, colonel, and general. By placing a given soldier somewhere in this system of categories, we have identified him in terms of rank. Identification in terms of broad social categories like military rank yields a person's *social identity*, as opposed to his *personal identity*, which is derived by identifying him in terms of a set of categories referring to unique individuals: categories like Sam Friedson of Pine Bluff, Arkansas; Henry Jones of Pitman, New Jersey; and the like. Personal identities serve as the pegs upon which social identities and personal biographies can be

---

New York: Random House, 1966; and Singer, *The Inner World of Daydreams,* New York: Harper & Row, 1975.

[3]For the best account of categorization and identification, see Jerome S. Bruner, Jacqueline J. Goodnow, and George A. Austin, *A Study of Thinking,* New York: Wiley, 1956, especially Chapters 1 and 2. For a fine application of these principles to the problems of human interaction, see Anselm Strauss, *Mirrors and Masks,* New York: Free Press, 1959, especially pp. 9–88.

hung.[4] If an individual could not be recognized from one occasion to another as the same person, no stable social relationships could be constructed, and therefore there would be no social identities at all. Both types of identification are vitally important in the process of human interaction.

As the reader will recall from our earlier discussions, we act toward things in terms of their implications for our plans of action, and therefore we have to discover the identity and meaning of every thing we encounter. For every plan of action, there is a classification of things in terms of their relevance to that plan. For the plan of "eating," for example, there is at the crudest level a classification of things into the broad dichotomous category set of "edible" and "inedible." (And, of course, for refinements of this basic plan, there are correspondingly refined classifications of things, ranging up through those constructed by gourmets and nutrition experts.)

Once one has properly placed some thing in such a system of categories, he knows how to act toward it from the perspective of the underlying plan of action. In this way, identification (as an act of categorization, placement, or naming) serves to release or inhibit certain acts toward things.

> It is just this future-oriented aspect of categorizing behavior in all organisms that impresses us most. It is not simply that organisms code the events of their environment into equivalence classes, but that they utilize cues for doing so that allow an opportunity for prior adjustment to the event identified. . . . Anticipatory categorizing, then, provides "lead time" for adjusting one's response to objects with which one must cope.[5]

As Bruner, *et al.*, point out, much of this categorizing on the part of lower animals takes place in terms of inborn categories,[6] whereas most of man's category systems are constructed or invented, to facilitate his greater repertoire of plans of actions.

[4]These two types of identity and their interrelations receive important discussion in Erving Goffman, *Stigma: Notes on the Management of Spoiled Identity*, Englewood Cliffs, N.J.: Prentice-Hall, 1963.

[5]Bruner, *et al., op. cit.*, p. 14.

[6]*Ibid.*, pp. 13–14.

In the case of identifying persons, these systematically related categories are referred to as *social positions* (or, by some authors, as "social statuses" or even as "social types").[7] A sprinkling of examples might include: wife, major general, third baseman, first violinist, Lutheran, Irishman, a Cabot, Fuller Brush man, "young man of great promise," plant manager, and the like. It is in terms of such categories that we place people in our identification of them.

By identifying persons we meet in terms of their social positions, we are afforded lead time in coping with them, for we may know what implications people in such positions have for our plans of action and we can modify our conduct accordingly. As some theorists have put it, we hold certain expectations toward the occupant of a given position, and these expectations exhibit a normative as well as an anticipatory aspect. The set of expectations held toward a given position is said to constitute the *social role* associated with occupancy of that position.[8] As suggested on pp. 6–7, this conception of "role" is in sharp contrast with our own.

The expectations that comprise a "social role" in this sense are entirely too vague, incomplete, and poorly specified in most instances to serve as genuine guides to action. The expectations held toward fathers, for example, are too ill defined to allow one either to act the part of a father or to predict in any detail the behavior of a specific father. Rather, they serve principally as very broad limits on the sort of behavior by fathers that will be approved, accepted, or tolerated by other people. The expectations or demands of a position are thus met by an astonishing variety of actual performances, which are judged as more or less appropriate to such a social position.

As we have argued earlier, the actual role-performance (or, as we shall call it here, the *interactive* role, as opposed to the *social* role) is not specified by the culture but is *improvised* to deal in

[7]See the review in Neal Gross, Ward S. Mason, and Alexander W. McEachern, *Explorations in Role Analysis,* New York: Wiley, 1958, pp. 11–20, 48–69. *Cf.* the concept of social type in Orrin E. Klapp, *Heroes, Villians, and Fools,* Englewood Cliffs, N.J.: Prentice-Hall, 1962, pp. 1–24.

[8]Gross, *et al., op. cit.,* pp. 11–20, 48–69.

some variable fashion with the broad demands of one's social position and one's character. Social position alone is not sufficient to specify role-behavior, for the demands of such a position are filtered through one's character or self-conception and are modified to blend with it.[9] The interactive role is a plausible line of action characteristic and expressive of the particular personality that happens to occupy the given position and represents that person's mode of coming to grips with the general expectations held toward someone in his position.[10]

ROLE-IDENTITIES

These considerations lead directly to our central concept, that of *role-identity*, which, in the dramaturgical language of Chapter 3, may be defined as the character and the role that an individual devises for himself as an occupant of a particular social position. More intuitively, such a role-identity is his imaginative view of himself *as he likes to think of himself being and acting* as an occupant of that position.[11]

This imaginative view of oneself in a position is usually rather idealized, incorporating standards of conduct and achievement that are unlikely to be consistently attained (or perhaps even approached) in the individual's actual day-to-day performances relevant to that role. Typically, this view of self is heavily freighted with all manner of more or less fantastic embellishments and exag-

[9]We are indebted to Michal M. McCall for suggesting this point in the present context. Compare also the related concept of "role-distance" in Goffman, *Encounters*, Indianapolis: Bobbs-Merrill, 1961, pp. 83–152.

[10]This conception of role will be elaborated further in succeeding discussions, but hereafter when we employ the bare term "role" we shall generally be referring to interactive rather than social role. See Ralph H. Turner, "Role: Sociological Aspects," in David L. Sills, editor, *International Encyclopedia of the Social Sciences*, New York: Macmillan, 1968, 13: 552–557.

[11]Research procedures for assessing role-identities are discussed on pp. 258–260. *Cf.* the conceptual treatment in George J. McCall, "The Social Looking-Glass: A Sociological Perspective on Self-Development," in Theodore Mischel, editor, *The Self: Psychological and Philosophical Issues,* Oxford: Blackwell, 1977, pp. 274–287.

gerations. The wealth of concrete detail that is included in these imaginations of self is astounding, ranging in many cases from fantasied heroic accomplishments and encounters right down to how one fancies he should posture and hold his head to communicate exactly the proper affect in a particularly dramatic engagement. This richness of imagery is not confined to exotic and merely aspired roles, as in the case of Walter Mitty,[12] but is typically encountered in people's thoughts of themselves in connection with their own mundane positions.[13]

These imaginations of self run heavily toward vicarious performances of the role in question. One imagines, and often actually play-acts in the inner forum, specific performances like writing a short story, building a boat in the basement, approaching the boss for a raise, asking the girl in study hall for a date, and catching one's limit of lunker bass on some faraway lake. An integral part of these imaginings is the reactions of other people to one's hypothetical performance: the look of envy by the office rival when he hears of one's promotion, the enthusiastic acclaim of one's newborn child by the girls at bridge club, and Mother's chagrin when she learns that her darling daughter has run off with that roguish scamp after all. Not all these other persons who figure in one's imaginary performances (as objects, accomplices, or audiences) are specific known persons, but perhaps most of them are. In this way, other persons—real, live individuals—are *built into* the very contents of one's role-identities.

As a consequence of these ties to specific persons and institutional contexts (like a particular company office), the content of a given role-identity continually changes as alters and institutions enter and pass out of the person's life stream.[14] Our imaginations

[12]James Thurber, "The Secret Life of Walter Mitty," in Thurber, *My World— And Welcome to It,* New York: Harcourt, 1942, pp. 72–81.

[13]Strauss, *op. cit.,* pp. 64–69; Alfred R. Lindesmith and Strauss, *Social Psychology* (rev. ed.), New York: Holt, Rinehart & Winston, 1956, pp. 206–212; and Goffman, *The Presentation of Self in Everyday Life,* Garden City, N.Y.: Doubleday Anchor, 1959, pp. 4–6, 252–253; and Singer, *op. cit.*

[14]Such changes in the content of an identity will be discussed in Chapters 7 and 8. Certain other types of change in contents are discussed on pp. 87–91 in this chapter.

of self reflect our interpersonal concerns[15] and tend to keep pace with our drift through this web of persons and associations.

Role-identities of this sort are not simply idle musings and entertaining daydreams; they exert important influences on daily life. In the first place, they serve as perhaps the primary source of plans of action. The vicarious performances that loom prominently in the substance of any role-identity serve as proving grounds and rehearsal halls for actual performances.[16] The imagined reactions of various others to these vicarious performances constitute important criteria for evaluating any possible plans of *overt* action similar in content to these vicarious performances.

Furthermore, the contents of a person's role-identities provide him with criteria for appraising his own actual performances. Those actions that are not consonant with one's imaginations of self as a person in a particular social position are regarded as embarrassing, threatening, and disconcerting; if possible, they will be discontinued and superseded by actions more in keeping with one's view of self.[17] Role-identities therefore constitute an important set of those perspectives or frames of reference for appraising one's thoughts and actions that we have previously called the "me."[18] In musing upon our role-identities we stimulate ourselves to smile, to frown, to become angry. Our whole daily routine is colored and embellished by them.

In fact, they give the very *meaning* to our daily routine, for they largely determine our interpretations of the situations, events, and other people we encounter. By providing us with plans of action and systems of classification, our role-identities go far to determine the objects of our environment, their identity and meaning.

[15]*Cf.* the somewhat clouded "looking-glass self." Charles Horton Cooley, *Human Nature and the Social Order* (rev. ed.), New York: Scribner's, 1922, pp. 183–185; and G. J. McCall, *op. cit.*

[16]Strauss, *op. cit.*, pp. 64–69; Lindesmith and Strauss, *op. cit.*, pp. 206–212; Singer, *op. cit.*; and Eric Klinger, *The Structure and Functions of Fantasy*, New York: Wiley, 1971.

[17]Edward Gross and Gregory P. Stone, "Embarrassment and the Analysis of Role Requirements," *American Journal of Sociology*, 1964, 70: 1–15.

[18]*Cf.* pp. 52–54.

This is particularly true of persons as objects, both ourselves and others.

Although the more or less autistic elaborations that form part of the content of one's imaginative view of self in a given social position are often somewhat bizarre, perhaps fantastic, it is important to note that role-identities are not at all purely idiosyncratic but actually include many conventional standards and expectations that would be held toward *any* occupant of that status. That is, among the contents of any role-identity are included those vague and abstract expectations we have discussed as social role.[19] It is through these conventional contents of one's role-identities, acquired in the socialization process, that one is irrevocably a member of his culture. Personal elaborations of these conventional contents are exceedingly important, yet they represent, in most cases, variations on culturally established themes. The conventional expectations provide the structural framework of a role-identity, whereas the individual embellishments put some human meat on these arid bones.

In interacting with strangers, we at first orient ourselves toward them in terms only of the ill-specified contours of their social roles. Such early interactions are, consequently, rather shallow, stilted, and uncertain. As we come to know them more personally, we are able to act toward them not merely in terms of their social roles but also in terms of their role-*identities,* taking into account their idiosyncratic interpretations and elaborations of those roles.[20]

Each role-identity of each individual thus has two aspects, the conventional and the idiosyncratic. The relative proportion of these two aspects varies from person to person, and from identity to identity for the same individual. Some people add little to the role-expectations they have learned; others modify and elaborate culturally defined roles to such extreme extents that the roles become unrecognizable to other people and the individuals are regarded as eccentric or mentally ill. Most of us, fortunately, fall somewhere between.

Because role-identities are idealized and rather idiosyncratic conceptions of oneself, the realities of life are constantly jarring

[19]See pp. 64–65.

[20]These differences receive considerable attention in Chapters 6 and 7.

them, raising difficulties and embarrassments for them. As a consequence of this jarring, we are always having to devise perspectives that allow us to *maintain* these views of ourselves, at some level, despite contradictory occurrences. As a creature of ideals, man's main concern is to maintain a tentative hold on these idealized conceptions of himself, to *legitimate* his role-identities.

Such legitimation is accomplished principally through *role-performances*, which are all those dramaturgical performances construed as relevant in some fashion to the particular role-identity in question.[21] If we conduct ourselves in a manner consistent with (and fulfilling of) the specific contents of our imaginative view of self, that view becomes a legitimate one. But, in speaking of such performances, we must remember always that much of human drama takes place in the head, in the inner forum. As mentioned above, many of our best role-performances take place purely in fantasy and imagination. A person who entertains the role-identity of a writer may never put a word on paper but may still partially legitimate this identity merely by toying with plot after plot purely in his mind. The reason that this kind of covert performance can be partially legitimating is that it is essentially a "dry run" or preparation for actual performance. It is, in this sense, the initial phase of an act and serves as a sign or gesture of what may come. To the extent that this is true, Mead has argued, one need not wait to see the rest of what is to come; the gesture stands for the entire act.[22] Therefore, this vicarious performance stands for an actual performance that may follow and, to the degree to which the connection is certain, provides the legitimation the act itself would have provided.

One might ask, then, why we ever bother with action at all, if we can (at least partially) legitimate identities simply through fantasy. Part of the answer,[23] of course, is that identities are not mere-

[21]Relevant research procedures are discussed on pp. 265–266. See also Turner, *op. cit.*

[22]*Cf.* pp. 51–52.

[23]Furthermore, if overt performances do not often follow one's vicarious performances, the latter becomes more uncertain as signs or gestures of the overt performances to follow. As this connection becomes more uncertain, the sign value (and therefore the legitimating value) of the vicarious performance becomes attenuated. And because particular persons are "built into" our imaginations of

ly for one's own consumption—other people demand that one claim some identity. If he does not, they are unsure how to classify him and, consequently, are not sure of how to act toward him. The result is that, if he does not claim some social identity, other people will *force* one upon him—perhaps one disadvantageous to him, for example, at the extreme, the identity of mental retardate or catatonic schizophrenic. Our bodies get in the way of other people, and they have to identify us before they can know what to do to get past us.

Yet if one does claim identities in this way, interpersonally, the legitimation of them is no longer so easy. He has not only to persuade himself that his views of himself are true enough, but he also has to act in such ways that the identities he has claimed before the other people are not disconfirmed in their eyes, for otherwise he is right back where he started—with no identity but in need of one.

This outcome leads to a consideration of what we call *role-support,* which is the expressed support accorded to an actor by his audience for his claims concerning his role-identity.[24] This support is not *simply* for his claim to the right to occupy the social position in question or for the conventional rights and duties of the accompanying social role, although role-support includes these points as a minimum. Nor is role-support to be equated simply with prestige, status, esteem, or social approval of one's conduct in a given social position.[25]

---

self, their reactions toward us are vital to the legitimation of these imaginations. Finally, in time, the accumulation of assessed reactions of others is effectively internalized into part of the "inner forum," so that we are "socially" motivated to do great deeds even though no one witnesses them. This process amounts to a kind of "reverse secondary reinforcement" (*cf.* Peter M. Blau, *Exchange and Power in Social Life,* New York: Wiley, 1964, pp. 42–43).

[24] Assessment procedures are discussed on pp. 266–267. See also Paul F. Secord and Carl W. Backman, "Interpersonal Approach to Personality," in Brendan H. Maher, ed., *Progress in Experimental Personality Research* (Volume II), New York: Academic Press, 1965, pp. 91–125.

[25] This fact is dramatized by the successful businessman or beautiful movie star who commits suicide, despite all the prestige and acclamation he has received. Though such people are apparently successful and "have everything to live for," the reactions of others simply have not supported the *specific* contents of their role-identities.

It is instead a set of reactions and performances by others the expressive implications of which tend to confirm one's detailed and imaginative view of himself as an occupant of a position. Role-support is centrally the implied confirmation of the specific *contents* of one's idealized and idiosyncratic imaginations of self. These expressive implications of others may be expressions "given" or expressions "given off," that is, intended or unintended.[26] The unwilling cries that escape the lips of a victim thus support the self-conceptions of the inquisitor as directly as do the flattering pleas of more pliable victims. And because it is the expressive *implications* of others' reactions that count as role-support, such support is not a thing to be simply perceived and weighed but is rather a matter of interpretation and construction. This fact gives rise to very important complications to be discussed in the concluding section of this chapter and in Chapter 5.

Such role-support is obtained from others primarily in response to one's own relevant role-performances. All kinds of people serve as audiences to one's performances and perhaps accord role-support in varying degrees, but their reactions are not given equal weight, just as in the theater itself the reactions of professional drama critics are taken more seriously than those of casual tourists visiting Broadway. Some audiences are recognized as having special competences and credentials. Others, like the family, are highly regarded on more general grounds; in fact, the reactions of some persons are taken more seriously simply because they have in the past tended strongly to support the very identity in question.

Nonetheless, all things being equal, each of us is his own most important audience, for, unlike other audiences, this one cannot be escaped. In the end, it is ourselves that we have to live with, and the role-support that we accord ourselves is most important.

In any case, taking the aggregate of the role-support accorded us by all the relevant audiences, there is almost always some discrepancy between the detailed content of the role identity and the role support gained from our performance; our overt role-performances are almost never brought off perfectly, and audiences are

[26]Goffman, *Presentation of Self,* pp. 2–6.

typically demanding. Accordingly, role-identities are seldom altogether legitimate. There is always some tension between the fostered reality of one's identity and discrepant impressions garnered from the external world.[27]

This discrepancy is exacerbated by the ephemeral nature of role-support. Like radioactive elements, role-support is unstable and decays as a function of time. An ample quantity of support today is no longer adequate tomorrow. This instability is a result of the volatility and fickleness of men. One's performance today is supported by others as entirely adequate, but tomorrow he must prove himself again, for his fellows (and he himself) recognize that skills, motivations, and resources often have a way of suddenly and inexplicably disappearing. "Can he still do the job? Is he losing his touch?" Past performances are an uncertain indicator of future capabilities, so that people cannot for long be taken on their laurels. Man's memory is no less fickle; yesterday's heroes are tomorrow's bootblacks. One quickly forgets his admiration and acclaim of another, who is thereby forced to impress us all over again. Besides, new audiences are constantly encountered who must of course be persuaded starting from scratch, and the evaluative criteria of old audiences are also subject to change.

Because of imperfect role-performances and the instability of role-support, then, identities are continually in need of legitimation. As proposed above, one of man's most distinctive motives is the compelling and perpetual drive to acquire support for his idealized conceptions of himself.

The need to legitimate one's role-identities encompasses something more than this search for role-support from others, however. Such support is merely a kind of social evidence shoring up one's claims to the identity, whereas the individual himself wishes to *enact* his roles, to fulfill his imaginings, to live according to his role-identities. The individual wants very much *to be and to do* as he imagines himself being and doing in a particular social position. As this congruence is seldom entirely possible, role-support—social testimony in support of his imaginings—takes on

[27]*Ibid.*, pp. 65–66.

considerable value to the person and may in fact become the major goal of a particular performance.[28]

Nonetheless, gaining role-support from others without actually enacting the role to its full extent can sometimes be very frustrating, haunting, and hollow. One seeks interactions and audiences, not only (and perhaps not even primarily) to obtain role-support from other persons, but also as opportunities for enactments whose intrinsic gratifications he may enjoy and through which he can give *himself* role-support from his more richly elaborated perspectives.[29] Men seek to live their lives and to live them in light of their role-identities. To the degree that they fail to do so, to the degree that their self-conceptions are thus not legitimate in the eyes of self or other, men yet strive to *foster the social impression* that they are so legitimate, through the acquisition of role-support.

We shall be following out these strivings in the remainder of the book, but it is first necessary to complicate the matter by considering the implications of the fact that each individual has a great many role-identities, not all of which are necessarily compatible or equally legitimate.

THE ORGANIZATION
OF ROLE-IDENTITIES

Everyone has, of course, a good many role-identities—one for each social position he occupies, aspires to occupy, or has fleetingly imagined himself occupying. These role-identities are not separate, each unto itself, but are woven into a complex pattern of identities. That is, they mutually influence one another and are organized into a more or less systematically interrelated whole. This organization of role-identities, as it exists at a given point in a

[28]This may be considered an instance of the "functional autonomy" of motives. *Cf.* Gordon W. Allport, *Pattern and Growth in Personality*, New York: Holt, Rinehart & Winston, 1961, pp. 226–257.

[29]We can, of course, give ourselves more exactly *relevant* support than can others for no one else is so familiar with the exact contents of our identities.

person's life span, corresponds to what many theorists have called the "ideal self."[30]

It should be emphasized that in speaking of "pattern" we do not imply the complementarity or integration of the constituent parts; indeed, it is a *variable* quality of considerable importance. What we do mean to imply is that the parts exist in relation to one another and that the relationships may be those of conflict as easily as those of compatibility. We shall see, in fact, that there is often a greater or lesser degree of conflict, even incompatibility, among the separate role-identities of a single individual.

The over-all organization of role-identities also varies in degree of *cohesiveness,* that is, in the extent to which separate role-identities are tightly or loosely interrelated. In most cases, they seem to "cluster" in smaller numbers of subpatterns. The basis for this clustering is ordinarily that several role-identities involve similar skills, have the same persons "built into" their contents, or pertain to the same institutional context or period of one's life. These clusters may themselves be linked more or less closely with other clusters or may be quite rigidly "compartmentalized" or dissociated from others.[31]

The feature of this organization of role-identities with which we shall be principally concerned in this book, however, is that these identities are also loosely patterned in a somewhat plastic hierarchy of *prominence*.

The relative prominence of a given role-identity is the resultant of many factors. Among these factors is the degree to which the person himself supports his own imaginative view of his qualities and performances as an occupant of the given position. He may well recognize that, in certain respects, this imaginative view of

[30]For a summary of work related to this concept, see Ruth C. Wylie, *The Self-Concept: A Review of Methodological Considerations and Measuring Instruments* (rev. ed.), Lincoln: University of Nebraska Press, 1974.

[31]Rigid compartmentalization is typically a less than conscious attempt to cope with latent conflicts among such clusters. The extreme case of such compartmentalization would be the supposed "multiple personality" cases reported in the psychiatric literature. See, for example, W. S. Taylor and Mabel F. Martin, "Multiple Personality," *Journal of Abnormal and Social Psychology,* 1944, 39: 281–300.

himself does not entirely square with even his own appraisals of his overt performances of the role, or, on the other hand, he may be quite pleased on the whole with his performances. Those identities that, from our egocentric perspectives, we more nearly manage to live up to are, in their rarity, very dear to our hearts.

Also involved, however, is the degree to which one's view of self has been supported by relevant alters—one's boss, peers, relatives, friends, experts—people whose evaluations and appraisals of this role could be expected to count. Not all these opinions carry equal weight, of course, for some audiences are recognized as more competent judges and some as personally more valuable to the individual. What is involved, then, is some sort of weighted average of the degrees of support from all these various audiences.[32]

Perhaps paramount among these determinants of prominence, however, is the degree to which the individual has committed himself to the particular contents of this role-identity, has gambled his regard for himself on living up to certain imaginations of self. If, for example, he has staked much of his self-esteem on becoming a recognized sculptor, that identity will loom prominently in his self-organization.

The same conclusion can be drawn with respect to more material investment of resources in a given identity. If one stakes his entire fortune or life's work on fulfilling a particular view of himself, that identity will be more prominent in the hierarchy, for one does not live by imagination alone. Man is still an animal and requires certain material resources to maintain pursuit of his various enterprises; these resources are not discarded lightly.

Accordingly, those identities and roles that materially benefit the individual by gaining him extrinsic rewards like money, labor, goods, favors, prestige, and the necessities of life itself will, other things being equal, weigh more prominently than those that gain him little or nothing.[33]

[32]For the operations that yield this weighted average, see p. 261.

[33]Complicating this distinction is the important fact that extrinsic rewards (as well as the intrinsic gratifications discussed in the following paragraph) can serve at the same time as *symbols* of less material rewards. The cash award known as the "Nobel Prize" or the lovers' first kiss is at least as important for its symbolic sig-

These rewards, however, must be contrasted with yet another determinant of prominence, the various *intrinsic* gratifications obtained from the performance of roles and the fulfillment of the corresponding role-identities. These gratifications differ from rewards like money in that they are not contingent concomitants of adequate performance.[34] Intrinsic gratifications include, to begin with, the sheer sense of efficacy in having done something with reasonable competence.[35] Animals are active, not passive, creatures, who enjoy activity and the exploratory challenge of many of their actions. More purely bodily gratifications must also be included in the category of intrinsic rewards, such as the sexual pleasure involved in certain roles, the pleasant body tone associated with athletic performance, and the soothing sensation of a cold drink consumed in connection with some sociable role-performance. Such intrinsic gratifications thus constitute another important link between the animal and the human worlds.

These several factors determining the prominence of a given role-identity—its degree of self- and social support, one's degree of commitment to and investment in it, and the extrinsic and intrinsic gratifications associated with it—undoubtedly differ in their relative importance. The weighting of these factors cannot be pronounced upon a priori, however, for the weighting almost certainly varies from person to person and would have to be empirically determined for each person under study.

Furthermore, for any one of these factors taken alone—for example, degree of social support—the relevant quantity is actually some sort of *average past level* of that factor.[36] That is, it represents

nificance with respect to certain role-identities as it is for its more material significance.

[34]Those gratifications that are thus contingent are *extrinsic* rewards. This distinction has interesting parallels with Blau's usage of the same terms to denote those rewards that are intrinsic to the particular interpersonal relationship and those that are essentially external or ulterior to that relationship. For Blau, the relevant unit is the interpersonal relationship, whereas in this book the unit is the performance. *Cf.* Blau, *op. cit.,* pp. 15–16, 35–38.

[35]Edward L. Deci, *Intrinsic Motivation,* New York: Plenum Press, 1975.

[36]It seems likely that this quantity is not a *simple* average of past levels but one that gives less weight to measurements taken in the more remote past, rather as Markov processes do. *Cf.* John G. Kemeny and J. Laurie Snell, *Finite Markov Chains,* Princeton, N.J.: Van Nostrand, 1960.

the *typical* amount of social support (or investment, commitment, and so forth) associated with the given identity up to the present time. The over-all prominence of a given role-identity is, then, actually a weighted average of the average past levels of several factors.[37]

Because of this fact, the prominence of that identity may eventually change over time if it should happen that events raise or lower the level of any of the several factors. For example, if one suddenly begins receiving a greater degree of social support for a given identity, this increase will in time serve to raise the average past level of that factor and thereby tend to increase the prominence of that identity, other factors remaining constant. These relatively long-term changes in the prominence hierarchy are of considerable importance and will be analyzed in Chapter 8, but they also raise considerations of more immediate relevance.

As the prominence hierarchy (or ideal self) is affected by time-linked changes in the factors underlying the prominence of a given identity, it is obvious that these factors are themselves somehow affected by the individual's continuing sequence of interactions.

Each and every interactional encounter calls forth some kind of role-performance that involves at least some of the individual's complement of role-identities. This activation of identities perforce increases his investment in (and usually his commitment to) those identities. Furthermore, the performance itself necessarily gains him *some* quantity (positive, negative, or zero) of self- and social support of the identities and of the intrinsic and extrinsic gratifications associated with their performance. These obtained quantities are then, of course, figured into the cumulative average level of these factors.

Where do these obtained quantities come from? Investment, commitment, and self-support of identities stem, of course, from the person himself—as performer and as audience, respectively. But the other quantities—social support of identities and many of the intrinsic and extrinsic gratifications deriving from their enactment—can be obtained only from others, the audiences before

---

[37]As might be expected, direct computation of this quantity is not altogether practicable, and a somewhat simpler procedure is recommended for actual research purposes at the present time. See pp. 260–262.

which the performance is staged. These other persons in turn, it must be remembered, also perform in the encounter and necessarily receive some quantities of these same factors. *Each* participant thus receives such quantities, and, if they can be obtained only from others, each must also give of them. In effect, then, the participants *exchange* varying quantities of these three factors; they reward others, and are rewarded by them, in the coin of social support of identities and of intrinsic and extrinsic gratifications.

In each human encounter, individuals are striving for rewards of these three types. As members of the distinctively human world, we seek social support of our identities. Primarily as members of the animal world, we seek intrinsic gratifications of role-performances. To bolster our capital resources for carrying out our various social enterprises, we strive for various extrinsic gratifications.

All three types of reward are at stake in every human encounter, and persons seek to maximize the rewards of given encounters across all three types. Or, to put it more accurately, they seek to maximize the *profits* to themselves in given encounters, for there are costs in interaction, as well as rewards. These costs include the investment of scarce resources to gain access to the encounter and the forgoing of alternative rewards, in addition to the varying quantities of social support and intrinsic and extrinsic rewards one must cede to the other participants. Once assembled in common presence, the participants in the encounter *bargain* and haggle over the kinds and quantities of these rewards that each will give the others in return for what he hopes to receive. This bargaining is not entirely ruthless and haphazard, of course, but is conducted with at least an eye toward certain rules of the market. These rules, like, for example, the principle of distributive justice, have been rather thoroughly explored in recent exchange theories of interaction.[38] We too shall treat of these rules in later chapters.

We wish here to emphasize, however, that our approach to social exchange and bargaining differs rather importantly from those

---

[38]*E.g.,* George C. Homans, *Social Behavior* (rev. ed.), New York: Harcourt, 1974; Alvin W. Gouldner, "The Norm of Reciprocity: A Preliminary Statement," *American Sociological Review*, 1960, 25: 161–179; and Richard M. Emerson, "Social Exchange Theory," *Annual Review of Sociology*, 1976, 2: 335–362.

of other theorists mentioned in Chapter 1. Among the several differences that will become apparent in later chapters, two are of particular relevance at this point: (1) We are as interested in how exchange proceeds in a single encounter as we are in the dynamics of enduring *relationships* of exchange; (2) we believe that any viable approach to social exchange must sharply distinguish among the three categories of rewards mentioned above and must examine the resulting types of *mixed* exchange (or barter of unlike kinds). (We shall try always in this book to give due weight to intrinsic and extrinsic gratifications as important categories of social rewards, but our primary emphasis will fall, nonetheless, upon the more distinctive category of support for identities.)

We shall take up the exchange processes characteristic of relationships in Chapter 7 and those characteristic of encounters, as well as the various types of mixed exchange, in Chapter 6. Many considerations of logistics, or allocation, typically regarded as part of the broader exchange process, will be treated in Chapter 9.

THE SELF AS A
DETERMINANT OF ACTION[39]

If, in the presence of others, one strives to maximize through his performance the possible profits in terms of these three categories of rewards, what should the content of that performance be?

As we have argued, each of the person's role-identities suggests (or contains within itself) many concrete actions or performances that he would like to stage, being the sort of person he likes to think of himself as being. Some of these suggested alternative performances are more central and important to the given identity than others, and many would be mutually incompatible in overt action at a single point in time. Nonetheless, each role-identity suggests a number of alternative lines of action.

[39]*Cf.* Mischel, *op. cit.*; Chad Gordon and Kenneth J. Gergen, editors, *The Self in Social Interaction* (Volume I), New York: Wiley, 1968; Gergen, *The Concept of Self*, New York: Holt, 1971; and Michael Argyle, *Social Interaction*, New York: Atherton, 1969.

Performances suggested by one role-identity, however, are often incompatible with certain performances suggested by other identities of the same individual. A partial solution to this dilemma is provided by the fact that role-identities themselves are not equally important to the individual but differ in their prominence. Other things being equal, performances strongly suggested by more prominent identities are more likely to be carried out than are those less clearly suggested by them or than are central suggestions of less prominent identities. In this way, the ideal self, or hierarchy of prominence, aids one in choosing among diverse projects of action.

Aside from this influence of the prominence hierarchy, what other factors cause certain of the person's role-identities, rather than others, to figure more saliently as sources of suggested performances in the situation? We propose that, broadly speaking, the relative need or desire for the various kinds and amounts of reward associated with enactment of a role-identity goes far in determining the salience of that particular identity. That is, a role-identity the enactment of which would probably gain the person greater rewards is more likely to be acted upon.

Separate calculi exist for each of the three categories of social rewards—for intrinsic and for extrinsic gratifications, as well as for social support of identity. *Within* each of these three categories, certain kinds (and amounts) of reward are momentarily more highly valued by the person. For example, the stranded motorist may at the moment more strongly desire assistance in starting his car than he desires a small favor from his employer, although this preference is subject to sudden change. With respect to intrinsic sorts of gratification, he may at one time desire sexual fulfillment more highly than he desires the pleasures of a fast game of tennis.[40] These momentary preferences for certain rewards cause some

[40]The calculi for intrinsic and extrinsic rewards, although of great importance, cannot be thoroughly developed in this book. A start has been made in this direction, however, by Homans, *op. cit.,* and by numerous personality and learning theorists. Let us re-emphasize that none of the reward calculi under discussion here are at all consistently or necessarily conscious or deliberate in their operation, though they may be quite rational indeed. *Cf.* S. I. Benn and G. W. Mortimer, editors, *Rationality and the Social Sciences,* London: Routledge & Kegan Paul, 1976.

role-identities to be correspondingly more salient than others, in that the enactment of those identities is judged more likely to obtain the more highly desired rewards.

A similar but somewhat more direct calculus exists with regard to the third type of social reward, support of one's identities. For example, a person may be more in need of support for his role-identity of handyman than for that of stamp collector. Accordingly, in order to obtain the more highly needed variety of support, he is more likely to act upon his identity of handyman than upon that of philatelist. Those identities most in need of support[41] are more likely to be acted upon, for we strive always to legitimate our conceptions of ourselves.

A related factor in determining the differential salience of role-identities as sources of possible performances in the situation is the *perceived opportunity structure* that this situation represents.[42] By ''opportunity'' we mean the opportunity to obtain various kinds and amounts of social reward, albeit at certain costs. The other persons and the situation itself are appraised in terms of potential profit to the actor (in terms of cost-reward ratios).[43] A person may be seen as a potential source of support for a role-identity badly in need of legitimation, if only one in turn allows him to enact one of his own or provide him with certain extrinsic rewards. Those identities whose enactments seem most profitable in terms of present opportunities are, *ceteris paribus,* most likely to be acted upon.   NB

The over-all salience of a given role-identity, then, is the resultant of five factors: (1) its prominence; (2) its need of support; the person's need or desire for the kinds and amounts of (3) intrinsic

---

[41]Need for support can be calculated basically in terms of the relationship between the average past level of support and the amount received in the very recent past. Certain complications arise, however, as discussed on pp. 85–86.

[42]This structure is discussed somewhat more rigorously on pp. 226–241.

[43]This assertion does not, of course, rule out the possibility of altruistic acts. As most of the exchange theorists have pointed out, the unilateral bestowal of reward is not infrequent, for it is adequately compensated by general social approval from third parties and the implicit promise of some kind of return favor from the recipient at some future date, even if it can take no more tangible form than sheer gratitude. Furthermore, for those persons whose conceptions of self involve altruistic bents, altruistic acts are directly profitable in terms of support for their self-conceptions.

and (4) extrinsic gratification ordinarily gained through its performance; and (5) the perceived degree of opportunity for its profitable enactment in the present circumstances. Again, these factors are not of equal importance in determining salience, and their relative weights must be ascertained empirically for individual cases.[44]

The resulting hierarchy of role-identities in terms of salience represents their relative order of priority as possible sources of performance in the situation.[45] In fact, we may usefully refer to this salience hierarchy as the "situational self" (as distinguished from the "ideal self" or prominence hierarchy). The individual tries to work into his actual performance those identities that are high in the order of salience and is less concerned with working in those that are low in the order.

It is of great importance to recognize that the actual performance of any person is *multiply relevant*, is relevant to, or involves, a number of the person's role-identities.

That subset which the person strives to incorporate in his performance in a given encounter constitutes the character (or persona)[46] he seeks to assume in that encounter. His performance before the other persons present is devised with the aim of acting in a manner consistent with and expressive of that character or set of role-identities, in order to legitimate them. In the terms employed earlier in this book, the individual thus improvises an *interactive role* for himself in the form of a line of conduct characteristic and expressive of a person with a particular self-structure (character). If the individual's actual performance is indeed consistent with and

[44]Procedures are discussed on pp. 262–264.

[45]See also Sheldon Stryker, "Identity Salience and Role Performance," *Journal of Marriage and Family*, 1968, 30: 558–564; and Jerrold Heiss, *Family Roles and Interaction*, Chicago: Rand McNally, 1968.

[46]"Persona," like character, is a dramaturgical term originally referring to the mask worn in Roman theater to express the personality or characteristics of the individual being represented. We shall use the term "persona" in referring to the character an individual repeatedly assumes in a given interpersonal relationship. *Cf.* Rom Harré and Paul F. Secord, *The Explanation of Social Behavior*, Oxford: Blackwell, 1972; and Helen Harris Perlmann, *Persona: Social Role and Personality*, Chicago: University of Chicago Press, 1968.

expressive of this self-structure, the audience is taken in and confers that character upon the performer. If the role is not well performed, on the other hand, the audience is not taken in and regards the performer as "out of character."

In this fashion, one's character and one's role are not entirely at one's discretion, to be chosen on the basis of one's salience hierarchy alone. Rather, these matters are considerably influenced by the audience, which may refuse to support a given role or to confer the corresponding character. Character and role are thus *social objects* determined jointly through the interaction of performer and audience. Each has certain preferences in the matter, but the resulting social objects typically represent compromises between performer and audience, compromises achieved through *bargaining* in terms of the various social rewards that may serve as inducements. These processes will be detailed in Chapter 6; the objective of the present section has been to gain some understanding of why the individual chooses a *particular* subset of identities to attempt to enact in a given situation.

We have introduced thus far quite a number of concepts having to do with self-structure, and it may be useful here to pause and summarize them. The essence of selfhood, we have argued, is the reflexiveness of one's thought and action; one is able to evaluate, and to act toward, one's own person in essentially the same manner as does any other person. We have, in Chapter 3, analytically distinguished three prime aspects of this reflexive process: the active aspect (self as performer), the reactive aspect (self as audience to that performer), and the phenomenal aspect (self as character performed).

Cross-cutting these *functional* divisions or aspects of the self are the structures of *content* discussed in the present chapter. That is, we have argued that the person does not think of himself abstractly but thinks *something about* himself. He develops quite specific and concrete images, attitudes, opinions, expectations, standards, and feelings toward his own person, just as he does toward other persons. Because any of these other persons plays a number of somewhat divergent social roles, ego's conceptions of that person are likely to be somewhat role-specific; he may think differently about his boss as a golfer or as a father than as an employer. Similarly, ego's conceptions of his *own* person are likely to be role-specific, and we have called these differential conceptions *role-identities*. These role-identities provide plans of action for the self as performer, evaluative standards for the self as audience, and phenomenal qualities for the self as character.

A person's set of role-identities is itself *organized* in complex fashion.[47] The most distinctive aspect of this organization is the hierarchical arrangement of the role-identities in terms of their individual prominence in the person's thinking about himself. Some of his identities are more important to him than are others, and the contents of these identities afford persisting priorities and dispositions that lend continuity of direction to the person's life. This hierarchy of prominence, sometimes called the "ideal self," is not the sole personal determinant of conduct, however, for, if it were, only the most prominent role-identities would ever be performed.

Other factors, closely linked to the person's short-run life situation, very often cause less prominent role-identities to become temporarily quite salient in the person's actions. We must therefore be careful to distinguish the very fluid hierarchy of identities in terms of salience (the situational self) from the relatively enduring hierarchy in terms of prominence (the ideal self). Furthermore, we must distinguish this situational self from *character*. The situational self constitutes merely the person's own preferences as to the subset of role identities he will enact in a given situation, whereas his character—being a social object—represents the subset that is actually interactively negotiated and ratified for him in the situation by all the participants. A character, in this sense, may also become a persona if it is repeatedly assigned to the individual in each encounter he has with a certain alter. That is, as we shall see

[47]G. J. McCall, *op. cit.*; and John E. Horrocks and Dorothy W. Jackson, *Self and Role: A Theory of Self-Process and Role Behavior,* Boston: Houghton Mifflin, 1972. See also the criticism of this notion in Chapter 9 of Arthur Brittan, *Meanings and Situations,* London: Routledge & Kegan Paul, 1973, and the rejoinder in George J. McCall, "Communication and Negotiated Identity," *Communication,* 1976, 2: 173–184.

in Chapter 7, a persona is to an interpersonal relationship as a character is to an encounter.

THE EFFECTS OF INTERACTION ON THE SITUATIONAL SELF[48]

As a result of one's performance in an encounter, he always receives some quantity (positive, negative, or zero) of each of the three types of social reward. As the salience of role-identities is determined in good part by the need or desire for various kinds and amounts of these rewards, it follows that the obtained rewards may alter the need or desire for them and, consequently, may in turn alter the salience hierarchy of role-identities.

Effects on Salience of Role-Identities

Considering first the intrinsic and extrinsic types of reward, we may ask what is the effect of obtaining such rewards upon the person's needs or desires, for such gratifications. If the obtained rewards are approximately of the kinds and amounts desired in the situation, immediate desire for further rewards of the same sorts ordinarily declines somewhat (although the decline is temporary in nature). If, on the other hand, the obtained rewards are *either* less than *or* greater than the kinds and amounts desired, the immediate level of desire for further rewards *increases*, through the operation of relative deprivation and relative enhancement effects. That is, the more a person is deprived of rewards relative to desires, the more he wants of them; the more unexpectedly bountiful the obtained rewards (for example, money or role-support), the more the person wants of them (the "windfall" effect). Furthermore, this increase will in general be more pronounced, the greater the discrepancy between obtained and desired rewards.

The picture with regard to the third category of social reward—support for one's identities—is rather more complicated. The ef-

---

[48]*Cf.* the references in footnote 39.

fect of obtained rewards of this sort on the immediate need or desire for further amounts of them takes the form of what mathematicians would call a *cubic* function (rather than parabolic, as in the case of intrinsic and extrinsic rewards).[49] That is, obtained support for an identity approximating the kind and amount desired in the situation does not increase immediate desire for further support. Moderate discrepancy between obtained and desired support, whether positive or negative in sign, serves to increase somewhat the desire for further support of this identity. More extreme discrepancies, however, produce opposite effects, depending upon the sign of the discrepancy. As before, obtained rewards that greatly exceed the kinds and amounts desired in the situation greatly increase the immediate desire for further such rewards. Obtained support *far below* the level desired in the situation, on the other hand, brings about a very sharp drop in the immediate desire for further rewards of this type, a drop that is explained in some detail on pp. 97–98 of the present chapter.

We have seen, thus far, that the social rewards obtained in an encounter affect in certain fashions the needs or desires for the three types of such reward. These three needs or desires are themselves, of course, three of the five determinants of the salience of role-identities. The fourth determinant, the perceived opportunity structure, is also affected by the rewards obtained in the encounter, in the bargaining process discussed in Chapter 6. In fact, only one of the five determinants, prominence, is *not* immediately affected by the outcome of a single encounter. In consequence, once the relative weighting of these five factors has been ascertained for a given individual, changes in the over-all salience hierarchy of role-identities (or situational self) can be specified as functions of the effects of the kinds and amounts of social reward obtained in the given encounter upon the underlying determinants of salience.[50]

[49]For a graphic representation of this function, see Hubert M. Blalock, Jr., *Social Statistics,* New York: McGraw-Hill, 1960, pp. 351–354.

[50]In subsequent writings we hope to be able to present such a thoroughly formalized model of the self, in the form of stochastic processes representing both the prominence and salience hierarchies as functions of these various rewards. At present, however, such a formalization would be relatively useless, for the constit-

Effects on Contents of Role-Identities

The rewards obtained through one's performance may be compared not only with the needs and desires underlying that performance but also with one's *expectations* regarding the performance. What the individual expects in and from interactions is determined, in the last analysis, by the contents of his role-identities.

If one has a highly idealistic role-identity, a performance that is considered quite adequate (or even superlative) by others may still so far diverge from the individual's standards for himself that he will consider it a failure.

> So we have the paradox of a man shamed to death because he is only the second pugilist or the second oarsman in the world. That he is able to beat the whole population of the globe minus one is nothing; he has "pitted" himself to beat that one; and as long as he doesn't do that nothing else counts. He is to his own regard as if he were not, indeed he *is* not. . . . (Our) self-feeling in this world depends entirely on what we *back* ourselves to be and do.[51]

Conversely, a role-performance that might be considered quite deficient by others may be judged quite adequate or even very successful by an individual with low expectations of himself.

Therefore, the objective role-performance itself is not the important thing; rather, it is the *perceived discrepancy* between the performance and one's ideal image (or role-identity) that forms the basis of one's judgment of success or failure in the performance.

These examples point up the further fact that there is no automatic or necessary correspondence between a person's evaluation of his role-performance and the evaluations made by his other au-

---

uent variables are being measured, not absolutely and directly, but relatively and often indirectly, as discussed in the Epilogue to this book. Nonetheless, as indicated on pp. 270–271, changes in the salience hierarchy as functions of rewards are already being exploited as tests of the theoretical framework, albeit less systematically than would be the case if the formalized model were currently practicable.

[51]William James, *Psychology: The Briefer Course,* New York: Harper Torchbooks, 1961, pp. 53–54.

diences. The two types of evaluation are, of course, not independent of each other, for our self-expectations are partly derived from the social expectations of our reference groups that we have internalized. Furthermore, our evaluations of self are in part derived from *our appraisal of* the very evaluations made by our audiences. But neither can we assume that the two types of evaluation are identical, or usually identical, as some theorists have seemed to imply.[52] The major point is that persons strive to fulfill their own expectations of themselves, not social expectations.

External social expectations are important in two ways: first, because self-expectations are to a greater or lesser extent derived from some amorphous average of social expectations and, second, because the self-expectation may call for a certain evaluation from one's audience, so that the person must take into account the social expectations of that audience if he is going to be successful in bringing about that desired evaluation. In both cases, social expectations are important but only as they are filtered through self-expectations.

The relationship between social expectations and self- expectations is variable and problematic in a number of ways. In the first place, social expectations, taken in the round, are equivocal and diverse so that the person can do a wide variety of things and still be "fulfilling social expectations." Appellations like "brave soldier," "decent girl," and "brilliant scholar" can be earned in a wide variety of ways. Such social expectations are only general prescriptions that provide but the bare outlines for conduct in concrete situations. In describing human activities as the fulfillment of role-expectations derived from the social positions interrelated in social systems, the theorist is therefore describing not social life but the silhouettes within whose shadowy bounds social life transpires.

In the second place, the individual is not simply a passive body whose direction of conduct is determined by the force of the social currents pushing against him. He can always, to some extent,

[52]This view is reflected in most such "psychology of adjustment" texts as L. F. Shaffer and E. J. Shoben, Jr., *The Psychology of Adjustment* (2nd ed.), Boston: Houghton Mifflin, 1956; and in most such structural-functional theories of socie-

screen himself from and open himself to different sources and aspects of social expectations. That is, although no one is completely immune to the expectations of his society and of those around him, neither is anyone completely "other-directed."

In the third place, the accuracy of the individual's perception of the social expectations and of the performance evaluations of others cannot be simply assumed; it is a variable, subject to systematic biases, as we shall see in the next chapter. Therefore, even if individuals were entirely motivated by the desire to fulfill the social role-expectations engendered by their positions in the social structure, even if these expectations were specific and unambiguous, and, finally, even if the person exerted no selectivity in responding to these pressures, it would yet remain true that social expectations and self-expectations would not correspond because of the problematic communication of these expectations and the subsequent evaluations of the person's performances. The fact that *none* of the above conditions holds true simply compounds the complexity and variability of interpersonal appraisals.

We must now inquire more closely into the nature of the self-expectations engendered by the individual's role-identities. Most of the characteristics of these expectations are derivable from the nature of the identities they are based upon. One thus has a number of complexes of self-expectations, which are ranked in hierarchies of prominence and of current salience, and the person (1) must seek situations that will provide the most efficient performance opportunities, and (2) he must sometimes sacrifice some self-expectations for the sake of fulfilling others. Like the identities they are concerned with, self-expectations have both conventional and idiosyncratic components, the relative force of which varies from person to person and from identity-expectation to identity-expectation for the same person. And like identities themselves, self-expectations are subject to changes through time, both in their relative importance and in their contents, as social experiences accumulate and are incorporated into them.

ty as Talcott Parsons, *The Social System,* New York: Free Press, 1951; and Ralph Linton, *The Study of Man,* New York: Appleton-Century-Crofts, 1936.

Self-expectations are an intrinsic constituent of the individual's role-identities. They are the components that form the major link between the individual and his social environment because they are the empirical gambles on which the individual stakes his self-conceptions. They are thus the major target of training and socialization efforts and of positive and negative sanctions.

Self-expectations tend, on the whole, to be rather more closely specified than do social expectations but are nonetheless better represented as a band or range of possibilities than as specific, easily delimited points. (At times, in fact, they are quite general, as in "having a good time" or "being happy.") In most cases, that is, a certain variety of alternatives suffice to meet the individual's expectations, and even when he is preoccupied with fulfilling some explicit expectation other behavior can, and sometimes does, serve as enactments of the role-identity.

Self-expectations, then, are the standards a person applies to his own empirical actions and their consequences. They represent a compounding of the contents of one's role-identities and one's assessments of the opportunities provided by the people, social objects, and situations available. One feels deprived, content, or elated in terms, not of empirical events themselves, but of the relationships between these events and the self-expectations based upon one's role-identities.

When we consider the relationship between self-expectations and the course of empirical events, four possibilities may be distinguished: Events may *fall short* of expectations, may *meet* expectations, may *exceed* expectations, or may qualitatively *differ* from expectations.

At first glance it might seem that all these possibilities would tend, in the long run, to converge into the second alternative, that of events meeting expectations, as the person is led by events to revise his expectations. This view provides the most widespread "model of adjustment" and indeed is the aim of psychotherapy. It is also the idealized model of the social structure, in which each "part" is perfectly trained into and contented with its positions and functions. These models assume that when expectations are exceeded they subsequently rise to meet events, that when expectations are not met they subsequently fall to the more modest level of actual events, and that the qualitatively different course of events subsequently becomes the expected course. These assumptions are quite reasonable from the point of view of these theoretical models, but they are not valid for living human beings.

Instead, as we have argued throughout this book, patterns of change in the contents of role-identities tend toward the case in which events in fact fall *short* of expectations, not meet them, for our identities are typically *idealized* conceptions of self.

Events that are repeatedly different from those envisioned in our expectations do tend to be incorporated into subsequent expectations, but more in terms of their optimal level of possible attainments, to the full reach of their possible implications, *not* merely to the level of what is statistically most reasonable. If a person's literary endeavors do not obtain the serious acclaim envisioned for them but instead receive attention as deadpan satire, the writer comes to think of himself as a satirist—not simply as a satirist but as a *good* one at that.

Events that actually meet our expectations do not thereby perpetuate these expectations but furnish grounds for *raising* our sights and serve thenceforth only as the baselines of minimal acceptability, as Blau has pointed out elsewhere.[53]

Events that exceed our expectations, as happens occasionally, tend to cause our expectations to rise in leapfrog manner *surpassing* what would serve as a "realistic" level of expectation.

These patterns of change reflect the vanity of man, but they also constitute his heroism. Men are seldom altogether realistic in their thinking about themselves but seek always to live beyond their individual means. In the process of living in the empirical world, then, one of man's most pervasive yet most difficult tasks is to handle in some fashion the persistent gap between self-expectations based on his identities and the actual course of events; that is, man must continually seek legitimation of his many role-identities.

[53]Blau, *op. cit.*, pp. 143–144.

MECHANISMS
OF LEGITIMATION

As we have suggested earlier, there is seldom any problem in imaginatively conceiving of performances that would be relevant to the content of a particular identity. The real problem in legitimation is to be found in the ever-present discrepancy between the role-identity itself and the role-support earned from various audiences by a particular role-performance. Our empirical performances almost always depart in some degree from the idealized images we have of ourselves in particular social positions. The central question of this section is: How do we deal with this discrepancy? How do we "make things right"?[54]

Many of our daily role-performances are, of course, so routine, even habitual, that we are scarcely conscious of them. Their crucial importance for some of our major identities may be brought home to us only when they are impeded, interrupted, or called into question. Only then do they pose real problems of legitimation. The smoothly executed habits that make up a fair proportion of our daily activities are therefore not considered in the following discussion, unless and until they have gone awry for some reason.

The first "mechanism" of legitimation, of coping with the discrepancy, is simply the fact that identities and support need not correspond completely or on each and every occasion. Serious legitimation problems usually arise only if the discrepancy is dangerously large during a single encounter or if it remains fairly large during each of a series of encounters. Most of us are realistic enough to be fairly satisfied with role-support that approaches rather than entirely meets the self-expectations engendered by our identities. We build up short-term credit, so to speak, both with ourselves and with others by occasional exceptional performances that leave a certain margin of social capital to gamble with or live

[54]Compare the somewhat similar approach in Paul F. Secord and Carl W. Backman, "Personality Theory and the Problem of Stability and Change in Individual Behavior: An Interpersonal Approach," *Psychological Review*, 1961, 68: 21–33. A more elaborated and empirically substantiated review of these ideas is found in Secord and Backman, *Social Psychology* (2nd ed.), New York: McGraw-Hill, 1974, pp. 528–548.

off for a time. The successful poet is thus allowed an occasional cliché, the good cook is free to experiment and to fail occasionally, and the brave man can indulge himself in an occasional flinch.

But habitual performances and the existence of a certain fleeting amount of interpersonal credit and tolerance form only the background for our more active strivings—albeit sometimes a quite pleasant background. They are, as it were, the open ground that lies before the person's first perimeters of self-defense.

At the level at which the individual must strive more actively for legitimation, we find, first of all, that people employ a good deal of *selective perception* of their own actions.[55] The individual knows in a general, though not necessarily consciously thought-out, sense what identities he is laying claim to and attempting to fulfill through his actions, and he can therefore ignore and disattend those features of his conduct that are not relevant parts of the performances of these roles. Unfortunately, the person's other audiences typically lack this knowledge, and consequently they can never be sure what is message and what is noise in the person's actions—at least until they are quite familiar with his particular dramaturgical idiom. In general, the person is able to pay most attention to a selected fraction of his own actions and the complementary actions of others, that fraction that is most favorable to his self-conceptions. The perceptual processes through which he does so will be taken up in detail in the next chapter.

There is a not too infrequent curious inversion of this first mechanism, in which the insecure or self-effacing person selectively perceives and exaggerates cues that are unfavorable to him. The psychological nuances of this strategy are very complex, but it seems usually to involve the handling of a threat to one's identities by "withdrawing from the race." That is, it seems to involve a subtle plea to be released from the standards of performance normally implied by others.

Second, there is a related mechanism of *selective interpretation* of the audience's response to our actions.[56] There are two charac-

---

[55]For a more thorough discussion of selective perception, see Chapter 5.
[56]Selective interpretation is discussed in more detailed fashion in Chapter 5.

teristics of interpersonal encounters that facilitate this selective interpretation. In the first place, audiences often respond in an equivocal manner that is open to a number of interpretations. In fact, the audience must sometimes reiterate its evaluations several times before they are brought home in a straightforward meaning to the individual. In the second place, the norms of propriety and polite discourse (which, in fact, is what much of our daily interactions are) dictate that we "nicify" our responses to the person. An example of this process is the common practice of prefacing a criticism with a complimentary or ingratiating remark; another is the etiquette of flattering hosts and guests. Such polite conduct on the part of others—whether or not they are really persuaded—may be interpreted by the performer as supportive of his performance.

These two mechanisms of selective perception and selective interpretation stand as the performer's first line of active defense. Not infrequently, however, the discrepancy between performance and role-identity is so great that it overwhelms these primary mechanisms, and the person must employ other measures to maintain a going concern, psychologically speaking.

If these mechanisms fail, the person may employ any one of a number of alternative strategies. Just which one or which combination of these strategies he uses depends upon his psychological predilections and interpersonal habits, as well as upon the situation and the audience. This group of mechanisms cannot be ranked, given our present state of knowledge about human beings, nor can firm generalizations be made about them. As their nature is still so poorly understood and as they are so difficult to define unambiguously, we shall only describe and briefly illustrate them in this book.

The individual may respond to the discrepancy by withdrawing from the interaction (what Lewin termed "leaving the field," *aus dem felde gehen*).[57] This response is a likely strategy, particularly in the early phases of the interaction, when the first hints of the outcome may be sensed but while the person has not yet staked his identities in it very deeply. The tentative nature of the early phases

[57]Kurt Lewin, *Field Theory in Social Science*, New York: Harper, 1951, p. 262.

of most interactions facilitates the employment of this strategy. If later phases of the interaction have already been reached, the individual may still partially withdraw from the obligation to make good his claims by lapsing into a more passive performance and perhaps ceding the spotlight to another actor.

The person may also handle the hinted threat of a discrepancy by switching to the enactment of another role-identity that he judges more likely to be successful in that situation. This strategy, rather than withdrawal, is likely to be adopted in interaction situations in which the person is under some formal or informal obligation not to leave, for example, when he is interacting with superiors, with guests, or with intimates.

The person may also employ what is termed *rationalization,* explaining away the discrepancy as having arisen from extenuating and unanticipated circumstances in the encounter that upset the performance. We may think of ourselves as fairly expert ping-pong players, for example, but have a bad evening "because of the bad background you have to hit against at Jason's house," or, thinking of ourselves as witty conversationalists, we may explain away our verbal ineptness during a particular exchange as having been due to the fact that we were too preoccupied with more pressing matters to devote ourselves to such repartee.

The individual may also resort to what is termed *scapegoating*, blaming someone else for his having failed to come through with a really impressive performance himself: The performance did not come off because others were too inept at performing the necessary counterroles or because those he was competing with used unfair practices. Who could be a good lover with such an unresponsive partner? How can you win against collusion? How can even a good parent bring up a boy who is bad by nature?

Sometimes, however, the fault does indeed lie with others, so we must be careful to distinguish between instances of scapegoating and examples of realistic perception by the individual. Often, of course, the individual's perception is neither clearly one nor the other but some admixture of the two. Students of subcultures and social classes tell us that these admixtures are frequently major aspects of group ideology. Unprivileged groups in particular tend to employ such beliefs in a sweeping, universalistic manner to account for their failures and tribulations. These beliefs usually contain some truth, of course, and often a good deal of it, but when they are employed to absolve group members automatically from striving to perform well, they appear to be scapegoating. (In a curious sense, scapegoating is thus a two-way street, with the majority group castigating the minority and the minority using the privileged majority as a means of excusing what are sometimes its own shortcomings.)

The individual threatened with a gross discrepancy between identity and support may also employ what is termed *disavowal* of the performance's serious relevance to the identity. In this strategy, he makes the claim that a seemingly relevant performance should not be taken seriously because he was only joking or caricaturing or because he was not really trying. Use of this strategy is facilitated by the fact that the person has some freedom to designate when he is frivolous and when his performances should be taken seriously.

A further mechanism one may employ when an audience other than himself is not sufficiently persuaded or is even unequivocally negative in its response to the performance is simply to *reject* or *deprecate* any audience that withholds role-support from him on the basis of that performance.[58] If the individual himself judges his performance to have been satisfactory and if he feels fairly self-confident about his judgment, it then follows that an unimpressed audience must be incompetent to evaluate him. The person may not put this appraisal to empirical test but may shun those audiences that he anticipates might not furnish him support if he were to go before them. And, simultaneously, he tends to underline his continuing allegiance to those alternative audiences that do confer full role-support or would, he thinks, if they were present. In general, this mechanism is employed perhaps more often in selecting audiences *before* the performance is staged than after

[58]*Cf.* E. J. Cleveland and W. D. Longaker, "Neurotic Patterns in the Family," in Alexander H. Leighton, John A. Clausen, and Robert N. Wilson, editors, *Explorations in Social Psychiatry,* New York: Basic Books, 1957, pp. 167–200, especially pp. 184–194.

the fact. But, as long as the person has alternative audiences to whom he can, in imagination, appeal, it is an available strategy when the audience present does not confer the required support.

Not only does this mechanism (that of rejecting the evaluations of the present audience and imaginatively referring a performance to other audiences not physically present) help one to deal with a gap between identity and support, but it also frees him to some extent from control by the social pressures of the immediate situation.

He may have no personal acquaintance with the hypothetical other audience; it may be only some group he wishes to emulate and aspires to join. The other audience may even exist only as a myth. But, real or not, the imagined reactions of other audiences provide him with a means of shifting perspective on his own performances. In a provocative discussion of this aspect of the relationship between reference groups and social control, Shibutani quotes Thoreau's famous lines: "If a man does not keep pace with his companions, perhaps it is because he hears a different drummer."[59]

But, in the course of every human life, there are times when all these mechanisms fail us and we cannot escape the awareness that an important audience judges us to have failed in a serious role performance. One of the ironies of our human existence is that some of our most important role-identities—like those involving the opposite sex, our careers, our parents, and our children—are, at the same time, the most vulnerable because we cannot take lightly these identities or the intimate audiences that judge the performance of them. The more involved we are, the more we have to gain, but the corollary of this assertion is that we also have more to lose.

If an important role-identity has been unequivocally threatened by loss of role-support from an important audience, one is likely to

[59]Tamotsu Shibutani, "Reference Groups and Social Control," in Arnold M. Rose, editor, *Human Behavior and Social Processes,* Boston: Houghton Mifflin, 1962, pp. 128–147.

experience misery and anguish. He may attempt partially to allevi-
ate this reaction by shifting his identity hierarchy, by giving higher
salience to his more successful role-identities. He deprecates the
threatened identity—chiding himself for being so obsessed with it
and derogating the audience that holds it to be so important. That
is, he tries to maintain a going concern psychologically by reduc-
ing his investment in the threatened role-identity. In a sense, he
thus sacrifices a role-identity in an attempt to save the standing of
the self as a whole.[60]

For most people, however, the salience hierarchy is not that
fluid, and therefore this defense is usually only partly successful. It
is likely to be a temporary "wild-eyed" reaction that fades within
a few days as the intensity of the anguish fades, and the salience
hierarchy tends to return to something like its precrisis form. In an
important sense, then, the individual often handles such a failure
by simply learning to live with it. Time does not exactly heal such
wounds; it tends rather to form scar tissue. "Once burned—well
learned."

Through such painful experiences, most of us learn to be more
cautious in committing ourselves so fully to given role performances with particular audiences; we hedge our bets; we adopt
a strategy of minimizing losses rather than of maximizing gains.
This change also involves an irony, because the very fact that we
commit ourselves less wholly means that we cannot succeed so
completely in realizing our ideal images through interactions.

If all these mechanisms fail, and on occasion they do, the individual may experience a generalized sense of self-derogation and
unworthiness if the threatened identity is a prominent one. This
feeling may be so painful that he believes he can resolve it only by
self-destruction. At the least, contemplation of suicide may be the
only background against which the self seems worthy to continue
to live; it may be the only reference point from which life seems
worth living. As Durkheim and other students have pointed out,
the likelihood of this extreme outcome increases if the individual

[60]This sacrifice is represented more specifically in the pronounced drop in immediate desire for support of that identity that results from an extreme negative
discrepancy between obtained and desired support, as discussed on p. 86.

lacks supportive interpersonal ties. Suicides resulting from loss of face, as documented by Durkheim and Malinowski, are the prototypical cases of this process.[61]

The frequency and intensity of such threats to one's role-identities are, however, fortunately diminished by *overevaluation* of performance, both on his own part and on the part of those closest to him, as Claude Bowman has so beautifully demonstrated.[62] A teen-age girl considers a poem, written for her by her swain, to be of real literary quality, whereas the very same poem, word for word, if written by a stranger, would be judged more realistically. As a further example, our friends are "spontaneous, fun-loving, and firm in their convictions"; our enemies are "irresponsible, self-indulgent, and pig-headed." We "discuss"; others "gossip." One of the major functions of "in-groups" seems to be the mutual maintenance and reinforcement of the members' self-conceptions. As Merton has so nicely pointed out, the very "virtues" of the in-group become vices when practiced by out-groups.[63]

This mutual overvaluation may occur by default, in a sense, out of sheer delight in finding another person who shares even the vocabulary associated with a given identity. This result is particularly likely when the opportunity structure is exceedingly limited or when the content of the identity is more idiosyncratic. In either of these cases it is far more difficult for the person to find satisfactory role partners, and anyone who is minimally adequate is likely to be treasured. The lonelier a girl is, the greater proportion of men who will be acceptable to her. Sometimes the person's choice of colleagues and acquaintances, or even of friends and spouse, is determined in part by this "default" process. Sometimes people become so starved for audiences who will help to confer role-support upon some of their more esoteric but treasured identities that they

[61]Emile Durkheim, *Suicide* (trans. John A. Spaulding and George Simpson), New York: Free Press, 1951; and Bronislaw Malinowski, *Crime and Custom in Savage Society*, New York: Humanities Press, 1926, pp. 77–80.

[62]Claude C. Bowman, "Distortion of Reality as a Factor in Morale," in Rose, editor, *Mental Health and Mental Disorder*, New York: Norton, 1955, pp. 393–407.

[63]Merton, *Social Theory and Social Structure* (rev. ed.), New York: Free Press, 1957, pp. 421–436.

set up what amount to reciprocal trade agreements in over-valuation. The sensitive young man thus has a charming admirer who has the intuition to recognize the merits of his poetry; a lonely girl has found a man whose phrases touch upon her daydreams. Each is richer for his overvaluation of the other.

> Whatever his position in society, the person insulates himself by blindnesses, half-truths, illusions, and rationalizations. He makes an "adjustment" by convincing himself, with the tactful support of his intimate circle, that he is what he wants to be and that he would not do to gain his ends what the others have done to gain theirs. And as for society, if the person is willing to be subject to informal social control—if he is willing to find out from hints and glances and tactful cues what his place is, and keep it—then there will be no objection to his furnishing this place at his own discretion, with all the comfort, elegance, and nobility that his wit can muster for him. . . . [He] need only be careful about the expressed judgments he places himself in a position to witness. Some situations and acts and persons will have to be avoided; others, less threatening, must not be pressed too far. Social life is an uncluttered, orderly thing because the person voluntarily stays away from the places and topics and times where he is not wanted and where he might be disparaged for going. He cooperates to save his face. . . .[64]

In the following two chapters, we shall examine the manner in which the person learns to perceive and to arrange those encounters in which he may safely enact the character he would like to be and to avoid those situations, acts, and persons that would threaten his role-identities. The emphasis in Chapter 5 is upon perception and appraisal and in Chapter 6 upon the negotiation of safe passage.

---

[64]Goffman, "On Face-Work: An Analysis of Ritual Elements in Social Interaction," *Psychiatry*, 1955, 18: 213–231. Quotation from p. 230.

Chapter 5

SOCIAL PERCEPTION AND APPRAISAL

The previous discussion of role-identities and their enactment in interaction situations has pointed up the crucial role that the perception and interpretation of other people and objects play in human affairs. Through this process of "social perception" we appraise the things and people around us and strive to assess what meanings they may have for the fulfillment of our role-identities. This statement does not mean that social perception is always selfish, for we often define others as people we want to help or love or make sacrifices for, but in the broad sense social perception is always self-centered.

As other people and objects are perceived and interpreted in terms of their meanings for us, it follows that our definitions and classifications only in part reflect the "real nature" of things. We create, as much as we define, the meanings of things, and, as we have seen, there is a large class of social objects that "exist" only as created and collectively understood meanings. No stolen base or flag can be found in nature.

The perception of other people and objects as opportunities, as threats, or as irrelevant—and the imputation of qualities to them more generally—is somewhat arbitrary from the standpoint of their "objective natures," and in many cases such meanings cannot be derived from knowledge of such objective qualities.

Beauty—and many other qualities of objects—is in the mind of the beholder.

It is in this sense that we can be said to interact, not with individuals and objects, but with *our images of* them. We do not, after all, deal with them directly as physical "things" but as *objects* that we have clothed with identities and meanings. We act toward them on the basis of their meanings for us, the implications they have for our manifold plans of action.

The meanings of persons as objects are much more difficult to discern than are the meanings of less intractable objects like animals and simple machines, simply because people are *aware* that they have implications for other people. Human beings, as opposed to inanimate objects, continually attempt actively to influence the meanings attributed to them by their fellows, for they too have plans of action. Accordingly, they conduct themselves in ways calculated to gain their own ends as far as possible.

Interpersonal appraisal therefore has a number of unique features, as well as features common to social perception in general.[1] In this chapter, the generic perceptual processes of identifying and interpreting objects will be taken up first, and then we shall turn to a detailed consideration of the more complex processes of interpersonal appraisal. And, as we go along, it should become ever more apparent that social perception is the two-way bridge between identities and interactions.

The process of perceiving objects, as we have repeatedly emphasized, is not a passive recording of external events. During each phase of the process, the perceiver actively intrudes upon the flow

---

[1] "Social perception" is the broadest of these concepts, referring to the perception and interpretation of social objects in general. "Person perception" refers to the perception and interpretation of that subclass of social objects known as persons and has been extensively studied. See, for example, Gustav Ichheiser, *Appearances and Realities: Misunderstanding in Human Relations,* San Francisco: Jossey-Bass, 1970; Peter B. Warr and Christopher Knapper, *The Perception of People and Events,* New York: Wiley, 1968; Henry Clay Smith, *Sensitivity to People,* New York: McGraw-Hill, 1966; and Theodore Mischel, editor, *Understanding Other Persons,* Oxford: Blackwell, 1974. "Interpersonal appraisal" refers to the perception and interpretation of persons *qua* opportunity-structures.

of data. Therefore, to understand what is "seen" we must understand the perceiver himself, as well as "what is really out there."[2]

Only a small, selected fraction of the data emanating from the world around us is ever perceived in any sense by the individual. And of this fraction, only a selected portion is in turn "chosen" in some sense by the individual to be interpreted. The phase of interpretation, of assigning meaning to this fraction, is largely determined by the accumulated experiences and the role-identities of the individual, and it is creative in the sense that the meanings assigned are compounds of the qualities of the objects perceived and the qualities of the perceiver. Each of these phases is further subject to biases, that is, to errors of omission and of commission.

These processes and their ramifications constitute the subject of the present chapter.

DIRECT PERCEPTION

"Nobody really understands me" is a complaint that has rolled down the ages, and it always contains some measure of truth. The perceptions we have of others, which form the bases for our interactions with them, are always incomplete and are also usually somewhat less than accurate.

> Organisms have a highly limited span of attention and a highly limited span of immediate memory. . . . In the interest of economizing effort we do three things . . . we narrow the selectivity of attention more or less to those things that are somehow essential to the enterprises in which we are engaged. Secondly, we "recode" into simpler form the diversity of events that we encounter. . . . Sometimes these recodings of information serve their economical function but lead to a serious loss of information. . . . *Not only is information lost, but misinformation is added.* Finally, we deal with the overload of information provided by the environment . . . by the use of technological aids.[3]

[2]See, for example, M. D. Vernon, *Perception Through Experience,* London: Methuen, 1970.

[3]Jerome S. Bruner, "Social Psychology and Perception," in E. E. Maccoby, T. M. Newcomb, and E. L. Hartley, editors, *Readings in Social Psychology* (3rd ed.), New York: Holt, Rinehart & Winston, 1958, pp. 85–94. Quotations from p. 86.

To understand the individual's appraisal of the people and situations he encounters, we must examine in detail this process of perception and recoding in which "not only is information lost, but misinformation is added."

Sensory Limits

The physical sciences describe our universe as a continuous and highly variegated kaleidoscope of particles in motion. The flux and swirl of events occur all along the breadth of the electromagnetic wave spectrum and involve all objects, from giant stars to the internal mechanisms of the smallest molecules. Every situation we step into contains a flood of these emanations. But the overwhelming proportion of these data makes no impression upon us whatever.

In the first place, there are the sense limitations of the individual as an animal. The physical characteristics of our sense organs impose limitations on both the breadth and the acuity of our perceptions. Even "normal" vision is sensitive to only a tiny fraction of the total electromagnetic spectrum, and our other senses are similarly restricted. Sight, as well as our other senses, is further quite limited in terms of the distance at which events can be detected and in acuity of perceiving small objects.

"Normal" sensitivity is therefore a relative and human-centered yardstick, and, from the standpoint of the total wealth of data that could theoretically be perceived, the entire race of man is quite severely handicapped. It would be genocentric and pretentious to assume that nothing important happens that lies beyond our sense limits.

Science has, of course, developed technological devices that vastly extend the range, acuity, and breadth of our sensory abilities. But these devices still fall far short of total sensitivity, and, furthermore, they can be employed only under special conditions.

Perspective

Beyond these sense limits, one's perceptions are limited simply by the perspective or position from which he does the observing.

His view is fundamentally colored by the position from which he looks, and it is therefore inevitably one-sided. While looking down the street, one, of necessity, misses what is going on up the street. Even a telescope, a microscope, or a television camera is bound by this same limitation of vantage point.

The bias of perspective that results from one's *social* positions is usually more extensive and more difficult to escape than are the effects of one's physical position in space. One's view of a university, for example, differs greatly, depending on whether he is a student, an administrator, or a naive taxpayer.

Accuracy of perception quickly diminishes with increasing "social distance," just as it does with increasing physical distance, as a large number of studies has shown.[4] We tend to perceive only the gross outlines of people and events that lie any distance from our own positions in the social structure. Our appraisals of the very rich, the very poor, the Bohemian, and the priest tend to be exceedingly superficial. Just as buildings block our view of the next street, so the relative insulation of strata and subcultures from one another partly obstructs the visibility of even those social positions that are fairly close to us. And finally, just as people employ closed doors and window shades to screen themselves from their physical neighbors, so do they also employ polite conversation, etiquette, and "public relations" to screen themselves from their neighbors in the social structure.

Selective Perception

Even more important than sensory limitations and the limits imposed by the position of the perceiver, perhaps, are the selective attention and selective inattention of the perceiver. A man driving a car through heavy traffic is selectively attuned to the movements of other cars and the colors of traffic lights and does not even "perceive" the movement of leaves on the trees along his path. The na-

---

[4]See, for example, Allison Davis, B. B. Gardner, and M. R. Gardner, *Deep South,* Chicago: University of Chicago Press, 1941, p. 65 and *passim.* Also, Milton Rokeach, *The Open and Closed Mind,* New York: Basic Books, 1960, pp. 166 *ff.*; and J. L. Simmons, "Tolerance of Divergent Attitudes," *Social Forces,* 1965, 43: 347–352.

tive of a jungle, however, would be keenly aware of such slight movements of leaves because they would signify the movements of animals through the underbrush.

On the basis of our earlier discussion of social objects and plans of action, we have seen that people tend to pay attention to those social objects that they think most relevant to their plans of action and tend to ignore those they judge irrelevant. "... [T]he significance of objects for men and women is, in the final analysis, what gives them the character of reality. For things are not real because they exist, merely, but because they are important."[5] Of course, the judgment of what perceptions are relevant and irrelevant is not necessarily or automatically accurate; foreign travelers have lost their lives because they ignored the twitching of leaves, and primitives have been impaled on hood ornaments for neglecting the significance of drivers' outstretched arms.

This example points up the fact that past training and experience have a great deal to do with how one perceives situations and other people. The learned cultural patterns, the perspectives engendered by social position, and the individual's personal history (discussed in Chapter 2) all enter into the determination of which subset of incoming stimuli one perceives and which he ignores.

Much of the socializing of a child and also much of the specialized training of youths and adults for skilled jobs involve teaching specific ways of looking at and listening to the world.[6] And a good deal of what we usually mean by "sophistication" is the ability to "read the signs" that portend the circumstances surrounding us.

Beyond all these considerations, the person's current hierarchy of role-identities differentially affects his sensitivity to stimuli. He selectively perceives those social objects that are most relevant to his currently salient roles; as he drives down the street, a hungry man is most likely to perceive an EAT or CAFE sign, and a man with

[5]Robert E. Park, "Human Nature, Attitudes, and Mores," in Kimball Young, editor, *Social Attitudes*, New York: Holt, 1931, pp. 17–45. Quotation from p. 35.

[6]Anselm L. Strauss, *Mirrors and Masks*, New York: Free Press, 1959, pp. 91–93.

a headache is most likely to perceive a DRUGS sign. A burglar appraises the same downtown street rather differently.

One's cultural belief system learned during socialization, the sum of one's experiences, and one's currently salient roles all contribute to the composition of what Bruner has called the individual's "expectancy set"; what he is set for perceiving in a situation and in other people.[7]

And the individual may sometimes be quite dogged in perceiving only those things congruent with his expectancy set. The force of external events can, however, break in upon one's expectancy set, and there are categories of stimuli—screams, explosions, shouts for help—that almost universally have this "breaking-in" property.

Less dramatically, the situation or the other people in it may present such an excellent opportunity for fulfilling a role-identity that is currently not salient that the individual's identity hierarchy and its corresponding expectancy set undergo change. One may come to complain about the noise of a party but stay to revel; an interruption becomes an encounter; the soldier joins the revolt.

The generalization, from the preceding chapters, that the animal actively *seeks* those stimuli that will fulfill his current needs or desires must now be qualified. Just as the animal can actively choose situations, so do situations sometimes have the power to "change the animal's mind."

INTERPRETATION

"Messages" from the outside world are even further altered as the individual *interprets* what he has perceived. He concentrates upon that subset of the incoming selected perceptions that seems most important to him and his current enterprises. This selective attention to some perceptions is in addition to the selective perception discussed before; that is, biased perception is further compounded by biased contemplation. One pays selective attention to

[7]Bruner, *op. cit.*

one's selective perceptions. The common case of two people arguing over the "facts" of a situation that each feels should be obvious to anybody becomes more understandable in this perspective.

All these remarks on limitations and biases in perception per se apply to the process of interpretation as well. A human being has sense limitations, but he has even greater limitations on the number of things he can consciously entertain simultaneously. The person's currently salient roles influence how things are interpreted and defined as objects even more than they influence perception, as we saw in Chapter 3. Furthermore, the sum of one's past experience affects both perception and the interpretation made of such perceptions.

Beyond these parallels, there is an additional factor involved in interpretations, that is, the "recoding" Bruner speaks of. *We simplify the waves of incoming perceptions by recoding their contents into summary categories.* A flux of visual perceptions along a certain segment of the light band is registered as "red"; the nerve transmissions from several hundred taste buds are registered as "salty"; the inundation of sensory data as we pass a girl on the street is registered as "pretty," or perhaps "slim, pretty, and lost in thought."

These categories—usually made up of words or images—are rather high-level abstractions; that is, the chain of inference from the raw sense data is quite long in most cases. The less concrete and descriptive the words, the greater the abstraction involved. The abstraction "red," as a summary of a few thousand nerve excitations on the retina, is fairly simple and straightforward. But many other abstract categories, like "pretty," "well-meaning," "prosaic," are not. The greater the level of abstraction of the categories into which incoming perceptions are recoded, the more chance there is for such factors as selective attention, perspective resulting from the sum of one's experiences, and the current expectancy set (stemming from the currently salient identities) to influence and color how these perceptions will be interpreted by the individual.

It must be emphasized that this process of matching categories with sense data is neither simple nor automatically correct. We have seen that the inference is always based only on a biased subset of the total sense data available. We have also seen that the perceptions are often only signs for invented social objects like a "stolen base" or "freedom." In addition, the data are often ambiguous, and the interpretations are therefore fairly arbitrary. At best, the signs are merely elliptical hints. It is in this sense that we remarked earlier that reality is not given but is "fragile and adjudicated—a thing to be debated, compromised, and legislated."

Particularly with the more abstract social categories that have been invented by man rather than named by him (particularly, that is, in the social realm), the organization and interpretation of incoming sense data are debatable. Most of what is commonly called description is actually interpretation, and people who think they are arguing over the facts are often actually arguing over how the facts should be interpreted.

These daily debates are engendered by the fact that people recode the sense data in different ways and into different categories. That is, people have divergent categories, and people also diverge on how they match data with categories. The pessimist sees that his glass is already half empty, and the optimist sees that his glass is still half full. The distinctive pattern of an individual's categories constitutes his belief system or world view, the perspective from which he tries to make sense of the world.

And it should be remembered that incompleteness, as well as twisting of facts, constitutes distortion. From a rather neutral conversation, one person selects those items that suggest positive reactions of others to him; another person selects those items that suggest rejection of that first person by the others. As the conversation includes both sets of items, each interpretation is based upon a true, but incomplete, perception and interpretation of the interaction.

Introduction of Misinformation

It is in the process of recoding sense data into symbolic categories that misinformation may be added. The process can be seen most clearly in identifying persons in terms of their *social* identities, the social categories to which they belong. Each major position (like "policeman"), as well as many important combinations of social positions (like "Irish policeman"), has attached to it in the popular culture a stereotype—a set of personal characteristics and behaviors that are expected of anyone who occupies that position.[8] These stereotypes ordinarily contain certain amounts of statistical truth in them and thus are useful in orienting people toward those who occupy such positions.

Few individual members of any category, however, are truly typical in terms of the stereotype. Some of the characteristics one would expect to find in a member of the category are actually missing in most concrete instances, and the individual has additional characteristics that are not included in the stereotype. The stereotype only partially fits the individual.

Consequently, when we appraise a stranger by identifying his salient social positions and ringing in the corresponding stereotypes, our expectations toward him include things that do not apply to him, and they omit important things that *do* apply to him. In recoding the sense data on this person into symbolic categories (social positions and the attached stereotypes), we thus introduce two important kinds of misinformation into our appraisal of him: errors of commission and of omission.

Stereotyping

These notions lead to a somewhat different perspective on stereotyping and "prejudice" and suggest that the popular condemnation of all prejudgments and stereotyped thinking is facile and unrealistic. All living creatures, it seems, must employ stereotypes to categorize and deal with the kaleidoscopic flow of events around them. Nor can they wait contemplatively until all the facts are in; they must prejudge the meaning of the whole on the basis of a few signs and must act upon this jot of knowledge.[9]

[8]Frances E. Aboud and Donald M. Taylor, "Ethnic and Role Stereotypes," *Journal of Social Psychology,* 1971, 85: 17–27.

[9]Eckhard H. Hess, "Ethology: An Approach Toward the Complete Analysis of Behavior," in Roger Brown, Eugene Galanter, and George Mandler, *New Directions in Psychology,* New York: Holt, Rinehart & Winston, 1962, pp. 157–266, especially pp. 179–187.

In addition to errors of omission and commission, however, stereotypes often have two further inadequacies. The generalities employed by all living things tend to focus upon and to exaggerate those qualities of the objects that are most relevant to their own plans and lives. Such qualities often include only fractional and very biased subsets of the total properties of those objects. For example, a young man may think of females almost exclusively as objects possessing some degree of the multidimensional attribute "desirability." He is surprised to learn that they must also budget their money, defecate, and have dental checkups, as he himself does.

There is yet another way in which our imputations may lead us astray. We tend to impute to objects fixed qualities, when in reality the objects are characterized by variables that wax and wane. No one is smart or pretty all the time, and, conversely, all of us have our moments. Nevertheless, our daily thoughts and conversations are filled with statements like "Jason's sure a bright fellow," "Gil's wife is very pretty," and "health food enthusiasts are out of it." These and a host of similar statements actually describe the statistical probabilities that objects will possess attributes at given moments, and we employ them because they are our best predictions of what we can expect from those objects in a series of encounters. But their validity is statistical rather than absolute.

In light of this perspective, stereotyping involves not merely the attitudes of rigid people discriminating against racial and ethnic outgroups. It is an inherent and inevitable aspect of every human appraisal of every person encountered.

It is therefore misleading to inquire about the presence or absence of stereotypes and prejudgments. Although all people employ these devices, the quality, objectivity, and validity of them vary tremendously, however. On one hand, there are the stereotypes of superstition and prejudice, based upon emotion and faulty information and unamenable to change by contrary evidence. On the other, there are the stereotypes called "scientific generalizations and theories," which are arrived at by the most objective techniques man has yet been able to develop and which are deliberately constructed to facilitate alteration or replacement by more accurate generalizations. It is true that many superstitions contain more than a little truth and that many scientific theories contain more than a little superstition and prejudice. But, despite this qualification, the contrast between the two types is basically the contrast between ignorance and knowledge. We must therefore inquire into the *quality*, not the existence, of stereotyping.[10]

Most individuals are aware, to some extent, that the stereotypes or categories they employ in coding incoming perceptions involve the hazarding of guesses. Consequently, people usually do not form instant judgments and hold them unalterably. Rather, they usually engage in a process of appraisal in which they seek further cues that will confirm, supplement, or refute their tentative first impressions. Often numbers of alternative judgments are simultaneously entertained, each of which is only tentatively held and each of which may be only tentatively discarded as further evidence accumulates. As evidence continues to accumulate, these alternatives are narrowed down, but often the process never reaches a final judgment. In this important sense, people are fundamentally ambivalent toward many of the people and objects around them. The individual acts toward the person or object in an equivocal way that takes some account of the various alternative evaluations he is entertaining; that is, he acts in such a way as to hedge his bets that any of the interpretations is actually valid, so that he is covered to some extent, whatever the outcome. And even though first impressions produce some selective perception and interpretation of the subsequent events, the person is still more or less prepared to change his mind.

In summary, then, the interpretation of incoming sensory perceptions by fitting them into abstract categories with attached stereotypes is altogether a gamble carried out by educated guesswork.

Nonetheless, it is often the best one can do, particularly in a first encounter. In mobile, pluralistic societies like our own, such

---

[10]Orrin E. Klapp, *Heroes, Villains, and Fools,* Englewood Cliffs, N.J.: Prentice-Hall, 1962, pp. 1–24; Joshua A. Fishman, "An Examination of the Process and Function of Social Stereotyping," *Journal of Social Psychology,* 1956, 43: 27–64; and Henry Clay Smith, *Sensitivity to People,* New York: McGraw-Hill, 1966, Chapter 8.

stereotypes attached to social identities are typically our sole source of orientation toward the majority of people we encounter. From visible clues to social identity, we connect strangers with stereotypes, so that we may predict their behavior and characteristics.[11]

Personal Reputations

Another device very much like stereotypes is the *personal reputation,* indirect knowledge about another person that preconditions one's view of him. Unlike a stereotype, which has to do with a person's *social* identity, a personal reputation has to do with *personal* identity. Reputations, then, are unique, whereas stereotypes are applied to any and all occupants of a given position.

Despite this difference, however, both devices function similarly by providing us with "prepackaged" appraisals of the other person, so that we need not start from scratch in deciphering the potential meaning of that other. Both also share the curious mixture of truth and error that stems from the partial overlap of category with person. That is, both stereotype and reputation (1) are incomplete and (2) contain a certain freight of misinformation about the person.

In fact, the two devices are seldom independent. In most concrete instances, the symbolic molds into which we recode incoming data about another person represent some kind of synthesis of impersonal reputation (the stereotypes associated with his social positions) and personal reputation. The relative contribution of the two varies from case to case, of course, including the oft-encountered extreme in which only the impersonal reputation is known. This situation is more frequent in *Gesellschaft* societies like our own than in small *Gemeinschaft* communities but it must be remembered that even in our own society we move in highly limited circles: Very often we have heard at least some fragmentary information about a particular person before we actually come in contact with him.

[11]Gregory P. Stone, "City Shoppers and Urban Identification: Observations on the Social Psychology of City Life," *American Journal of Sociology,* 1954, 60: 36–45; and Lyn Lofland, *A World of Strangers,* New York: Basic Books, 1973.

In light of the importance of reputations, we should consider the manner in which they are formed and employed.

INDIRECT PERCEPTION[12]

The reputations we associate with persons are fundamentally indirect perceptions of them. We hear anecdotes, epithets, and characterizations of people from third parties, and through them we form impressions of these people without ever having met them. Therein lies the economy of reputations and their liability.

Presumably the third parties have had direct contact with alter and are speaking from personal knowledge, at least in part. As we have seen, even direct appraisal of persons is a hazardous and inherently somewhat inaccurate process. A third party's direct knowledge of alter in itself represents a simplified, distorted, and selective distillate of those limited data about alter that he has managed to take in.

But, more important, what this third party in turn *tells* us about alter represents only a biased sample of his own limited knowledge. The things this third party decides to tell us are influenced by his own feelings about alter, his perceptions of what our own goals toward alter might be, and the sort of feelings he wishes us to have toward alter.

Nor does distortion end there. We, in turn, selectively perceive and interpret this biased transmission of information. The message received is not the same as the message sent. What we make of it depends on its congruence with other information we may have about alter, on our estimates of the third party's reliability and allegiances, and so forth.

Consequently, personal reputations are thrice cursed from the point of view of dependable knowledge of alter. Yet reputational knowledge is priceless, for, despite its deficiencies, it does allow us

[12]Perhaps the majority of the person perception research has focused on indirect perception, usually through an impression formation paradigm. See, for example, Albert H. Hastorf, David J. Schneider, and Judith Polefka, *Person Perception*, Reading, Mass.: Addison-Wesley, 1970; and Richard R. Izzett and Walter Leginski, "Impression Formation as a Function of Self Versus Other as Source of Information," *Journal of Social Psychology*, 1972, 87: 229–233.

to orient ourselves toward alter *before* we actually encounter him; it affords us "lead time" in dealing with him. It would ordinarily require a number of meetings to obtain the kind of information about alter, however incomplete and distorted, that is contained in his prepackaged reputation. Very often this utility of reputations, like that of stereotypes, outweighs the risks attendant upon their use.

PECULIARITIES OF PERSONS AS OBJECTS

As we have seen, perception is generically a most difficult enterprise and one that is rewarded with varyingly mediocre success. The perception of persons, as a particularly important special case of this process, is subject to certain unique difficulties that arise from some peculiarities of persons as objects.

In the first place, no other object can purposefully and differentially conceal or reveal certain of its characteristics. Being a self-conscious animal, man—like no other object—modifies his behavior in view of the fact that he is under observation. He hides certain facts about himself and advertises others, in an attempt to influence our appraisals of him. We are all engaged in public relations for ourselves. Furthermore, to another observer in a quite different relationship to him, the person adjusts this concealing and revealing behavior, hiding some things that have been previously revealed and advertising some that have been previously hidden.

Consequently, a person is never quite the same object to any two observers. Knowledge of a person is relative to the relationship in which one stands with him. What is truth from the perspective of an observer in one relationship to him is error from the perspective of another observer in a different relationship to him. In this pragmatic sense, his nature as an object is not determined by himself as an individual but rather in interaction with another.

Of course, this analysis is not the whole story. His tactics of concealment and revelation are not completely effective. Those data about himself that he purposely reveals or permits to be discovered (what Goffman calls "expressions given")[13] may not be the only data that the observer receives. The person's expressive control is never total; unconscious gestures, attitudes, habits, and slips reveal things without his conscious effort (which Goffman calls expressions "given off"). Furthermore, the observer may have learned from others certain facts about the person that the latter thought he had effectively concealed.

Beyond these problems of information control,[14] by which we mean control of expression of information, there is often a discrepancy between expressions transmitted and the impressions received. An act, gesture, or sentence is often amenable to more than one interpretation, so that the impression received by the observer may not be the one intended for him to receive.

The person as object has still another peculiar means of controlling appraisals of himself, however. Persons, unlike other objects, purposively reward the observer for making certain appraisals and punish him for making others. Through differential sanctions, the person thus helps to bring about the desired image of himself in the eyes of the observer, reinforcing the effects of concealment and revelation tactics.

THE ROLE OF PERCEPTION IN INTERACTION

Altogether, then, it appears that our appraisals of people are considerably less than completely accurate. But if identification of objects, especially persons, is so crucial to interaction (see pp. 58–60), how can we proceed on the basis of such faulty appraisals? It is certainly true that we would do better in interaction if we had more and better information about the other persons, but we have seen that the pictures we receive of others necessarily contain mix-

[13]Erving Goffman, *The Presentation of Self in Everyday Life,* Garden City, N.Y.: Doubleday Anchor, 1959, pp. 2 *ff.*

[14]See pp. 187–194. Also, *cf.* Goffman, *Stigma: Notes on the Management of Spoiled Identity,* Englewood Cliffs, N.J.: Prentice-Hall, 1963, especially Chapter 2 ("Information Control and Personal Identity").

tures of truth and error. These pictures bear only probabilistic correspondence to the other persons themselves.

In consequence, we must act always on the basis of incomplete evidence. We cannot wait for an illusory sense of certainty, for life moves too swiftly; we must continually gamble that our appraisals of others are fairly accurate.

There are two kinds of error that can befall us in these gambles: We may be overly cautious and reluctant to bet upon our appraisals, or we may too rashly assume that our superficial images of the others are essentially correct. Individuals no doubt differ rather characteristically in the types of error that they are prone to make, some being rashly bold in interaction and others being timidly overcautious in acting on their appraisals.

But even when we manage to avoid either of these gambling errors by taking only tentative action, on the basis of moderate evidence, our images of alter are still incomplete and somewhat misleading. Nevertheless these images are all we have; accordingly, we are really acting toward our images rather than toward the metaphysical realities that somehow lie behind them.[15] We *impute* to the real him all those characteristics, goals, and motives that constitute our image of him, *and then we act toward him in terms of those imputed features.*[16]

If our images are not minimally accurate, we cannot have successful social lives, yet there is a wide gap between this sort of minimum and complete accuracy. The relative worth of these images reflects the extent to which they contain that information most relevant to the particular interaction situations in which we encounter alter and the extent to which the freight of misinformation is either pragmatically irrelevant to those particular situations or is cleared up by alter in response to our actions toward him.

In general, the greater the breadth and the duration of our experiences with alter, the more accurate our images of him become. Yet this clarification process is not an automatic one, for, although

[15]Ichheiser, *op. cit.*

[16]Kelley G. Shaver, *An Introduction to Attribution Processes,* Cambridge: Winthrop, 1975; and E. E. Jones *et al.,* editors, *Attribution: Perceiving the Causes of Behavior,* Morristown, N.J.: General Learning Press, 1971.

accurate appraisal of persons is rewarding to the individual in that it helps him deal more effectively with the world, this reward factor motivates him only up to the point where he *thinks* he is getting along well with alter. It does not motivate him to strive for greater accuracy of perception beyond this point.

In fact, this reward factor may be counteracted by rewards for maintaining a particular inaccurate image of alter. Ego-defense needs, for example, may necessitate believing that alter thinks highly of one or denying that alter knows more about cabbages or kings than ego does.

By various mechanisms ego may thus actively strive to maintain his distorted view of alter.[17] He may selectively ignore data about alter that are at variance with his view of him, and, when this method fails, he may explain away the incongruous data as resulting from factors like temporary mood or unusual circumstances. For example, the informal gaiety of a "dull, bookish professor" may be explained away as the result of a break in the rainy weather or a publication acceptance, so that one's image of him remains intact. This sort of thing may be supported by others who share the same motives, reinforcing one's image of alter regardless of what alter may actually do.

Whether or not his initial inaccurate image of alter is functional for ego, he may actually cause it to become accurate, an instance of what is known as a "self-fulfilling prophecy."[18] That is, by proceeding as though his image of alter were true, the person may effectively force alter to behave in a fashion that supports the person's image of him. This process might be described by the following paradigm:

A. Ego makes an inference about alter.
B. Ego acts toward alter in terms of this inference.
C. Alter makes inferences about ego in terms of his action.
D. Alter tends to react toward ego in terms of his inference.
E. Thus ego's inferences tend to be confirmed by alter's actions.

[17]Simmons, "On Maintaining Deviant Belief Systems: A Case Study," *Social Problems,* 1964, 11: 250–256.

[18]Robert K. Merton, "The Self-Fulfilling Prophecy," in Merton, *Social Theory and Social Structure* (rev. ed.), New York: Free Press, 1957, pp. 421–438.

. . . To choose an example among many possible ones, my informant rented a room for several days from a middle-aged woman. After seeing her only briefly, and before he had spoken with her, he "intuited" that she was a warm accepting person who was filled with psychic strength and goodness. When he first talked with her a couple hours later, his manner was far more friendly and patronizing than usual. He showed interest in her collection of antiques, asked about her children, and ended up by saying he felt she was a wonderful person and he wanted to rent from her, partly because they would have a chance to talk together. During the next few days, the writer had a chance to question other tenants and neighbors about the landlady. They described a fairly caustic gossiper who was unreasonably strict about the use of electricity, and of her property and grounds. Her attitude toward the writer was taciturn. But she responded graciously to my informant's open friendliness. She sought him out to talk with on several occasions, she inquired if there was enough light in his room for late reading and supplied him with a table lamp, etc. In her behavior toward him, my informant's intuition certainly seemed correct.[19]

Just such a paradigm lies at the heart of the currently fashionable *labeling theory* of deviant behavior.[20] A policeman, for example, infers that a streetcorner youth is a delinquent troublemaker and acts toward him on that basis, perhaps taking him to the juvenile authorities. Having been more or less officially labeled as a delinquent troublemaker, the youth may come to view himself as one and to act accordingly, thus confirming the policeman's inference, however inaccurate it may have been initially.

The inevitable conclusion we must draw from our consideration of person perception, however foreign it may seem to commonsense realism, is that our images of people will always contain some admixture of truth and error but that this must be a *workable* admixture. That is to say, it must contain just enough of the relevant truth about alter to allow us to take minimally successful action toward him. Seldom are we truly *en rapport* with

[19]Simmons, "On Maintaining Deviant Belief Systems," p. 253.

[20]E.g., Edwin C. Lemert, *Social Pathology*, New York: McGraw-Hill, 1951; Howard S. Becker, *Outsiders*, New York: Free Press, 1963; and Edwin C. Schur, *Labeling Deviant Behavior*, New York: Harper & Row, 1971.

him, for we do not truly know him. Ordinarily, we understand him just well enough to work out a sort of fumbling, on-again, off-again accommodation in which we manage to get along with, and past, one another without serious conflict. Only rarely, and then most often in quite intimate relationships, do we truly communicate and interact in harmony. More will be said about such cases of "empathy" in later chapters.

We shall take up in the next chapter the processes by which persons, having appraised one another for personal meanings, actually work out these mutual accommodations by striving for some sort of shallow consensus upon the meanings attached to one another.

Chapter 6

THE DYNAMICS
OF
INTERACTIONS

"Social interaction" is one of the most widely used concepts in the social sciences, yet comparatively little is actually known about the concrete processes of face-to-face interaction. We are all steeped in interaction experiences, yet this pan-human store of experience remains largely untranslated into explicit scientific knowledge.

How do persons modify their conduct when they encounter one another and go on to engage in more or less sustained interactions? Each brings a distinctive set of identities, goals, and problems to an encounter; how do they conduct themselves so that their own concerns are advanced (or at least not significantly damaged) without so jeopardizing the others' concerns that the very fabric of the interaction itself dissolves?

Man, both as animal and as dreamer, is highly dependent upon interaction with his fellows. His daily life, which takes place in the intersection of these two worlds, must be lived in consort with the other humans on the scene. Through what means does this consort take place?

Despite the centrality of this question for understanding social man and his behaviors, little is known about its answers. In this chapter, drawing upon the scattered insights of others, we shall attempt to frame a partial answer to the HOW of interaction. We must emphasize that it is only a partial answer, for face-to-face interaction is a richly faceted and multiplex phenomenon containing many simultaneous and intertwined strands.[1] We shall be able to consider only a handful of the major processes involved: those of symbolic interaction, negotiated exchange, social influence and power, and task performance. Many others of nearly comparable importance, like social control, conflict, social integration, and the like, are regrettably omitted here.

IDENTIFICATION AND INTERACTION

When people encounter one another, they pose problems for one another all around. Other people are always somewhat unknown quantities, for they are complex, flighty, changeable creatures of mood and impulse. A woman, to be sure, is a "sometime thing." And who knows for sure whether or not that nice man downstairs may someday invade one's chambers armed with an ax and bent on mayhem? It happens somewhere every day. People can never be taken quite for granted, for one never knows what they may do. Even the lowliest "worm" may turn, and every "dog" has her day. As a consequence, we find that we must ever be appraising anew our friends and our lovers, our parents and our children. And we, in turn, are as much enigmas to others.

We try to judge others in terms of their significances for us, their implications for our plans of action. Literally, we do not know what to do with respect to another person until we have established his meaning for us and our meanings for him. The arduous, haphazard, and generally less than successful processes involved in such appraisal of persons have been, of course, explored in the previous chapter.

But we must now consider the fact that, in a concrete interaction situation, *every* person must appraise *everyone else,* and the pic-

[1]*Cf.,* for example, Adam Kendon, Richard M. Harris, and Mary Ritchie Key, editors, *Organization of Behavior in Face-to-Face Interaction,* The Hague: Mouton, 1975; John Laver and Sandy Hutcheson, editors, *Communication in Face to Face Interaction,* Baltimore: Penguin Books, 1972; and Michael Argyle, *Social Interaction,* New York: Atherton, 1969, for analyses of intertwining linguistic, paralinguistic, kinesic, and proxemic coordinations in interaction.

tures they come up with must all be at least roughly consensual, else some interactors will be acting in quite groundless fashion and at cross-purposes with the others. This latter outcome, of course, not infrequently occurs.

More important, however, it is still true that in the great majority of interactions people do manage to attain some fumbling consensus on the situations and the warm bodies within them, and they thus go on to conduct their respective businesses. It must be emphasized that such ''consensus'' does not mean real agreement on all appraisals among all the actors. Rather, consensus is defined here as the lack of impeding disagreements. *All that is needed is a sufficient lack of disagreement about one another for each to proceed in some degree with his own plans of action.*

This achievement is, in itself, no mean feat, however. It is a complex and quite problematic accomplishment. In the early sections of this chapter we shall examine the processes by means of which people are able to achieve such rough and ready ''working consensuses'' on the identities and meanings of the persons present. Later in the chapter we shall inquire how, social identities having been thus established, these persons carry out and mutually adjust their individual lines of action, how interactive roles are devised and performed.

Structured Situations

We are all aware that things are easier to understand when they are seen in context. A deformed tree becomes understandable within the context of a wind-swept plateau, and some of the ambiguities of foreign movies disappear when we have learned something of the cultures that produced them.

The same is true when it comes to judging persons. We can usually better understand them and their behavior when we know the contexts of their actions. Behavior that seems at first glance bizarre and irrational often becomes eminently reasonable when we know the web of circumstances in which it occurred. Behavior, even extreme behavior like suicide, gang delinquency, and paranoia, is ''reasonable'' from the perspective—the definition of the situation—of the behaving person.

The context or *situation* whithin which people encounter one another often affords excellent clues to their meaning for one another's plans of action.[2] In fact, much of socialization involves learning to define, at a glance, the more common situations of the immediate society and the limitations and opportunities they entail. For example, if we walk into a theater and find a man in non-military uniform standing expectantly at the door, we know automatically that he is a ticket-taker and that we must present to him valid tickets if we wish to continue into the theater. The ticket-taker is not so labeled, nor is his uniform particularly distinctive, yet we do not have to ask why he is is blocking our entrance, because the situation itself is so standardized in our culture that it provides sufficient clues as to the mutual implications of the persons involved. This and a host of other recurring and conventional situations themselves tell the contemporary American how he must conduct himself.

But this clarity of circumstance does not obtain in every human encounter or even in the majority of them. In fact, it is most likely to occur in precisely such routine and superficial interactions as the exchange of a ticket for entrance to the theater. And even then, the interaction may "spill over" from the specified into other exchanges and responses if the ticket-taker has a curious haircut, is an attractive girl, or is the son of one's insurance man.

Unstructured Situations

In most human encounters the contexts or situations are to some degree ambiguous and unstructured; that is, the situations are not clearly defined in the eyes of the interactors. The degree of unstructuredness results either from the uncertainty of the actors about which of their identities will be involved or from ambiguities in the meanings of the situation for the identities that have already become involved (or, not uncommonly, both of these factors).

[2]See the compilation on situational factors in Norman S. Endler and David Magnusson, editors, *Interactional Psychology and Personality*, Washington, D.C.: Hemisphere, 1976.

Typically, the problem in such cases is not that there are no available interpretations but rather that there are two or more *alternative* interpretations that could be placed upon the situation, each of which implies a somewhat different and perhaps conflicting meaning for the persons involved. If the alternative interpretations are held by different actors, a "situation-defining phase" is likely to occur.[3]

For example, the ticket-taker may also be a very close friend. The significance of this warm body, its implications for one's plans of action, is rather different if it is only that of a ticket-taker than it would be if it were only that of a close friend. In the first case, he will simply reach out for the tickets, tear them, and return the stubs, perhaps throwing in a mechanical "thank you." In the second case, he would stop any other activities (at least momentarily) to greet one warmly, inquire into one's present health, and engage in some idle conversation.

But as he is actually both ticket-taker *and* friend, it is not clear which of these patterns one should expect. If he is a very close friend, there may even be some consideration that he should let one into the theater without demanding a ticket. Rival interpretations of the situation, as being one of an impersonal encounter between theater official and patron or as being one of an encounter between warm friends, are competing for acceptance in this concrete case.

Between the two parties, an agreement on which interpretation to accept must be worked out quickly and unobtrusively. They must decide between them which scene to stage here, the meeting of official with patron or the meeting of friend with friend. They must decide, in effect, which identities are to be honored.

This decision is, of course, seldom an either-or decision even in "simple" situations like that described. Most often some sort of compromise interpretation is negotiated so that both sets of iden-

---

[3]See Donald W. Ball, "The Definition of the Situation: Some Theoretical and Methodological Consequences of Taking W. I. Thomas Seriously," *Journal for the Theory of Social Behaviour,* 1972, 2: 61–82; and R. S. Perinbanayagam, "The Definition of the Situation: An Analysis of the Ethnomethodological and Dramaturgical View," *Sociological Quarterly,* 1974, 15: 521–541.

tities receive partial recognition in the situation without either completely prevailing to the exclusion of the other.

In the typical concrete interaction, the "working consensus" arrived at is such that several identities of each of the interactors are involved. Usually the several identities are so blended together in the unfolding interaction that they can be separated only analytically.

The means by which these identities are "negotiated, legislated, and adjudicated" are quite complex, and we shall group them into two categories: the cognitive processes and the expressive processes.

COGNITIVE PROCESSES IN INTERACTION

This group of essentially covert processes has a certain logical priority in the complex flow of interaction, for these processes have to do with judging the identities that the various interactors (including onself) are likely to claim in the situation. Working from subtle clues and faint impressions, one attempts to discern the identities relevant to each of the several participants.

Imputation of Role to Alter

A person's social identities are not ordinarily to be physically perceived but are to be inferred from his appearance and, especially, his actions. The man in blue uniform may not be a policeman but an actor or a bus driver; the man in shirtsleeves may not be a customer but a captain of detectives. Even sexual identification is subject to error and deception. Social identities are seldom simply read off from a person's appearance but must be inferred from visible clues and from his behaviors.

When we use a person's behaviors as the basis for our inferences about his identities, we are employing the process of *role-taking*, a process that has been very widely discussed in the social-science literature.[4] Role-taking is but a special case of the general process of appraising persons that was discussed in the preceding chapter. The distinctiveness of role-taking as a perceptual process lies in its aim, which is to discover not the qualities of a person but the role he is performing before one and, thereby, his operative social identities.

An interactive role is, it will be remembered, the characteristic and plausible line of action that flows from, is truly expressive of, a distinctive character. The same person, of course, takes on different characters under different circumstances, and his roles, accordingly, also differ. His conduct at any moment is behavior organized under the influence of his current role, that is, the line of action that flows from and expresses his current character.

In role-taking, then, one is not trying to see through to a person's true self (his prominence hierarchy); one is merely trying to discover the contours of the role the other is currently projecting and the character (salient subset of identities) that underlies it. One is trying to see through the other's specific acts to discover the line of action that gives them direction, coherence, and meaning.

> Behavior is said to make sense when a series of actions is interpretable as indicating that the actor has in mind some role which guides his behavior. . . . The isolated action becomes a datum for role analysis only when it is interpreted as the manifestation of a configuration. The individual acts as if he were expressing some role through his behavior and may assign a higher degree of reality to the assumed role than to his specific actions. The role becomes the point of reference for placing interpretations on specific actions, for anticipating that one line of action will follow upon another, and for making evaluations of individual actions. For example, the lie which is an expression of the role of friend is an altogether different

[4]Ralph H. Turner, "Role Taking, Role Standpoint, and Reference Group Behavior," *American Journal of Sociology*, 1956, 61: 316–328; Turner and Norma Shosid, "Ambiguity and Interchangeability in Role Attribution: The Effect of Alter's Response," *American Sociological Review*, 1976, 41: 993–1006; Robert H. Lauer and Linda Boardman, "Role-Taking: Theory, Typology, and Propositions," *Sociology and Social Research*, 1971, 23: 137–147; and Jean M. Guiot, "Attribution and Identity Construction: Some Comments," *American Sociological Review*, 1977, 42: 692–704.

thing from the same lie taken as a manifestation of the role of confidence man.[5]

The unity of a role cannot consist simply in the bracketing of a set of specific behaviors, since the same behavior can be indicative of different roles under different circumstances. The unifying element is to be found *in some assignment of purpose or sentiment to the actor.* Various actions by an individual are classified as intentional and unintentional (relevant and irrelevant) on the basis of a role designation. . . . Role-taking involves selective perception of the actions of another and a great deal of selective emphasis, organized about some purpose or sentiment attributed to the other.[6]

In trying to discern alter's role, then, we impute to him certain purposes or motives in the light of which alter's actions appear coherently organized as a recognizable line of action. "The key to person perception lies in our attention to what he is *trying to do.*"[7]

To understand, explain, or justify specific actions, then, we impute (or avow) *motives.* If we were so crude as to grill alter about why he did a certain thing in a situation, he would try to explain his behavior, to justify his conduct, by avowing certain motives or purposes for those actions.[8] Men, unlike other animals, are always under the scrutiny of their fellows and are potentially held accountable for their every action, as we have noted before. Consequently, they must always be prepared to avow the motives that justify their every act, past, present, and future.

They do not have complete freedom of choice in this avowal, however. "Institutionally different situations have different vo-

[5]Turner, "Role-Taking: Process Versus Conformity," in Arnold M. Rose, editor, *Human Behavior and Social Processes,* Boston: Houghton Mifflin, 1962, pp. 20–40. Quotation from p. 24.

[6]*Ibid.,* p. 28.

[7]Gordon W. Allport, *Pattern and Growth in Personality,* New York: Holt, Rinehart & Winston, 1961, p. 520.

[8]Marvin B. Scott and Stanford W. Lyman, "Accounts," *American Sociological Review,* 1968, 33: 46–62; Phillip W. Blumstein *et al.,* "The Honoring of Accounts," *American Sociological Review,* 1974, 39: 551–566; and Rom Harré and Paul F. Secord, *The Explanation of Social Behaviour,* Oxford: Blackwell, 1972.

cabularies of motive appropriate to their respective behaviors.''[9] That is, there is only a finite and small number of motives recognized in the culture for avowal or imputation, and these few motives are differently associated with certain situations and certain social positions. Therefore, a motive avowed in one type of situation may constitute a perfectly acceptable justification of one's acts, whereas the very same motive avowed in a different type of situation would not be accepted as a justification. For example, a person caught in a lie can often justify his conduct by claiming to have been trying to protect a friend's feelings, but, if he is caught in the same lie in a courtroom situation, this motive will not persuade the judge.

In our pluralistic society with its competing groups, each of which fosters its own distinctive perspectives on the world, there have developed divergent vocabularies of motive. The homosexual may be able to justify his conduct to the ''gay'' world but not to the courts. A medieval monk avowed that he gave food to a poor but pretty woman because it was ''for the glory of God and the eternal salvation of his soul,'' but the Freudians would question this avowal and impute frankly sexual motives to him.

> What is reason for one man is rationalization for another. The variable is the accepted vocabulary of motives, the ultimates of (justificatory) discourse, of each man's dominant group about whose opinion he cares.[10]

If we are to understand a person's behavior, to discern a role through it, we must try to discover for which audience he is avowing and imputing motives, and whether or not the vocabulary in terms of which he does so is an acceptable one to that particular audience. Once we decide whom he is playing to, so to speak, we can usually discern the motives or purposes that are organizing his line of action. If we do not share the vocabulary of motives held by that particular audience, however, we may be totally unable to make sense of alter's actions.

[9]C. Wright Mills, ''Situated Actions and Vocabularies of Motive,'' *American Sociological Review*, 1940, 5: 904–913. Quotation from p. 906.
[10]*Ibid.*, p. 910.

These remarks and our daily experiences point up the fact that role-taking is at least as complex and uncertain a process as is social perception generally. A number of researches—and, again, our daily experiences—shows that people vary markedly in the "breadth," the "depth," and other aspects of their role-taking abilities.

A modicum of role-taking ability is widespread in every population because most interactions pertain to only a fairly small number of types of social identity, and most members of the population have had at least some experience with each. In the course of our lives, most of us experience at least something of all the fundamental human themes and relationships. Most of us have had at least fleeting experience with being leader and follower, poet and performer of repetitive routines, active manipulator and passive recipient, idealist and opportunist, success and failure. The extent and the content of experience with these archetypical identities and themes vary tremendously, of course, but some experience with the forms, at least vicariously, is probably fairly universal within a given culture.

Each individual therefore has, incorporated into his "inner forum," a repertoire of many different perspectives and vocabularies of motives, albeit in different proportions and balances. This repertoire, and the use of analogies, enables us to take roles. The analogies, so common in literature and daily discourse, enable us to relate an initially unfathomed human action to our own repertoire and thus to gain insight into it: "Riding in a small plane is no more upsetting than riding a ferris wheel, and flying in a jet-liner is like sitting in your living room—after a fast elevator ride up."

We can take another's role, then, if some components of our own "inner forums" are at least generally similar to the identities that are salient in his actions. We temporarily and hypothetically "stretch" our own hierarchies of identity-perspectives until the situation is viewed from a vantage point, opportunity structure, and motivations similar to those of alter. If we and alter are "like-minded" or "see eye to eye," role-taking is relatively easy. But we shall never completely match alter's perspective, and the more dissimilar he is from us the more "elastic" our own perspectives must be to catch even a glimpse of his own point of view.

It must be emphasized that "role-taking" is a metaphor. We do not and cannot literally "take" alter's role. When we "project" ourselves into his situation and imagine how we would feel, we are sometimes impressed by the intensity and realism of our own feelings, but these feelings are *ours*, not his, and the accuracy of our role-taking remains uncertain.

The variables that determine the accuracy, breadth, and depth of our role-taking abilities in interaction situations derive from the nature of the role-taking process itself.[11] The first and most important are the amount and breadth of our experiences. We learn role-taking not only from our own accumulated direct experience with various roles but also, to a lesser extent yet more broadly, from observing the counterrole performances of those who have interacted with us. In this manner, for example, persons develop some insight into the perspectives of the opposite sex, and children have some glimmering of what it means to be a parent. The information accumulated from observing those who are in counterroles to ourselves is one of the major avenues of "anticipatory socialization" more generally, as we shall see in Chapter 8.

Role-taking ability can thus develop both from "subjective" experience with similar roles and from more "objective" experience in observing others in these roles. Professionals often develop a great deal of this "objective" knowledge about their clients, and the latter are often surprised by what seems to them uncanny familiarity with their own points of view. Such knowledge on the part of the doctor, the teacher, the official points up the fact that "empathy" must not be confused with sympathy or emotional involvement of any kind; the professional is often quite aloof and "clinically distant" from his client.

Role-taking ability is also affected by the conventionality of the identities and performances involved. In fact, role-taking is almost

[11]For a systematic review of evidence on the factors determining accuracy of role-taking and person perception, see, for example, Allport, *op. cit.*, pp. 497–548. Also, Claudia Hale and Jesse G. Delia, "Cognitive Complexity and Social Perspective-Taking," *Communication Monographs*, 1976, 43: 238–245.

always a partial and selective process that focuses upon the more superficial and conventional aspects of the other person's identities. This incompleteness is present of necessity, as these conventional aspects are the "common denominators" of imagery and motivation in that social grouping.

And finally, role-taking ability is subject to the degree of familiarity with the other person. This familiarity may be direct, through long interaction with the particular person, or indirect, through a good deal of interaction with other but similar persons, which is why role-taking ability tends to decrease with social distance and why interaction with foreigners poses such problems.

Role-taking is altogether, then, a variable and uncertain business, but it is a crucial aspect of negotiating interactions.

Improvisation of a Role for Self

Once we have discovered what we (rightly or wrongly) conceive to be alter's current interactive role, we modify our own lines of action on the basis of what we perceive alter's implications to be with respect to our manifest and latent plans of action. That is, having imputed a role to alter, we devise (or improvise) our own roles in the light of what alter's putative role means for us.

This description must not be taken to imply that alter's role (lover, for example) determines our own role in the simple sense that we are thereby led to play the corresponding counterrole (Juliet to his Romeo). Instead, we devise our roles in terms of how we can best make use of alter's line of action; if alter's imputed role happens to be one that is unfavorable to our plans, we devise our role in terms of how we can induce alter to *change* his line of action to one more profitable to us.

In other words, the interactive role that we believe we discern in alter's behaviors is appraised in terms of the *opportunity structure* this role presents for us. Perceived opportunity structure, it will be recalled, is one of the important determinants of our own salience hierarchies, or situational selves. It is in this fashion that the role we impute to alter influences the contents of our own roles, by making certain of our role-identities (those for which alter's role constitutes opportunities) more salient in the situation. As discussed in Chapter 4, we attempt to work into our situational performances, or interactive roles, those identities that are currently most salient. Given the salience hierarchies and the perceived opportunity structure, our purposes or aims in the encounter are relatively clear cut: We wish to enact certain contents of the salient identities with the aim of obtaining certain kinds and amounts of social reward—role-support and intrinsic and extrinsic gratifications. Of course, we do not necessarily expect to receive these rewards from alter himself; we may be performing toward alter but *for* such alternative audiences as bystanders and spectators or even absent third parties in terms of whose perspectives we ourselves can appraise our performances and thus receive vicarious social support.

Alter, meanwhile, must also attempt to discern these roles of ours (and, consequently, to modify his own). He must endeavor to identify which audiences, identities, and vocabularies of motives are relevant to our improvised roles. Once he has imputed interactive roles to us, he can proceed to devise and revise his own role.

If the parties are to achieve any kind of rudimentary accommodation in the situation, each party's improvised role must be at least roughly in line with the role imputed to him by the other parties. In all but the most standardized situations, this rough correspondence is entirely problematic. The chances of crossing one another up are very great, especially in those cases in which one is reluctant to go along with alter's role or with the role alter imputes to one. A person's imputed and improvised roles must be somehow squared with one another, through communication with alter, who faces the same problems.

This process of communication takes place through another, more overt set of processes, the expressive processes.

EXPRESSIVE PROCESSES IN INTERACTION

The imputation and improvisation of interactive roles are purely cognitive or perceptual matters, involving the identification of persons and lines of action, and are passive in nature. Even the improvisation of one's own role is purely a matter of thinking about oneself and one's course of action, a matter of identifying who one is or would like to be in the current situation. It does not involve doing anything about it.

The expressive processes to which we now turn are, on the other hand, not covert and operating upon received impressions, are not cognitive and responsive. They are instead overt processes involving expression of information in active attempts to affect situations. These processes are those employed to bring the imputations of one party into line with the improvisations of another party through the expression of images of self and other.

Presentation of Self

The first of these expressive processes is the selective presentation of self, the tactics of which have been very thoroughly explored by Erving Goffman.[12] By carefully controlling one's expressive behaviors one can convey to alter an image of the character one desires to assume in the situation. If this control is exercised skillfully, if one's performance thoroughly sustains one's role and character, alter will have little ground for denying one's claims to identity (at least in terms of the information available in the encounter itself; if alter is able to examine one in a broader context he may, of course, be more able to expose one's claims).

In the case of such skillful performances, ego virtually constrains alter to accept ego's claim to character and to conduct himself toward ego in the fashion appropriate when in the presence of such a character. That is, when an individual "makes an implicit or explicit claim to be a person of a particular kind, he automatically exerts a moral demand upon the others, obliging them to value and treat him in the manner that persons of this kind have a right to expect."[13] In effect, then, an individual's presentation of

---

[12]Erving Goffman, *The Presentation of Self in Everyday Life,* Garden City, N.Y.: Doubleday Anchor, 1957. See also Eugene A. Weinstein and Lawrence S. Beckhouse, "Audience and Personality Factors in Presentation of Self," *Sociological Quarterly,* 1969, 10: 527–537; David J. Schneider, "Tactical Self-Presentation after Success and Failure," *Journal of Personality and Social Psychology,* 1969, 13: 262–268; and Part I in Harré, ed., *Life Sentences: Aspects of the Social Role of Language,* New York: Wiley, 1976.

[13]Goffman, *op. cit.,* p. 13.

self tends to become a self-fulfilling image (as discussed in Chapter 5). By conducting himself as if he were a certain kind of person, he exerts leverage on others to *act toward him* as if he were that kind of person and thus to support his performance and his claims. If a person claims to be a writer or an expert fisherman or a topflight golfer *and if nothing about his talk or performance enables us to dispute that claim,* we have no choice but to go along, at least publicly, with his claim to that identity, at least for the time being.

It is precisely this leverage on others that allows us to maintain our conceptions of ourselves in some degree, as long as we can avoid tripping ourselves up through our own performances. People are obliged to give us the benefit of the doubt as long as the case against our claims is not established *beyond* reasonable doubt.

Because this leverage tempts us to exploitation, however, the others tend privately to be quite skeptical and to develop subtle tactics for testing our performances for signs of deception.[14] We, in turn, attempt to counter these tactics with dramaturgical techniques of our own, so that the most ordinary encounters come to resemble the maneuverings of highly developed intelligence and counterintelligence agencies.[15]

Nonetheless, until the evidence is in, each must accord the other the benefit of the doubt.

Altercasting

The second expressive process, that of altercasting,[16] resembles presentation of self in its form but differs in its point of applica-

[14]Paul Ekman and Wallace V. Friesen, "Nonverbal Leakage and Clues to Deception," *Psychiatry,* 1969, 32: 88–106.

[15]Goffman, *Strategic Interaction,* Philadelphia: University of Pennsylvania Press, 1969. See also Eugene A. Weinstein, "Toward a Theory of Interpersonal Tactics," in Carl W. Backman and Paul F. Secord, editors, *Problems in Social Psychology,* New York: McGraw-Hill, 1966, pp. 394–398; Blumstein, "Audience, Machiavellianism, and Tactics of Identity Bargaining," *Sociological Quarterly,* 1973, 36: 346–365; and John P. Hewitt and Randall Stokes, "Disclaimers," *American Sociological Review,* 1975, 40: 1–11.

[16]Weinstein and Paul Deutschberger, "Tasks, Bargains, and Identities in Social Interaction," *Social Forces,* 1964, 42: 451–456; Weinstein and

tion. Not only does our performance express an image of who *we* are, but it also simultaneously expresses an image of whom we take *alter* to be. This image, too, has a tendency to become self-fulfilling, for we act toward alter as if he were indeed the sort of person we take him to be, and we may continue to do so regardless of what alter actually does. The enthusiastic salesman may treat a person as if this other were an eager customer, and the protestations and denials of other may be interpreted as merely coy expressions of such eagerness, thus confirming the salesman's image of other and perpetuating his line of action toward him. And, in fact, casting him in this manner *may* actually lead other eventually to adopt this role of eager customer. Therein lies the eventual utility of this expressive process.

Yet neither presentation of self nor altercasting necessarily or automatically brings into line the roles and characters that we devise for ourselves with those imputed to us by alter. These processes only serve to express to alter the results of our cognitive processes, to express the roles we have imputed to alter and the roles we have devised for ourselves. Alter may not even "read" these expressive messages correctly, for it is a long leap from expressions sent to impressions received. Whether accurately read or not, the expressed roles for self and alter may not be acceptable to alter in terms of his own hierarchy of role-identities.

In such a case, one's expressive processes do not serve to structure the encounter but only suggest to alter the direction in which one would like to modify the roles of each party. Alter, in turn, will employ these processes to indicate to one the somewhat different direction in which he would like to modify the interactive roles. If neither party is willing to give on these issues, both will continue to talk right past each other, acting profitlessly on incompatible bases.

Typically, however, the two parties will negotiate some sort of compromise, each acceding somewhat to the other's demands,

Deutschberger, "Some Dimensions of Altercasting," *Sociometry,* 1963, 26: 454–466; Raymond P. Perry and J. Edwin Boyd, "Communicating Impressions of People," *Journal of Social Psychology,* 1972, 86: 95–103; and Edwin C. Schur, *Labeling Deviant Behavior,* New York: Harper & Row, 1971.

though seldom in equal degree. Labeling theorists have emphasized such inequalities between the altercasting by social control
agents (e.g., policemen or psychiatrists) and the presentation of self
by private citizens in delicate encounters. Even there, however, the
putatively delinquent or insane person will seldom simply acquiesce in the agent's altercasting but will continue to attempt to
present a more favorable character, seeking against heavy odds to
negotiate a more desirable compromise.[17]

THE NEGOTIATION
OF SOCIAL IDENTITIES[18]

This compromise definition of the role and character of each is
not executed in a single step but is the eventual result of a complex
process of negotiation or bargaining. There are essentially two
stages in this bargaining: the negotiation of social identities and
the negotiation of interactive roles. That is, agreement must first
be reached simply on the broad outlines of who each party is in
terms of social categories like doctor, lawyer, and Indian chief
before bargaining can begin on the specific contents of the present
behavior of such characters. We shall confine ourselves to this first
stage of the negotiation in this section and return in subsequent
sections to the negotiation of the actual contents of interactive
roles.

At both stages of the negotiation, the moves of each party are
motivated by cost-reward considerations but take the form of in-
sinuations about identities. At base, that is, the negotiation is a

---

[17]See, *e.g.*, R. C. Prus, "Resisting Designations: An Extension of Attribution
Theory into a Negotiated Context," *Sociological Inquiry*, 1975, 45: 3–14; Joseph
W. Rogers and M. D. Buffalo, "Fighting Back: Nine Modes of Adaptation to a
Deviant Label," *Social Problems*, 1974, 22: 101–118; and Mordechai Roten-
burg, "Self-Labelling: A Missing Link in the 'Societal Reaction' Theory of Devia-
tion," *Sociological Review*, 1974, 22: 335–356.

[18]See Blumstein, "An Experiment in Identity Bargaining," unpublished
Ph.D. dissertation, Vanderbilt University, 1970. *Cf.* the views of Arthur Brittan,
Meanings and Situations, London: Routledge & Kegan Paul, 1973; and Lothar
Krappmann, *Soziologische Dimensionen der Identität*, Stuttgart: Klett, 1969.

process of bargaining or haggling over the terms of exchange of social rewards, yet it does not assume the outward appearance of a crude naming of prices. Rather, it takes the form of an argument or debate over who each person is; the tactics of rhetorical persuasion or dramatic arts are more evident in the process than are those of the market place. Each move is presented as a change (or a refusal to change) in the presentation of self or in altercasting. If the move is in a direction acceptable to the other party, he will alter his expressive behavior in a manner that tacitly signals his concurrence and his concession (or perhaps signals his demand for still further concessions in the same direction from his partner). If the move is not acceptable, it is countered by a studied and emphatic persistence in his line of altercasting and presentation of self. Among the socially skilled, this rhetoric has sometimes been elevated to a high art form (as in the manuals of Stephen Potter),[19] and encounters between particularly adept performers often become legendary.

Nonetheless, considerations of exchange underlie the process. Each person seeks to incorporate into his performance in the situation those identities that are uppermost at the moment in his salience hierarchy of role-identities. The negotiation is basically a process of settling which, how many, and how much of his salient role-identities each person will be allowed to incorporate into his performance. Weinstein and Deutschberger[20] have pointed out that there are not one but two bargains to be struck in this connection, one with oneself and one with alter.

In our terms, one must, first of all, somehow reconcile the role he improvises for himself (in response to the role imputed to alter) with the demands of his own salience hierarchy. He is seldom allowed by others to perform exactly the interactive role he would like; he is seldom able to comply exactly with the preferences established by his own salience hierarchy but will have to settle for the most profitable compromise. (This necessity for compromising with one's own situational self is, incidentally, a prime cause of

[19]*Inter alia,* Stephen Potter, *One-upmanship,* New York: Holt, Rinehart & Winston, 1955; and Potter, *The Theory and Practice of Gamesmanship,* New York: Holt, Rinehart & Winston, 1954.

[20]Weinstein and Deutschberger, "Tasks."

the omnipresent discrepancy between the role-support gained from a particular performance and the demands of the identities themselves.)

Second, he must also reconcile his improvised role toward alter with the demands of *alter's* salience hierarchy. The content of one or more of alter's salient role-identities may dictate that the person act toward him in an altogether different fashion than indicated by his own improvised and expressed role.

The first stage in this process, as mentioned, is to negotiate the social identities of each participant, to come to agreement simply upon the relevant social categories and social positions to which each person belongs for purposes of the present encounter. This agreement represents essentially a *working agreement* on which the parties can stand while they continue to bargain, negotiating the specifics of their interactive roles. The form of such a working agreement is schematically represented in Figure 1.

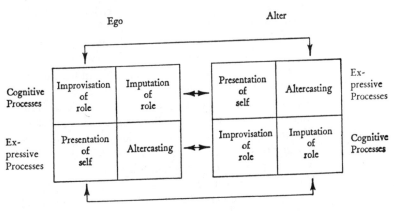

Figure 1.   The Working Agreement

A working agreement can be said to exist when the cognitive processes of one person, with respect to social identities, are not in gross conflict with the expressive processes of the other person. It exists, that is, when the altercasting of one party is not greatly inconsistent with the improvised role of the other party and when the presentation of self by one party is not in conflict with the role imputed him by the other, as in Figure 1.

Such an agreement is problematic in its attainment and far from stable. The process of negotiating such an agreement is splendidly portrayed in John Barth's novel *The End of the Road*. A young man has just made a pick-up at the beach and is overhastily seducing the lady, who protests:[21]

"Don't you understand how you make me feel? Today is my last day at Ocean City. For two whole weeks not a soul has spoken to me or even looked at me, except some horrible old men. Not a *soul!* Most women look awful at my age, but I don't look awful: I just don't look like a child. There's a lot more to me, damn it! And then on the last day you come along and pick me up, bored as you can be with the whole thing, and treat me like a whore!"

Well, she was correct.

"I'm a cad," I agreed readily, and rose to leave. There was a little more to this matter than Miss Rankin was willing to see, but in the main she had a pretty clear view of things. Her mistake, in the long run, was articulating her protest. The game was spoiled now, of course: I had assigned to Miss Rankin a role of Forty-Year Old Pick-up, a delicate enough character for her to bring off successfully in my current mood; I had no interest whatever in the quite complex (and no doubt interesting, from another point of view) human being she might be apart from that role. What she should have done, it seems to me, assuming she was after the same thing I was after, was assign me a role gratifying to her own vanity—say, The Fresh But Unintelligent Young Man Whose Body One Uses for One's Pleasure Without Otherwise Taking Him Seriously—and then we could have pursued our business with no wounds inflicted on either side. As it was, my present feeling, though a good deal stronger, was essentially the same feeling one has when a filling-station attendant or a cabdriver launches into his life-story: as a rule, and especially when one is in a hurry or is grouchy, one wishes the man to be nothing more difficult than the Obliging Filling-Station Attendant or the Adroit Cabdriver. These are the essences you have assigned them, at least temporarily, for your own purposes, as a tale-teller makes a man The Handsome Young Poet or The Jealous Old Husband; and while you know very well that no historical human being was ever *just* an Obliging Filling-Station Attendant or a Handsome Young Poet, you are nevertheless prepared to ignore your man's charming complexities—*must* ignore them, in fact, if you are to get on with the plot, or get things done on schedule. . . . Enough now to say that we are all casting directors a great deal of the time, if not always, and he is wise who realizes that this role-assigning is at best an arbitrary distortion of the actors' personalities; but he is even wiser who sees in addition that his arbitrariness is probably inevitable, and at any rate is apparently necessary if one would reach the ends he desires.

It is important to recognize the considerable strain that this unre-solved difference in identification of self and other has placed upon the interaction. Until the two come to an agreement, neither can safely pursue his own course with respect to the other. Perhaps he will prove more persuasive under the circumstances, perhaps she. Or they may be forced to agree to be, not simply pick-ups nor yet quite lovers, but some special category of noncasual sex part-ners instead. Whatever the direction of the resolution, it must be attained in one of the several fashions we have portrayed. Indeed, Barth's novel goes on to detail the succession of rhetorical and dramaturgical moves through which the two negotiate an eventual and rather unequal compromise.

If a pattern of interaction has been established between two par-ticular actors—if an "interpersonal relationship" has developed—this first phase of agreement can perhaps be assumed, but, if the relationship changes or the actors are thrown into new situations, these rudimentary interaction processes begin anew.[22]

Such a working agreement, in which the expressive processes of one party are in rough agreement with the cognitive processes of the other and vice versa, constitutes the "definition of the situa-tion." In routine and standardized encounters, this agreement is readily attained; in the more typical situation, it must be ham-mered out through this process of negotiation. Despite the claims of some theorists, it must be emphasized that the attainment of such a "definition of the situation" does not settle the matter of

[22]Barney Glaser and Anselm Strauss, "Awareness Contexts and Social Interac-tion," *American Sociological Review*, 1964, 29: 669–679.

identities and the meaning of persons for the remainder of that encounter. On the contrary, it is only the beginning, an agreement on which the parties can stand while they continue to negotiate the finer points of their roles and characters through many more rounds of bargaining.

We must take certain exception, for example, to the views of Erving Goffman on this point.[23] Goffman has argued that such a "definition of the situation" serves as a set of boundary rules governing the subject matter that can be admitted to that particular encounter and that these rules must be treated with utmost gravity, for a threat to them is a threat to the structure of the entire encounter. Reaching such a working agreement is, after all, a social act, generating social objects—the consensual roles and characters of the people present. If any one person should then act out of character, the selves of all would be threatened and restorative measures required.

This analysis is certainly valid;[24] the working agreement is assuredly a delicate balance of interactive processes and is easily tipped. What Goffman omits is that there is every pressure to continue the struggle over one's character and role, to bring them more into line with one's role-identities. As a natural consequence, someone will occasionally push too hard in this struggle and upset the working agreement, spoiling the encounter and embarrassing the character of everyone present. This risk is always present in the bargaining process, but it is one that is very often taken by at least one party to the negotiation, in the hope of winning greater opportunity to fulfill his role-identities.

If the working agreement, the definition of the situation, is upset in this fashion, it is neither the end of the world nor necessarily the end of the encounter. Very often a new agreement is negotiated, perhaps itself to be upset and superseded. A single encounter, then, often presents the appearance of successive *phases*

---

[23]Goffman, *Encounters,* Indianapolis: Bobbs-Merrill, 1961, pp. 7–81.

[24]Michal M. McCall, "Boundary Rules in Relationships and Encounters," in George J. McCall, Michal M. McCall, Norman K. Denzin, Gerald D. Suttles, and Suzanne B. Kurth, *Social Relationships,* Chicago: Aldine, 1970, pp. 35–61.

of interaction, each marked by the negotiation of a new working agreement.[25]

A working agreement is so easily upset simply because it is a precarious balance of processes, the balance that has been portrayed in Figure 1. It is an agreement only as long as the expressive processes of one party roughly correspond with the cognitive processes of the other. These processes do not cease when an agreement is attained but go on as long as the parties are in contact. The persistence of the working agreement depends upon the continuing correspondence of the constituent processes. One must continually monitor the expressive implications of his behaviors so as not to contradict alter's images of him and alter, and alter must do the same. If an act should contradict one of these images, it must be successfully explained away, or the working agreement will at once collapse. We shall have more to say about this problem shortly.

TASKS AND INTERACTION

Our emphasis thus far on identities in interaction must not be allowed to obscure the obvious fact that more is involved in encounters than skirmishes over identity. After all, people do much of their work in the company of other people, and in fact an increasing proportion of jobs consists entirely of doing things to, for, with, or against other people. Play, too, is typically an interactional endeavor, as are family life, politics, and most of our other social institutions.

The establishment of identities within an encounter is usually little more than a necessary prerequisite to the execution of other social tasks. It is a necessary but seldom an exclusive task in face-to-face encounters. Many complex activities are carried on in the presence of other people, and in most instances these activities (rather than the establishment of identities) are the main focus of the en-

[25]*Cf.* Anselm Strauss, *Mirrors and Masks,* New York: Free Press, 1959, pp. 44–88.

counter. The negotiation of identities is the *first* task of interaction, and, although it is never completely settled, it ordinarily fades into the background as a working agreement, in terms of which the interactors can turn to the main business of the encounter, can go on to build canoes, make love, or eat dinner.[26]

This task focus can assume an infinitude of forms, as we have seen in Chapter 2. It may be a merely sociable conversation, it may be the negotiation of a military surrender, it may be a game of craps, or it may be the purchase of a girdle. It may be entirely nonverbal, as in the case of underwater demolition experts rigging a charge, or it may consist entirely of talk, as in the case of psychiatrist and patient.

Whatever the task, *it* is ordinarily "figure," and the negotiated identities are the "ground" in the encounter. Occasionally, however, something may call into question this working agreement on identities, causing a figure-ground reversal, so to speak.[27] If, in a team of professional carpenters, one should happen to strike his thumb rather than the nail or if a league bowler should happen to throw a gutter ball or two, these errant task performances raise to prominence the legitimacy of his claims to the identity that has previously been accepted by all present. To choose a rather different sort of example, it may develop that, in the course of buying a pair of shoes, the customer's casual remark reveals that he is the brother-in-law of the clerk's Thursday-night bridge partner; this remark then leads to a renegotiation of the identities that had underlain the encounter.

These "figure-ground reversals" stem from the fact that the cognitive and expressive processes are carried on *throughout the*

[26]M. M. McCall, *op. cit.*

[27]For readers to whom this allusion to illusion may be unfamiliar, see, for example, M. D. Vernon, *The Psychology of Perception*, Baltimore: Penguin Books, 1962, pp. 40–46 and *passim.* Contrasts and shifts between task-focused and identity-focused interaction are discussed more fully in Ralph H. Turner, "The Self-Conception in Social Interaction," in Chad Gordon and Kenneth J. Gergen, *The Self in Social Interaction* (volume I), New York: Wiley, 1968, pp. 93–106; Turner, *Family Interaction*, New York: Wiley, 1970; and George J. McCall, "Communication and Negotiated Identity," *Communication*, 1976, 2: 173–184. *Cf.* Shelley Duvall and Robert A. Wicklund, *A Theory of Objective Self-Awareness*, New York: Academic Press, 1972.

encounter, even after rough accord has been reached between them. The working agreement can be called into question whenever the expressive implications of one person's task-oriented actions come to differ from another's accepted image of him. Task performance will then be largely suspended until the working agreement can be restored (for example, through joking, disavowal, explanation, or apology) or renegotiated.[28] Far from being an unusual and destructive occurrence, such occasional oscillation between interactional concern for the task and concern for the working agreement appears to be more the norm than the exception.[29]

Nonetheless, it remains true that this occasional shift of focus does engender a certain strain in the encounter, for the two concerns are somewhat incompatible. If attention must be diverted from the ongoing task to reconsideration of the negotiation of identities, the task performance necessarily suffers in the meantime. If the execution of the task has implications for the role of one of the participants, the performance necessarily threatens the negotiated agreement. Therefore, there is ordinarily a certain amount of strain between these two concerns in any encounter.

This strain, however, is a variable quantity, being more intense in certain types of encounter. Perhaps the polar types in this res-

[28]Goffman, "Embarrassment and Social Organization," *American Journal of Sociology,* 1956, 62: 264–274; Edward Gross and Gregory P. Stone, "Embarrassment and the Analysis of Role Requirements," *American Journal of Sociology,* 1964, 70: 1–15; André Modigliani, "Embarrassment and Embarrassability," *Sociometry,* 1968, 31: 313–326; Goffman, "On Facework: An Analysis of Ritual Elements in Social Interaction," *Psychiatry,* 1955, 18: 213–231; Bert R. Brown, "Face-Saving Following Experimentally Induced Embarrassment," *Journal of Experimental Social Psychology,* 1970, 6: 225–271; W. Peter Archibald and Ronald L. Cohen, "Self-Presentation, Embarrassment, and Facework as a Function of Self-Evaluation, Conditions of Self-Presentation, and Feedback from Others," *Journal of Personality and Social Psychology,* 1971, 20: 287–297; and Marvin B. Scott and Stanford W. Lyman, "Accounts," *American Sociological Review,* 1968, 33: 46–62.

[29]Compare, for example, with Bales's concept of the "equilibrium problem" in the context of small group interaction. R. F. Bales, "The Equilibrium Problem in Small Groups," in Talcott Parsons, Bales, and Edward A. Shils, editors, *Working Papers in the Theory of Action,* New York: Free Press, 1953, pp. 111–161.

pect are a sociable party and a personal quarrel. In the case of the party, as Simmel has pointed out,[30] the task itself is essentially nothing more than identity negotiation, so that the task concern is virtually identical with the concern for the working agreement. In the personal quarrel, on the other hand, the demands of the encounter itself (to negotiate a working agreement on which to stand) run counter to the demands of the task proper, which is to deny and demolish the assumed role of the other person. The two concerns of the encounter are thus quite antithetical. Most encounters, of course, are intermediate between these two extremes in relation to the strain between the two interactional concerns.

THE NEGOTIATION OF INTERACTIVE ROLES[31]

Granted that the working agreement on social identities may at times be called into question, it nonetheless constitutes the ground upon which the participants may stand as they proceed to negotiate the specific shape and content of their respective interactive roles in the encounter.

As already argued, we try to shape or control the other's behavior in the direction most profitable to our own desires, and we do so by offering (or withholding) certain rewards. These rewards are typically embodied in our own behaviors *vis-à-vis* alter; our behaviors may directly provide him with sexual pleasures, task assistance, or support for his self-conceptions. Performances thus constitute the *medium* of social exchange.

We do not, however, ordinarily stage rewarding performances of this sort until we have received some indication that alter will,

[30]Georg Simmel, *The Sociology of Georg Simmel* (trans. Kurt Wolff), New York: Free Press, 1950, pp. 40–57. Also, Jeanne Watson, "A Formal Analysis of Sociable Interaction," *Sociometry*, 1964, 21: 269–280.

[31]*Cf.* William J. Goode, "A Theory of Role Strain," *American Sociological Review*, 1960, 25: 483–496; Brittan, *op. cit.*; and Bruce Kapferer, editor, *Transaction and Meaning: Directions in the Anthropology of Exchange and Symbolic Behavior*, Philadelphia: Institute for the Study of Human Issues, 1976. At a more general level, see Jeffrey Z. Rubin and Bert R. Brown, *The Social Psychology of Bargaining and Negotiation*, New York: Academic Press, 1975.

in return, stage a performance rewarding to us. A bargain must be struck before the goods will actually be allowed to change hands, so to speak.

This implicit bargaining, too, takes place through the medium of dramaturgical performances. Our actions are tailored to convey, through expressive implications, hints of what we are willing to do, if only alter will accept certain detailed contents of our altercasting and presentation of self. A prototypical example of all these processes is the courting situation. If the girl's behavior gives the impression that she is a normal, red-blooded dating girl, the boy is willing to ask her to the movies on the implied promise of a little hand-holding and a goodnight kiss. If she then welshes on the implicit bargain, he will attempt to negotiate it more firmly by casting her in the role of gold-digger or prude; if he attempts to go beyond the terms of the implicit bargain, she will continue the bargaining process by casting him in the role of wolf or cad. The bargaining process is, as we have argued, carried on through the medium of the expressive processes: altercasting and presentation of self.

Let us examine more closely the manner in which social rewards are thus employed in shaping the interactive roles of the participants in an encounter.

Extrinsic Gratifications

Social scientists are most familiar with the role of extrinsic gratifications in this respect, thanks to the advanced development of economic theory. Certain events and objects are gratifying to the individual simply because they are useful to him in pursuing his various endeavors. Money, labor, information, material goods, privileges, favors, social status, all these elements and more may be helpful to him in carrying out his various enterprises. As a consequence, they acquire certain value of their own, and he may be willing to incur certain costs simply to acquire them.

If through his performance a person provides alter, or implies that he will provide him, with such gratifications, alter may be willing to act in a manner that is in turn rewarding to ego. Of course, it is not necessarily the case that alter's performance will be rewarding to ego in the sense that it repays him in kind, through affording him extrinsic gratifications of some sort. Very often, in fact, it will be rewarding in that it provides ego some other category of valuables, so that the exchange of rewards is a *mixed* exchange, an important type that will be discussed later.

Intrinsic Gratifications

Many actions or performances are gratifying in themselves, as we have seen in earlier chapters. They may be gratifying in that they bring us various bodily pleasures or relieve certain bodily discomforts, or they may be gratifying in that they afford us simply a sense of efficacy, of having done something in the world. These performances are enjoyable in themselves, as witnessed by the fact that a person is willing to suffer certain costs simply to be allowed to perform them.[32]

Again, if through his actions ego provides, or implies the provision of, an opportunity for (or cooperation in) the enactment of these activities, alter in turn may be willing to act in a manner that is rewarding to ego. In many cases, of course, as these enjoyable activities are often social acts involving more than one person, his rewarding action may simply involve allowing ego to engage in the activity with him. This need not be the case, however; he may instead allow ego to enact some *other* activity that is enjoyable to ego (and perhaps not at all enjoyable to him). Or, again, he may provide some different category of reward in a mixed exchange.

Support of Role-Identities

Undoubtedly man's most distinctive type of gratification is support for his various role-identities. Men seek to live and act in the manner in which they like to imagine themselves living and acting or, failing that in some degree, at least to be able to continue thinking of themselves in that same manner.

[32]These intrinsic gratifications and their reward values have been extensively studied, of course, by many behavioral psychologists. See, for example, J. S. Brown, *The Motivation of Behavior,* New York: McGraw-Hill, 1962; and especially Edward L. Deci, *Intrinsic Motivation,* New York: Plenum Press, 1975.

If one's performance allows or promises to allow alter to act in such a manner, thereby enabling alter to sustain his self-conceptions, alter is gratified. Ego's performance may go no further in this respect than to imply expressively that alter is in fact the sort of person he imagines himself to be, yet alter is still gratified by it. In order to obtain such a performance by ego, he is typically willing to act in a manner that is rewarding to ego, whether by supporting in turn ego's own role-identities or by providing him with some other category of reward. Let us treat the former case, however, before turning to mixed exchanges.

There are perhaps two major strategies that may be employed in an attempt to exchange role-support for role-support, each of which implies a somewhat different tacit reciprocity.

First, ego may try to obtain role-support from alter primarily on the merits of role-performance itself. This approach is basic, and it involves an unspoken agreement among the parties present that each will serve as a reasonably cooperative but more or less honest audience for the other. Each, that is, agrees to evaluate the other's performance as objectively as is consistent with ordinary tact and to confer upon him whatever role-support is warranted by this evaluation.

Needless to say, this approach always entails a certain risk for the performer, as his performance often does not merit role-support sufficient to match completely the standards incorporated in his role-identity. This risk is especially present with respect to his more unrealistic role-identities, in which he likes to think himself capable of performances and qualities that are in fact somewhat beyond the limits of his abilities.

The risk is also greater to the degree that the role-identity is heavily freighted with idiosyncratic contents. The situation may be too conventional to allow for enactment of such autistic elements, or the alters may be incapable of serving either as role partners or as competent audiences for these less conventional aspects of one's role-identity. In such cases, the individual can merely accept apathetically, and perhaps with quiet desperation, the enactment and support of only the more commonplace (and therefore less valued) aspects of the identity.

There are, then, two dimensions to the risk involved in enacting a given role-identity: its loftiness and its autism. But even if the individual recognizes this risk, recognizes, that is, that his role-identities are not altogether realistic, he may be unwilling or unable to withhold them from the interaction.

In that event, the person may try to resort to a second and more devious strategy, that of outright bartering for role-support. He may attempt, that is, to negotiate a tacit agreement to support alter's more vulnerable role-identities *come what may*, in return for the same favor: "I'll scratch your back if you'll scratch mine."[33] This strategy is seen most frequently at either extreme of social relatedness: in very close relationships, bordering on *folie à deux,* and in very fleeting encounters between strangers.

Two persons very close to each other may come to expect each almost automatically to support the other's performances and claims, regardless of other factors, simply as his due for participation in such a solidary unit. This phenomenon involves the *overvaluation* of performance by intimates that was discussed in Chapter 4.[34] This bartering strategy is also frequently seen, strangely enough, at parties and mixers that bring together numbers of strangers who are likely never to see one another again. We are all familiar, in this context, with the tragicomic figure who runs from person to person, presenting the same "come-on," seeking (often desperately) someone who will, for the duration, allow him to pretend to be what he is not. If he is lucky enough to encounter someone in the same fix (very often someone of the opposite sex), the two may quickly negotiate this sort of "scratch my back" understanding. The resulting suspension of critical evaluation of each other, though transparent to outsiders, allows them to gain a fleeting modicum of support for their starving role-identities.

Most actual encounters, however, seem to involve combined strategies, drawing upon elements of each of these two major approaches. Most of our relevant role-identities are, after all, just

---

[33]For a more colorful and conceptually germane phrasing of this bargain, compare Bob Dylan's concluding interjection in "Talking World War III Blues," *The Free-Wheelin' Bob Dylan,* Columbia Records CL 1986.

[34]See pp. 99–100 and references.

realistic enough so that we demand a real judgment from alter. They are not so realistic, however, that a truly objective judgment from alter would actually be entirely consistent with our views of ourselves. Therefore, we most often compromise the "honest evaluation" agreement just a bit with a certain amount of barter, for insurance's sake.

Mixed Exchanges

Almost all concrete encounters are mixed exchanges, in that more than one type of gratification is employed as a reward in shaping the other person's conduct. Almost any performance has implications for each category of the other person's gratifications—extrinsic, intrinsic, and role-support. The concrete combinations are literally innumerable. Some are frowned upon in a given society, as when role-support is exchanged, not for kind, but for certain extrinsic rewards. This sort of thing is seen, for example, in flattery for ulterior motives; the subordinate may supply his superior with extravagant quantities of role-support in the hope of gaining promotion or special treatment in return. Similarly frowned upon are some exchanges of extrinsic rewards (money) or great quantities of role-support (flattery) for certain intrinsic rewards (sexual intercourse).

What seems to be protested in some of these mixed exchanges is not that they are mixed (for marriage is also a mixed exchange) but that they are mixed in an utterly unbalanced fashion. Large quantities of one category of reward are being exchanged, not for comparable quantities of the same type, but for large rewards of some other category. A rule of the market place seems to be that the obtained rewards of each party must be at least somewhat comparable *within each category of reward:* extrinsic rewards for extrinsic, intrinsic for intrinsic, and role-support for role-support. (The rewards need not be identical, of course, for otherwise it would be bootless to exchange; money may be exchanged for labor, or support of the identity of husband may be exchanged for support of the identity of wife. They must, however, be rewards of the same broad category.)

A further rule of the market place in such social exchanges is the rule of distributive justice, that one's investments, rewards, and costs should all be roughly comparable. If one's costs are higher, for example, one's rewards ought also to be higher, so that the profits (rewards less costs) will be roughly equal among all the parties to the exchange.[35]

Within the framework of (1) these and other rules of the market place and (2) the working agreement on social identities, individuals can then proceed to negotiate their interactive roles.

To begin with, they must come to some sort of agreement on the *task focus* of the encounter. Contrary to the implications of some theorists, such an agreement is neither identical with nor implied by the working agreement on social identities. Many possible tasks or social activities are open to persons with given sets of identities; they must decide not only who they are but what they are doing there. Two friends, for example, convened for a sociable evening, must choose between many alternative activities: conversation around the kitchen table, fishing, bowling, golf, billiards, a game of cards, and so on. Perhaps, for the sake of illustration, they eventually choose to go bowling.

Having done so, they must proceed to make a host of further collective decisions to implement this chosen task focus, to narrow it down and specify it into meshing interactive roles. Somehow, tacitly or explicitly, decisions must be reached on who will drive them to the bowling alley, who will pay for the rented shoes, who will bowl first, who will keep score, who (if anyone) will buy the beer, and so forth.

Every one of these decisions on the task and its specifications into behavior, as well as on the task-related objects (shoes, beer, car, and so forth), has *symbolic significance* in relation to various

[35]The rules of mixed exchanges are best discussed in Uriel G. Foa and Edna B. Foa, *Societal Structures of the Mind,* Springfield, Ill.: C. C. Thomas, 1973. Rules of distributive justice are discussed in George C. Homans, *Social Behavior* (rev. ed.), New York: Harcourt, 1974, pp. 241–268. See also Richard M. Emerson, "Social Exchange Theory," *Annual Review of Sociology,* 1976, 2: 335–362, for other rules of exchange.

gratifications and identities. That is, each has differing implications, simultaneously, for many specific kinds of gratification.[36]

Let us consider, for example, a person's calculus of extrinsic gratifications. The decision to do the driving or the scoring implies a certain amount of labor and risk on his part. Monetary considerations are involved in deciding whose car will be taken, who will rent the shoes and buy the beer, and how many lines they will bowl. Aside from actual expenditures, there is the matter of forgoing opportunities for remunerative activities. Status is also involved in the decisions on who will drive, who will bowl first, and so on.

These same negotiations also have implications for one's intrinsic gratifications. Who will have the pleasure (if it be such) of driving and scoring? Shall athletic pleasures be allowed to prevail over opportunities for rest and relaxation? Perhaps the cool night air at the ball park would be more desirable than the stuffy atmosphere of the bowling alley. Shall the person spurn the greater sense of competence obtained through golfing in favor of the much lesser sense of competence that arises from his less adequate performance at bowling?

The calculus of role-support is also involved in these decisions. Does the decision to bowl or to buy the beer agree with his conceptions of himself? If so, is such a decision more gratifying in terms of his legitimation needs than the decision to golf or to discuss the latest international crisis would be?

Every facet of one's performance, and of that of alter, must be weighed in terms of all three calculi simultaneously, in order to determine its over-all profitability. Buying the beer costs money but brings status, provides a refreshing drink, and is perhaps congruent with one's conception of self as friend. Is it, on balance, worth doing? This consideration underlies our every act *and every act of alter's.*

If an act, whether one's own or alter's, does not appear to be sufficiently profitable for his own concerns, he will, other things being equal, propose some more desirable alternative. In the light

[36] See Kapferer, *op. cit.*

of emerging conditions, he has to strike a bargain, not only with himself, but also with alter as to how much he is willing to settle for in the encounter.

Note once more that these complex calculations, though they may be quite rational, are seldom very conscious or deliberate.

If two parties cannot agree upon a pair of interactive roles sufficiently profitable to each, they may break off negotiations and end the encounter, departing for more profitable alternative encounters. Most often, however, they do manage to strike some minimally adequate bargain. This bargain can be achieved in either of two ways. First, they may compromise upon the roles they would ideally like to perform in the situation. If one person wants to golf and the other wants to bowl, they may compromise by discussing their golf games at great length before going out to bowl. Or, second, they may strike a bargain not in terms of the present encounter but in terms of a *series* of encounters. That is, they may agree to bowl tonight on the implicit promise of golfing on some future occasion. To borrow a phrase from the grain market, this negotiation of a bargain for the current encounter in terms of promises for different bargains in later encounters might well be called "trading in futures." It is this tactic that constitutes the most distinctive feature of exchange in established social relationships, a point to which we shall return in Chapter 7.

EXCHANGE AND POWER IN INTERACTIONS

In concrete encounters, the people involved seldom have altogether equal voices in shaping the nature and course of the interaction. In most cases, one actor (or coalition of actors) will be in a position to drive a harder bargain for his definition of the situation and his plans of action. The distribution of power among actors in an encounter varies between two limits: complete equality or peerage and absolute control. A closer examination will reveal, however, that these theoretical limits seldom if ever occur, for, on one hand, there are always some resources and choices open even to the most abject of slaves, and, on the other hand, the exact balancing of resources, determination, identity-involvements, abilities to estimate costs and rewards, and vulnerability is a highly improbable event. Peers may exist in age, occupational level, and legal status, but they do not exist in interpersonal encounters.

Most discussions of power, because they have focused on power in continuing relationships, must therefore be qualified in discussing power in a given encounter. Power is said to arise from an imbalance in exchange resources.[37] If one person needs something from alter but alter has less need of anything from that person, alter is in a better bargaining position, has power over that person.

The peculiarities of power in encounters stem from the nature of the resources relevant to encounters, which differ in important respects from the resources relevant to relationships. Money, status, authority, knowledge, equipment, sex, strength, skills, and so on are obviously potential resources in both encounters and relationships. They remain relatively constant over a series of encounters, however, and may be outweighed in a given encounter by more transitory resources, like isolated and atypical pieces of information, momentary determination, transient advantages in energy level, and the like. Such factors, which may be ephemeral aspects of relationships, may become determinants in specific encounters. A person who is dominant over the long run of a relationship may thus find himself temporarily dominated by alter in a particular encounter if he is ill or tired or bored while alter is at normal efficiency. We shall return to these peculiarities of power in encounters very shortly, but in the meantime we must pay due respect to the common features of the two types of power.

Exchange resources, whether manifested in one or in a series of encounters, are largely the same and consist of role-support and the various intrinsic and extrinsic rewards. No priorities can be set regarding the relative efficacy of these rewards, for they take on value only in relation to the shifting needs and desires of the individuals. Now one thing, now another, may be more highly valued.

[37]See, for example, Richard M. Emerson, ''Power-Dependence Relations,'' *American Sociological Review*, 1962, 27: 31–41; and Wally D. Jacobson, *Power and Interpersonal Relations*, Belmont, Calif.: Wadsworth, 1972.

All we wish to point out here is the great importance of that category of rewards that has been largely ignored in other exchange theories, namely, role-support and the opportunity to enact cherished role-identities. If one person provides an unusually fine opportunity in this respect, whereas alter is not an especially important audience or role-partner for any of *his* identities, that person can drive a hard bargain regardless of other resources. In fact, it is this sort of power differential that is usually behind an unbalanced mixed exchange, for alter may not be able to provide enough valuable role-support to make exchange worth the other person's while. Consequently, alter may be led (or forced) to accord him extravagant rewards of other types in order to receive the desired role-support in return.

It is rarely the case that one actor completely dominates the course of a given encounter; the most dependent of alters ordinarily has at least some veto powers. And in fact, in the typical interaction, the "advantage" tends to pass successively from participant to participant, ordinarily accompanied by (and often on the basis of) shifts in events and activities that call forth different role-identities. This fluctuation does not necessarily dismay the momentarily "disadvantaged," for each can expect to gain or regain his moment in the spotlight.

The prolonged and continued exercise of power, however, often leads to resentment and opposition toward the party who drives the bargain and sets the terms of the exchange. As a result, power often seeks to become legitimate *authority;* the power-wielder seeks to forestall resentment and opposition by claiming to act, not as a merely avaricious party seeking private ends, but as an agent of a larger body exercising legitimate claims on everyone in the situation. That is, the power-wielder may claim to be acting as a representative of the relevant profession or institution whose interests are involved in the encounter, may claim greater competence in the matters involved, may claim higher status, or may even claim supernatural sanction.[38] Such authority, backed by power, produces more compliance than does simple power (al-

[38] Max Weber, *The Theory of Social and Economic Organization* (trans. A. M. Henderson and Parsons), New York: Free Press, 1947, pp. 324–329.

though authority alone, of course, can be overcome by superior naked power).

As can be seen from this discussion, authority, unlike power, never lies in interaction but must always derive from factors outside the encounter itself. As a result, authority makes itself felt in encounters only through the medium of social relationships that happen to be involved in a given encounter.

An additional type of influence on encounters, beyond those of power and authority, is what might be called *social skill*. That is, some people are more knowledgeable and skillful in the basic processes of negotiation than are others.[39] In general, one's skill at "manipulating" various types of interaction to serve one's own ends tends to increase with greater breadth and depth of social experience. A situation that is "unstructured" in the eyes of the more innocent and naive actor may be highly predictable from the perspective of the more worldly actor.

The socially skilled actor, or "operator," has learned to make use of certain principles of interaction. One such rule of interaction in our society, for example, is that, when one person proposes a course of action, alter must either acquiesce or give a cogent reason for declining. Furthermore, there is some pressure on the original proposer to accept at face value alter's avowed reason for declining, for the offered reasons are often not alter's real reasons for declining. The verbalized reason is, rather, tailored to alter's appraisal of the proposer and what would be acceptable to him in light of the situation, social desirability, and so forth.

The socially skilled "operator" can make use of this rule in either or both of two ways. First, knowing the types of reason that alter may offer for declining, he can frame his proposal in such a way that the ordinary stock reasons for declining cannot be used, leading alter to invent some still flimsier reason. Second, the operator is often able facilely to discount or to knock down the flimsy reason alter offers. The operator recognizes that, in such cases, it is

[39]For a social skill model, see Michael Argyle, *The Psychology of Interpersonal Behaviour*, London: Methuen, 1967. For a discussion of manipulativeness, see Phillip W. Blumstein, "Audience, Machiavellianism, and Tactics of Identity Bargaining," *Sociological Quarterly*, 1973, 36: 346–365.

often easier for alter simply to acquiesce than to give his real reason for originally refusing.

Furthermore, the operator is keenly aware that most actors, in most situations, are relatively equivocal, ambivalent, and hesitant in their negotiations. In such cases, the more determined, positive, and unequivocal one actor is, the more completely he will be able to shape the interaction through structuring the situation for the others. This structuring is accomplished through interpreting ambiguous cues for others, suggesting courses of action when others hesitate to commit themselves, and resolving choices through presenting the others with *faits accomplis*.

Through all these and other tactics, the operator is often able to manipulate encounters in directions favorable to his own ends. It often happens, of course, that a person of power and authority is also socially skilled in the ways of interaction, though he need not be an "operator" in the pejorative sense. Perhaps equally often, however, the person of power and authority is himself confronted or challenged by just such an operator. In such cases, what is loosely termed a "power struggle" is almost certain to take place within the encounter, and each antagonist may compete for the allegiances of other persons, giving rise to coalitions in the bargaining.

MULTIPERSON ENCOUNTERS

For the most part, we have been speaking until now as though there were only two persons involved in any encounter. This assumption is, of course, a presentational simplification, for we very often engage, face to face, a number of people simultaneously. This eventuality enormously complicates the negotiation of encounters, for the character and role of each person must still be ratified by all. As a consequence, when there are more than three or four persons, the characters and roles assigned to each are depicted even more sketchily and equivocally than they are in the two-person case we have been discussing. First of all, each person is necessarily allotted a shorter amount of time in which to express his views of self and other and can only concentrate on the major points. Second, human obtuseness being what it is, the greater the number of judges to be persuaded, the greater the difficulty of attaining even a rough consensus on identities and roles.

In such situations, some of the people involved may effectively delegate their expressive time to a representative, who thus negotiates for a coalition and speaks more or less for all its members. This process is often seen when several members each of several organizations or categories are brought together in an encounter and informal leaders or spokesmen emerge to speak and question for their fellows. Such delegation by no means ensures a more realistic or satisfactory negotiation, for the views expressed by a spokesman are usually more nearly his own than truly representative of the less dominant members of his coalition.

Because of the exaggerated crudity of the consensus in a multiperson encounter, as well as the power potential of emerging coalitions, the likelihood of a truly fruitful accommodation of persons is significantly smaller than in a dyadic encounter. This likelihood is perhaps the major reason that larger interactions like sociable parties frequently break up into smaller, somewhat autonomous encounters.

Another frequent pattern of interaction when more than two persons are involved is what might be called "simultaneous performances." That is, the individual enacts, through a single dramaturgical performance, more than one role in the technical sense, each directed at a different alter. The teen-age boy, for example, when confronted at once by his mother and his self-consciously masculine buddy, must enact somewhat conflicting roles and characters. He must sustain the simultaneous impressions of intimate socialized respect for his mother and of "no-nonsense" bravado for his friend. Each of the alters may thus be serving as a specific role-partner and audience for only part of the spectrum of identities ego is currently performing. The complexities of giving a competent performance increase geometrically with the number of specific simultaneous involvements, so that a limit is soon reached on this sort of thing. As this limit is approached, there is again a tendency for the interaction to break up into several smaller encounters, simply to ease the strain upon the performers. Furthermore, such exaggerated breadth of performance ordinarily precludes the intensity and depth of involvement frequently found in dyadic encounters. Simultaneous performance necessitates only a stylized and truncated enactment of each role; a gesture must do for an acknowledgment of close friendship, and the wisp of a smile must convey flirtation.

There is a third form that multiperson encounters frequently take, in which one actor is the central performer and the others engage in more or less joint dialogue with him. Communications flow almost exclusively from the central figure to others and from others to him but not among the others. These others are constrained to enact only those identities that are germane to the identity and actions of the central figure. This sort of pattern is most likely to emerge when one person commands inordinate resources or power in the current encounter; examples of such central figures include one's boss, persons of great fame or status in the society, a stunningly attractive girl, a fascinating character, and someone who is being honored or questioned.

Imbalances of interactional resources may characterize "groups," as well as individuals, of course. In multiperson encounters, some of the participants may band together, tacitly or explicitly, as a coalition to influence the bargaining process in the encounter as a whole.[40] They may do so in an attempt to coerce others into granting certain concessions in return for the particular resources controlled by that coalition; at an elementary level, this behavior can be seen in gatherings with unequal sex ratios, which place the scarcer sex in a favorable bargaining position. Coalitions may also form to protect individuals' common investments in an identity that they legitimately share but that is now claimed by an unproven outsider; if a party includes a number of political scientists, for example, and some other person begins to hold forth very knowingly on the political crisis of the day, the political scientists are quite likely to cooperate tacitly in putting him in his place. These reasons are but two of those for which coalitions may form

[40]Theodore Caplow, *Two Against One: Coalitions in Triads*, Englewood Cliffs, N.J.: Prentice-Hall, 1968.

in an encounter, but, whatever the reason, it remains true that coalitions more easily acquire power than do individuals through
such "restrictions of free trade."[41]

In fact, in many cases, exchange in encounters can more profitably be viewed as taking place between rival coalitions than
among disparate individuals. This fact has occasionally been recognized in the group-dynamics literature, and Goffman has taken
some tentative steps toward analyzing this phenomenon in his
discussions of dramaturgical "teamwork."[42] A thoroughgoing
treatment of the problem, however, still lies in the future of interaction analysis.

THE INDIVIDUAL
AND ENCOUNTERS

We have seen in this chapter the numerous constraints placed
upon the individual's preferred line of action in a social encounter. Although his salience hierarchy of role-identities provides
him with reasonably definite preferences as to the character and
role to be assumed in the encounter, the necessity for bargaining
with the other participants typically forces him to settle for
something less and something else. Others seldom allow him to
perform a role exactly as he would like to, thus creating (or exacer-
bating) a discrepancy between his performance and his conceptions of himself. There is, then, a chronic need for legitimation of
these conceptions of self; few interactions are altogether satisfying
in this respect.

Particular interactions are also less than satisfying in the respect
that only a few of one's many role-identities can be worked into a
given encounter. Large segments of one's self-structure are forced
to go unhonored in any particular gathering, because they would

[41]*Cf.* Peter M. Blau, *Exchange and Power in Social Life*, New York: Wiley,
1964, pp. 187–194, on additional factors restricting free competition.

[42]For example, John Thibaut, "An Experimental Study of the Cohesiveness of
Underprivileged Groups," *Human Relations*, 1950, 3: 251–278; Goffman,
Presentation of Self, pp. 77–105 and *passim*.

not be particularly compatible with one's emerging role in the encounter as shaped by the negotiation process.

For these reasons, the individual cannot safely stake his self on a single encounter but must evolve means of staking it on an indeterminate *series* of encounters. These problems will be discussed more fully in Chapter 9, but we must consider here two of the most important such means: the construction of agendas and the formation of interpersonal relationships.

As no single performance can satisfy all a person's needs and desires, a series of qualitatively different performances must be staged in order to cover all these needs. As they are different in content, some of these performances may be less than compatible and will at least differ in the types of audience, resources, and other elements that they require for successful staging. To cope with these incompatibilities and differential requirements, the person must set up *agendas,* or schedules of performances.[43]

These agendas (or life plans) come in all different sizes, some roughly covering the remainder of the life span, some covering only the rest of the week, and some (perhaps the most important) covering the remainder of the day. In constructing these agendas, priority is given, as far as possible, to one's more salient identities, and the others are worked into the remaining time as far as resources and the opportunity structure permit. Once the agenda is tentatively set, one moves from stage to stage according to schedule, staging *this* performance in the setting most favorable to its success and staging *that* one over there.[44] The course of daily movement through space and time is largely determined by the dramaturgical exigencies of staging role-performances most effectively.

But of course this kind of agenda is not entirely ours to establish, for performances typically require audiences and supporting

[43]See p. 265 for operational specifications and Chapter 9 for further substantive discussion of agendas.

[44]Manford H. Kuhn, "Major Trends in Symbolic Interaction Theory in the Past Twenty-five Years," *Sociological Quarterly,* 1964, 5: 61–84, especially p. 73. See also George A. Miller, Eugene Galanter, and Karl H. Pribram, *Plans and the Structure of Behavior,* New York: Holt, Rinehart & Winston, 1960.

casts, which in turn implies dramaturgical discipline on all our parts to show up at the right place and time, ready for our cooperative endeavors. Agendas, like performances themselves, are interactively negotiated and not necessarily with equal voice by each participant. Duly established agendas, requiring dramaturgical discipline, are nonetheless often disrupted by accidents, unpredictable events, and the competing demands of other encounters. In the case of such disruption of one's agenda, whether by others or by himself, his whole enterprise of identity legitimation is threatened until he can work out a new, "next best" answer to the staging problems posed by his variety of desired role-performances. We shall have more to say on these topics in subsequent chapters.

Even though a given performance is always relevant to more than one of our identities, no single performance or daily agenda of performances can serve to legitimate all our role-identities; there are simply too many of them, and they have to be tended all the time. What a moment ago was accepted as a legitimate claim to an identity may no longer be, for we recognize that people are most fickle and changeable indeed.

Identity, like freedom, must be won and rewon every day. Each identity must continually be legitimated. Legitimating one's self-structure is like dusting a huge old house: If he starts by dusting the parlor, by the time he gets to the upstairs guest room, the parlor is already badly in need of dusting again. Woman's work is never done, nor is that of maintaining the self.

Agendas, then, must be arranged in such a way as to provide continual legitimation of each of one's various role-identities.[45] Because of this constantly recurring need for legitimation, one seeks stable, dependably recurring *means* of such legitimation. Typically, such means are to be found in *interpersonal relationships,* in which at least one and usually both parties can usually be

---

[45]It should be emphasized that such legitimation can be only continual, rather than continuous, for the variegated nature of the self requires that any given role-identity be omitted from one's performance, at least on occasion, as incompatible or irrelevant.

counted upon to aid in the legitimation of one or several of the other person's role-identities, on a somewhat routine basis and for a succession of interactions over a substantial period of time. These dependable sources of rewards greatly simplify one's agenda-construction, though it remains a necessarily complicated business, as we shall see. These complex interrelations between encounters and human relationships constitute the subject of the chapter to which we now turn.

Chapter 7

THE CAREER
OF A
RELATIONSHIP[1]

The aim of man, the dreamer, is to live in terms of his role-identities. But it is not so easily done, as we have seen. To enact and fulfill his self-conceptions he must retailor the purely animal aspects of his nature, he must ferret out and successfully guess a minimum of information about the world around him, and he must allocate his resources in a shifting and uncertain empirical market place. To live in any human sense—and perhaps to live at all—he must succeed in his allocations and negotiations at least to the extent that he reaps a certain minimum of extrinsic and intrinsic rewards.

In addition to all these difficulties in enacting his identities, he must, as a necessary prerequisite or poor substitute, legitimate them by gaining a modicum of corresponding role-support from self and others. And role-support, as we have seen, is a scarce and fragile commodity. Not only must such support be achieved; it must be more or less continually *maintained*. One's image of oneself in a particular role may be quite solidly established through the support of those around him, only to have its legitimacy

[1]Many of the problems, concepts, and propositions in this chapter, as in Chapter 6, receive considerable amplification in George J. McCall, Michal M. McCall, Norman K. Denzin, Gerald D. Suttles, and Suzanne B. Kurth, *Social Relationships,* Chicago: Aldine, 1970; and G. J. McCall, "A Symbolic Interactionist Approach to Attraction," in Ted L. Huston, editor, *Foundations of Interpersonal Attraction,* New York: Academic Press, 1974, pp. 217–231. See also the

thrown into question by a single isolated incident. Or a new but patently relevant judge may come upon the scene and openly dispute one's claims to this identity. But even if such contingencies do not arise, role-support, like other unstable elements in nature, tends to decay as a simple function of time. Without at least periodic substantiation, role-support dissipates.

Identity must be won and rewon continually. Audiences are fickle, and we must continually induce them anew to support our roles and legitimate our claims to particular identities. The athlete who does not stay in shape very quickly becomes "the former athlete," a spouse cannot rest upon the laurels of honeymoon romance and intimacy to hold her mate, and a person cannot have friends without continuing to be a friend himself. The struggle to legitimate one's identities is never-ending, and we shall see in this chapter that identities must be won and rewon during the career of each relationship with others, or such relationships will go awry.

Role-support is therefore a precious commodity, not cheaply bought or easily earned, nor is it available on every hand. How do human beings resolve this difficulty? By what means do they manage to procure more dependable supplies of role-support and intrinsic and extrinsic rewards?

In every human society this fundamental problem of social exchange is resolved, at least partially, by establishing *interpersonal relationships*. As a consequence of our recurring needs for role-support and the other commodities of social exchange, we are disposed to seek dependably recurring *sources* of them. And when we locate or are thrown together with individuals or groups that, for whatever reason, are able, willing, and ready to afford us supplies of such exchange commodities, we are disposed to "corner the market" by establishing more durable bonds with those alters, that is, by establishing interpersonal relationships. As we return to these sources of support and other rewards, our interactions with these alters begin to take on distinctive contents and patterns.

closely related approaches of Ralph H. Turner, *Family Interaction,* New York: Wiley, 1970; Murray S. Davis, *Intimate Relations,* New York: Free Press, 1973; and Thomas J. Scheff, "On the Concepts of Identity and Social Relationship," in Tamotsu Shibutani, editor, *Human Nature and Collective Behavior,* Englewood Cliffs, N.J.: Prentice-Hall, 1970, pp. 193–207.

Perhaps unknowingly—or even unwillingly—we have become involved in sequences of processes that make up the careers of relationships.

As Max Weber pointed out,[2] a relationship, in its most generic sense, is the existence of a substantial probability of interaction between two or more persons. This definition is too broad for our purposes, however, as it would encompass any distinguishable connectedness between any two parties: for example, that between any two persons who take the same streetcar or between the Premier of Russia and any American child living in a city the former is capable of having bombed.

An *interpersonal* relationship must be defined as one that necessarily involves each participant as a personal entity. That is, each of the parties must *recognize* the other as a distinctive individual of whom he has some prior knowledge. Interpersonal relationships are literally relationships between persons (although in their dynamics they are actually relationships between personas).[3]

Interpersonal relationships can be classified according to the basis for the probability that the two parties will "personally" interact. The basis may be mere propinquity, as in the case of streetcar riders; it may be legal, as in the case of parolee and probation officer; it may be institutional, as in the case of fellow employees. In fact, the range of possible bases is wide indeed, as we shall see. In this chapter, however, we shall be concerned primarily with those interpersonal relationships in which at least part of the probability of interaction rests on the fact that one (or both) of the parties believes that he may gain role-support from the other. Intrinsic and extrinsic rewards may of course also be involved, and they will be given some consideration. But to understand distinctively human relationships we must focus upon the distinctively human commodity of role-support.

[2]Max Weber, *The Theory of Social and Economic Organization* (trans. A. M. Henderson and Talcott Parsons), New York: Free Press, 1947, pp. 118–120.

[3]George J. McCall, "The Social Organization of Relationships," in McCall *et al., op. cit.,* pp. 3–34. *Cf.* Steven W. Duck, *Personal Relationships and Personal Constructs: A Study of Friendship Formation,* New York: Wiley, 1973.

THE NATURE OF
INTERPERSONAL TIES

These remarks point up the fact that *reward dependability* is central to interpersonal relationships and is, in fact, a major reason for their existence and continuation. People seek one another out repeatedly, in order to "use" one another as dependable sources of role-support for prominent identities and for the other exchange rewards. This adherence is quite similar to our reliance upon certain name brands of consumer goods and our habitual consumption of certain genres of mass media. And in both cases we may do some "shopping around" or even "switching." The major differences are that habits of interpersonal "consumption" involve mixed exchange rewards and that we must usually negotiate for them with others, rather than simply buying them.[4]

But such reward dependability is not the only tie in interpersonal relationships. At least four other components can be distinguished.

Beyond this first factor of reward dependability, there is also an element of *ascription* in many relationships. The prototypical case is of course those interpersonal relationships based upon blood relationships or kinship. Murdock and other anthropologists have asserted that the very shapes and contents of many interpersonal ties are defined by the culturally ascribed relations between the persons involved.[5] In more complex societies, the force of kinship seems to become attenuated, but there too individuals inherit many ties and have many others foisted upon them by their social

[4] At this point it is useful to recall certain peculiarities of negotiated exchange in established relationships, as opposed to less structured single encounters. First, there is often no need to *develop* a working agreement on social identities but only a need to reinvoke and maintain a previously established agreement. Second, there is a good deal more leeway in striking a bargain for any single encounter in terms of interactive roles, as one party may agree to settle for less in the encounter on the implicit promise that he will do better in some future encounter with the other party; this phenomenon we have called "trading in futures." Third, exchange in a relationship is more dependable and calculable than exchange in a single encounter, for exchange resources relevant to the former are more stable and predictable than are those relevant to the latter.

[5] E.g., George P. Murdock, *Social Structure*, New York: Macmillan, 1949.

groupings. For example, many teacher-pupil, supervisor-employee, and colleague or peer relationships are, in this fashion, ascribed.

In addition to these passive types of ascription, persons actively *strive* to achieve a large number of social "ascriptions." That is, they seek to have many of their relationships legitimated and consecrated by being conferred upon themselves and alter by officials of their social groupings. Many of the social positions thus ascribed—a doctorate, a licensed occupation, a military rank—exist and are defined largely in terms of specifying the ascriptive component of a whole set of relationships to other positions.

Third, there is the factor of *commitment* in many if not most relationships. To a varying extent, the person has privately and publicly committed himself or been committed to honoring a restrictive covenant, a trade agreement, with the other party. He has pledged the semi-exclusive use of the other party as a source of certain specified role-supports and other exchange rewards. He has committed himself to the legitimation of certain aspects of certain of his role-identities by endorsing the other party as a partner in their enactment and as an audience whose opinions about his performances of these identities are given primary weight.

Commitments are a strategy for increasing and ensuring the dependability of a source of exchange rewards. But they are much more. They are frequently entered into through moral convictions, as well as, or even instead of, through opportunism or sheer desire. If there are no elements in a relationship but commitment based upon moral convictions, the relationship is literally only a duty. Even if the commitment is not *made* on moral grounds, the person is under some moral obligation to fulfill it. To have made a commitment is to have bound oneself, and it requires a very good excuse to withdraw from alter without losing face. Even interpersonal relationships are thus at least partly public affairs.

Although ascriptions and commitments often blend and are, in fact, the social and personal sides of the same coin, we must be careful to distinguish between them. Persons often enter into what they think are commitments only to discover later that they have recruited themselves into ascribed relationships that they cannot dissolve without the formal consent of their social groupings. Marriage is a major example, but it is not the only one. Marriages are actually legal contracts, not only between two people, but between the couple and the state. Whenever there are laws governing interpersonal relationships—and there are such regulations more often than we recognize—the ties have elements of ascription in them.

Fourth, there is the factor of *investment*. When a person has expended such scarce resources as money, time, and life chances in establishing and maintaining a relationship, he cannot afford to throw away such investments without realizing substantial returns from them. The normative standards involved in most relationships—sometimes termed the "norm of reciprocity"[6]—demand that we also show some consideration for alter's investments as well, for the tie is, after all, a joint venture. The social grouping regulates and ensures this reciprocity to some extent through ascriptions, and a large bulk of the moral teachings of any group further bolster the likelihood of reciprocity by engendering strong senses of commitment in many relationships. We are thus taught to honor our parents, to be true to our spouses, and to do a day's work for a day's wage. And the society applies further informal social pressure and formal injunctions to see that we do so.

Finally, and most important for the person's identities, in most cases, is the factor of *attachment*. Attachments to others are formed as the individual's identities evolve and change. One's dreams of oneself, the idealized pictures he has of himself in certain social positions, are seldom constant over very long periods of time. As a person faces new tasks and new alters, these tasks and alters become incorporated into his daydreaming about himself in these social roles. Consequently, *specific persons and their behaviors get built into the contents of role-identities* and become crucial to the legitimation and enactment of these identities. This building of specific others into the very contents of role-identities is what we mean by becoming "attached" to particular alters.[7]

[6]Alvin W. Gouldner, "The Norm of Reciprocity: A Preliminary Statement," *American Sociological Review*, 1960, 25: 161–179.

[7]For further analysis of attachment and its determinants, see G. J. McCall, "A Symbolic Interactionist Approach to Attraction," *op. cit.*

Such attachments make the individual vulnerable to the decisions, reactions, and whims of the others and to all the physical and social vicissitudes that may befall these others. As the Buddhists put it, to become involved with another is to surrender a hostage to the fates. It is thus another irony of human life that those intimate relationships that give so much pleasure and meaning to our daily round have the simultaneous potential of giving us so much grief.

When one becomes attached to a particular other, the resulting relationship also tends to become "nontransferable." Any competent clerk or repairman will do, but one cannot so easily go looking for another mother, another brother, another child. The less transferable a relationship, the more vulnerable one is.

These five elements, then, are some of the important ties that bind two persons together, making it likely that they will continue to interact on a personal basis in the future. Reward dependability, ascription, commitment, investment, and attachment are the social psychological glue that cements individuals into social units, interpersonal relationships.[8]

These factors usually blend and run together in most continuing interpersonal relationships. Nevertheless they are distinct factors; they are present in different amounts in different relationships, and they often vary independently of one another. For example, we sometimes have commitments that differ from those ascribed to us; we frequently forgo the potential rewards of exchanges because of "prior commitments"; we fret over interpersonal investments that have not yet yielded dependable reward sources; we seek to secure our attachments through mutual commitments and formal ascriptions; and conversely, we may resignedly fulfill commitments that no longer reflect our attachments.

Individuals are most preoccupied with their attachments, but the societies they live in are most concerned with their ascriptions and commitments. At the least, social forces seek to produce in the individual a set of commitments that correspond to and imple-

[8]*Cf.* the analysis of interpersonal bonds in Turner, *op. cit.*; and in Frank E. Millar and L. Edna Rogers, "A Relational Approach to Interpersonal Communication," in Gerald R. Miller, editor, *Explorations in Interpersonal Communication*, Beverly Hills, Calif.: Sage Publications, 1976, pp. 87–103.

ment his ascriptions. If ascriptions, commitments, and attachments are all aligned, conventional social opinion regards this as
even better. But the person is not simply left on his honor in these
matters. Such ascriptions and commitments, once made, are en-
forced by a host of informal social pressures and formal social controls, and ordinarily the individual cannot seriously violate them
without incurring retribution.

A wide divergence between one's commitments and one's attachments is likely to engender a good deal of personal discontent,
and the person will be motivated to reduce the divergence, either
by giving up his attachments or by changing his commitments—
his job, his spouse, his style of life. But neither of these strategies
is easily brought off, and most of us carry around some freight of
discontent and restlessness because the two sets of factors are not
mutually aligned. Most frequently we attempt compromise solu-
tions of moderate divergences by negotiating redefinitions of the
contents of the commitments and by reshuffling the intensities of
our attachments.

Persons tend to make investments on the basis of their attachments, particularly in the early phases of relationships, in attempts to secure commitments from the other parties as dependable sources of exchange rewards. In later phases, however, a
person must often continue to invest in the relationship even
though his attachments may have shifted to some extent or even
though alter proves somewhat unreliable as a source of reward.
This is so because his resources are quite limited, as we have seen,
and hence he cannot afford simply to throw away what he has
already ''put into'' the relationship and start anew. This dilemma
is, in fact, particularly common in many of one's deepest and most
intimate associations, like marriage, parenthood, and many ties
based upon career. After a certain point, many such investments
are virtually irreversible. ·

In many ways, then, an interpersonal relationship can make
demands upon a member even when these demands are not particularly agreeable to him as an individual *or necessarily to his
partner.* And such demands are, of course, hallmarks of social
structures. Through the intentional or unintentional development

of these five types of interpersonal tie, individuals give rise to the most elementary form of social structure—an interpersonal relationship. The two persons are no longer merely disjoint individuals but constitute a unit, a collective unit of which they are the members. As members, they are at times subject to demands, not only from their partners, but also from the relationship itself, as we have seen.

Like other social structures, an interpersonal relationship is a social unit capable of *collective action as a unit*, not merely the joint action of its members as individuals. A man and a woman, as individuals, are not capable of adopting a child, for example, although a married couple is. A social unit is capable of actions that are beyond the efforts of the people who belong to it.

Not all types of social structure are entirely identical in their properties, however, and it is important to recognize some of the peculiarities of interpersonal relationships in this respect. Many social structures (for example, the group in the full sense of that term) are distinguished by the members' own perceptions of it as a collective unit; the members perceive the structure as a reality beyond themselves as individuals, as a unit to which they merely belong. They recognize, for example, that, were any of them to die tomorrow, the structure would persist and would merely recruit replacements for them. They recognize, that is, that they are only members and therefore replaceable, substitutable, interchangeable.

This feature is less clearly developed in interpersonal relationships. The awareness of the relationship as a unit beyond the members is much more prominent under certain circumstances than under others. Typically, such awareness is heightened when the members are dealing with or are oriented toward the larger social world, which tends to treat them as a unit. Married people are invited to events not as persons but as couples; social considerations extended to one person are often extended to his close friend as well, in recognition of their close relationship. The members themselves, recognizing their shared interests and shared fate in dealing with the larger social world, tend to act in concert rather than as individuals. Married couples, friends, colleagues typically act toward outsiders as *teams*, cooperating to maintain proper fronts. (These phenomena of dual participation and pair-centered interaction have received insightful discussion by Willard Waller.)[9]

Nevertheless, when dealing with matters more internal to the relationship than external, this awareness of the relationship as a superordinate unit diminishes and often disappears. This fact, its causes, and its consequences were brilliantly analyzed by Georg Simmel, who recognized that, under certain circumstances,

> . . . each of the two feels himself confronted only by the other, not by a collectivity above him. The social structure here rests immediately on the one and on the other of the two, and the secession of either would destroy the whole. The dyad, therefore, does not attain that superpersonal life which the individual feels to be independent of himself. . . . This dependence of the dyad upon its two individual members causes the thought of its existence to be accompanied by the thought of its termination much more closely and impressively than in (a social group), where every member knows that even after his retirement or death, the group can continue to exist. . . . A dyad, however, depends on each of its two elements alone—in its death, though not in its life: for its life, it needs *both*, but for its death, only one. This fact is bound to influence the inner attitude of the individual toward the dyad, even though not always consciously nor in the same way. It makes the dyad into a (social structure) that feels itself both endangered and irreplaceable, and thus into the real locus not only of authentic sociological tragedy, but also of sentimentalism.[10]

The intrinsic sentimentalism brought out by Simmel is one of the most distinctive features of an interpersonal relationship and can be seen in a number of forms.

First of all, it is seen in the sense of *uniqueness* that the participants often feel, that there has never been a relationship (a

[9]Willard Waller, *The Family: A Dynamic Interpretation*, New York: Dryden, 1938, pp. 383–389. See also Erving Goffman's discussion of "teamwork" in his *The Presentation of Self in Everyday Life*, Garden City, N.Y.: Doubleday Anchor, 1957, pp. 77–105.

[10]Georg Simmel, *The Sociology of Georg Simmel* (trans. Kurt Wolff), New York: Free Press, 1950, pp. 123–124. Much of the following discussion is derived from pp. 118–135.

love or a friendship, for example) quite like theirs. This feeling is a natural consequence of the awareness of the fragile and irreplaceable nature of an interpersonal relationship, and it leads the participants to place some emphasis on uniqueness.

Closely related to this feature is the sense of *intimacy*, of giving or showing certain things only to one other person and to no one else. This emphasis is congruent with the emphasis on uniqueness, but Simmel also pointed out how it can come, like a cancer, to destroy a relationship. That is, the parties may come to share only trivia (because these small things are not shared elsewhere and are therefore intimate) and may thus come to exclude from the relationship other parts of themselves that are more widely shared but also more important to their self-structures. The relationship itself thus becomes trivial and unsatisfying.[11] Another danger posed by the sense of intimacy is the possibility of its disruption—which we call "jealousy" and which stems from our knowledge or our fear that some of these intimate facets are *not* being given to us and to us alone.[12]

Yet a third aspect of the sentimentalism intrinsic to relationships is a sense of *consecration* that stems from the fact that each of the parties knows all too well that he can depend only upon the other, and upon no one else, in matters pertaining to their relationship. In a group, by way of contrast, a person's failure or odious act can be hidden behind the front of the group; he can claim to have been acting not as an individual but as an arm of the group. In an interpersonal relationship, on the other hand,

> neither of the two members can hide what he has done behind the group, nor hold the group responsible for what he has failed to do. Here the forces with which the (social structure) surpasses the individual . . . cannot compensate for individual inadequacies, as they can in (groups). There are many respects in which two united individuals accomplish more than two isolated individuals. Nevertheless, the decisive characteristic of the dyad is that each of the two must actually accomplish something, and that in case of failure only

[11]*Ibid.*, p. 127.

[12]Michal M. McCall, "Boundary Rules in Relationships and Encounters," in G. J. McCall *et al., op. cit.*, pp. 35–61; Davis *op. cit.*; and Richard Sennett, *The Tyrannies of Intimacy*, New York: Knopf, 1976.

the other remains—not a super-individual force, as prevails in a group even of three.[13]

And, as a final aspect of this semtimentalism of the dyad, there is the unsurpassed *purity of reciprocity*. In the interpersonal relationship, in which there is no one else to hide behind or to use as a distraction, the revered norms of reciprocity in exchange, of distributive justice, can be seen to work unimpeded by other persons. This observation does not mean, of course, that imbalances in exchange, which we ordinarily call "power" and "exploitation," do not occur in such relationships, for they do occur frequently, as we shall see. The purity of reciprocity entails only that such imbalances are much more difficult to conceal or legitimate than they are in more complex social structures.

In forming an interpersonal relationship, then, by continuing to seek out a particular alter as a source of scarce role-support, a person lets himself in for more than he may have bargained for. This seemingly simple action actually entails the recruitment of alter, and of himself, into a fairly inviolable social structure that, once entered, binds both parties in a complex web of obligations and sentiments.[14]

Indeed, the course of a relationship may be quite different from that intended by either party. Relationships may grow without the conscious intent or even the awareness of the persons involved, through benign circles of exchange favors[15] or through being thrown together repeatedly. Conversely, relationships may fail to form despite the intent of one or more of the persons involved. For example, various types of "incompatibility" may arise independently of the efforts of the parties. Even more frequent per-

[13]Simmel, *op. cit.*, p. 134.

[14]The volume by G. J. McCall *et al.*, *op. cit.*, offers a thorough sociological analysis of dyadic relationships as a quite distinctive form of social organization. In the analysis of this form, special attention is given to peculiarities of social structure, culture, organizational dynamics, organizational change, inter-organizational relations, and functions of relationships.

[15]That is, in a casual encounter, one person may allow the other the better of the exchange, assuming that this other will reciprocate sometime—the phenomenon of "trading in futures." In this way, he makes a claim for a future en-

haps is the situation in which the full-blown relationship is *different in content* from that originally intended by the participants. The counselor becomes a lover, the rival a friend, the client a partner in duplicity. The course a particular relationship takes is the result of the interdependence of the factors mentioned and the influence of additional factors we shall soon discuss.

But first we must note that, as Simmel has argued and as many of us have learned from experience, social order defies the ordinary laws of order, in that it does not obey the law of entropy.[16] That is, interpersonal relationships are relatively easy to create (indeed neither party may realize that one has been created until after the fact), but they are exceedingly difficult to destroy because of the strength of the bonds that are involved.

In the remainder of this chapter we shall examine, first, the processes by means of which relationships are created, maintained, and cultivated and, then, the more taxing processes by means of which they may come to be destroyed.[17]

THE INITIATION OF RELATIONSHIPS

There are three principal modes in which a person may come to enter into an interpersonal tie.

1. He may be born into, inherit, or otherwise be ascribed a relationship. Some of the most fundamental human ties, like kinship and even marriage in some societies, begin in this manner, al-

counter, and the norm of reciprocity serves as a starting mechanism to establish some sort of relationship. *Cf.* Gouldner, *op. cit.*; and Peter M. Blau, *Exchange and Power In Social Life,* New York: Wiley, 1964, p. 16. Trading in futures imposes a commitment upon alter to reciprocate, and ego himself often effectively makes a "side bet" that alter will do so. *Cf.* Howard S. Becker, "Notes on the Concept of Commitment," *American Journal of Sociology,* 1960, 66: 32–40.

[16]Simmel, *op. cit.,* p. 380.

[17]Compare the approaches developed in Theodore H. Newcomb, *The Acquaintance Process,* New York: Holt, Rinehart & Winston, 1961; Paul F. Lazarsfeld and Robert K. Merton, "Friendship as Social Process," in Morris Berger, Theodor Abel, and Charles H. Page, editors, *Freedom and Control in Modern Society,* Princeton, N.J.: Van Nostrand, 1954, pp. 18–66; John W. Thibaut and

though it is usually assumed that corresponding commitments and attachments will grow from them. The course of the relationship will, of course, depend to a great extent upon whether or not such commitments and attachments actually do develop and upon the specific forms they take. Therefore, only the bare skeleton of a relationship can actually be ascribed.

2. The relationship may be reputation-mediated; that is, prior knowledge of one person on the part of the other (or mutually) leads to a substantial change in the probability that the two will personally interact and form a tie. This change may occur in a number of ways. A person may deliberately seek out a particular alter because alter's personal or impersonal reputation suggests that he could provide role-support for a particular identity and would perhaps be a source of other rewards. Or other parties may "bring the two together" on the basis of their reputations, for example, in the widespread practice of introducing eligible men and women to each other. A person may also seek out alter because he seems promising for one identity, despite a reputation that bodes ill for other identities. Or a person may seek out another as relevant to one identity but come in time to relate to him in terms of other identities, for example, when the kindly doctor becomes the family friend. The forms that such mediations may take are quite numerous, but in each case it is the personal reputations and stereotypes of the participants that have set the process in motion.

3. The participants may be brought together (or thrown together) by circumstance, with neither having any personal knowledge of the other. This occurrence is particularly likely when the persons themselves are highly mobile or when social conditions are in flux as in wars, revolutions, and rapid social change. These con-

---

Harold H. Kelly, *The Social Psychology of Groups,* New York, Wiley, 1959, pp. 64–79; and William J. Chambliss, "The Selection of Friends," *Social Forces*, 1965, 43: 370–380. Especially relevant are the closely related views presented in Charles D. Bolton, "Mate Selection as the Development of a Relationship," *Marriage and Family Living,* 1961, 23: 234–240; Turner, *op. cit.*; Davis, *op. cit.*; Duck, *op. cit.*; Irwin Altman and Dalmas A. Taylor, *Social Penetration: The Development of Interpersonal Relationships,* New York: Holt, 1973; and Miller, *op. cit.* Our own analysis is, of course, further developed in McCall *et al., op. cit.*; and G. J. McCall, "A Symbolic Interactionist Approach to Attraction," *op. cit.*

ditions have occurred in the lives of a great many people in our century. The majorities of whole populations have been refugees for much of their lives, meeting only strangers or cohorts from the same home provinces or officials from former camps. Population statistics show that, in our own country too, a sizable proportion of the population has moved and moved again. Such sweeping movements of large numbers of people are more frequent and extensive than we usually recognize, but we must also recognize that, even under conditions of high social disorganization, the majority of the relationships that develop between persons is reputation-mediated, at least in terms of impersonal reputations.

The importance of reputation in bringing people together is often underestimated, for we seldom enter into sociable encounters without already knowing something about alter (as discussed in Chapter 5). It is through reputations that we typically learn of existing opportunity structures and decide whether or not to take advantage of them. This pervasiveness of reputation-mediated interaction is brought home to us most dramatically when we come face to face with someone we know nothing about, and who knows nothing of us, and we are obliged to sustain some kind of civil interaction with him.

In their first encounter, unacquainted people face the problem of identification in its purest and most agonizing form. Who is the other person? Who am I in this situation? Who *could* I be? What do I *want* to be? Who does *he* want me to be? The processes of interaction discussed in the previous chapter attain the zenith of their difficulty and importance in first encounters. Each party must read the person with extra care for any clues to identity that he may give or give off. If either party has any reputational knowledge of the other, it serves to guide the process of reading clues. In either case, however, each party is sensitized to a much wider range of possible identities than in more ordinary interactions, for neither has much idea who alter may turn out to be, nor is either acquainted with the little idiosyncrasies of alter's particular dramaturgical idiom.

And, while trying to read alter, each must also present a self, lay claim to a character. Being unable—and unwilling—to claim blatantly *all* one's identities in a first encounter with a more or less unknown stranger, each must select from his identity-set a subset that represents his "opening bid," so to speak.

How is this selection made? Typically, each selects a subset of identities that, on the basis of his tentative reading of alter, are "safe" identities, that is, identities that will be acceptable to alter and to which ego can fairly easily validate his claims. Yet this subset, which is the character he wishes to claim, or the persona he presents to alter, must not be *too* safe, or else he will not seem interesting to alter, nor will he stand a chance of gaining support for any of his less conventional role-identities. Each must cautiously, very tentatively and subtly, hint at some of the less commonplace aspects of his identities while anchoring his performance on his "safe" identities—a distinction that is only relative, to be sure.[18]

From cues given and given off in this manner, the person may sense that alter shares one of his less safe identities, and both may hunger for legitimation and enactment of this identity. Yet, ordinarily, neither dares come right out and claim that identity openly, for fear that he may have misread the signs and will spoil the interaction.

Potential concurrence (on such an identity) is always problematic and innovation or the impulse to innovate (is) a stimulus for anxiety. The paradox is resolved when the innovation is broached in such a manner as to elicit from others reactions suggesting their receptivity; and when at the same time, the innovation occurs by increments so small, tentative and ambiguous as to permit the actor to retreat, if the signs be unfavorable, without having become identified with an unpopular position. Perhaps all social actions have, in addition to their instrumental, communicative and expressive functions, this quality of being *exploratory gestures.* . . . By a casual, semi-serious, non-committal or tangential remark I may stick my neck out just a little way, but I will quickly withdraw it unless you, by some sign of affirmation, stick *yours* out. I will permit myself to become progressively committed but only as others, by some visible sign,

[18]*Cf.* Blau, *op. cit.,* pp. 69–76. The necessity of venturing beyond the thoroughly "safe" is more pointedly developed in Gerald D. Suttles, "Friendship as a Social Institution," and in Norman K. Denzin, "Rules of Conduct and the Study of Deviant Behavior: Some Notes on the Social Relationship," both in McCall *et al., op. cit.,* pp. 95–135 and 62–94, respectively.

become likewise committed. . . . Each actor may contribute something directly to the growing product, but he may also contribute indirectly by encouraging others to advance, inducing them to retreat, and suggesting new avenues to be explored. The product cannot be ascribed to any one of the participants; it is a real ''emergent'' on a group level. We may think of this process as one of mutual conversion. The important thing to remember is that we do not first convert ourselves and then others. The acceptability (of claiming an identity) to oneself depends upon its acceptability to others. Converting the other is part of the process of converting oneself.[19]

But this process of cautious mutual exploration and conversion in search of legitimation and an opportunity of enacting one's less conventional identities is one that takes a good deal of time, ordinarily spread over a series of encounters. On the basis of his first tentative identifications, in his first encounter, he may detect enough promise in alter to want to continue the exploration process. On the other hand, he may become alienated from the tentative, potential relationship at any point in this process of mutual exploration.

First encounters, then, may have any of several possible outcomes, on the basis of first impressions:

1. First impressions of alter may correctly convince ego that alter has little to offer him. In this case, ego makes himself unavailable for further encounters.

2. First impressions may mistakenly lead ego to be disinterested in further interaction with alter even though he *would* be interested if his initial reading of alter had been more accurate. Under conditions in which mobility is high and sociometric webs are loose, ego is unlikely to have any further encounters with alter, and an opportunity is lost.

Sometimes, however, work associations, residential propinquity, or daily routines may continue to throw ego and alter together despite ego's wishes, with the result that ego picks up further information about alter that leads him to change his initially unfavorable evaluation of alter. It should be pointed out, however,

[19]Albert K. Cohen, *Delinquent Boys,* New York: Free Press, 1955, pp. 60–61.

that the initial negative impression produces a biased and selective definition of alter—and, as a consequence, selective attention to information confirming that view—so that it takes a good deal of evidence indeed to change ego's evaluation. It does happen, though, and some of our most significant others may be acquired in precisely this fashion.

3. Initially favorable impressions may be disconfirmed in the process of subsequent exploration, so that ego is no longer interested in spending further time and effort in developing this relationship. The pretty girl turns out to be a strident prude, and the apparent bohemian soon reveals himself as childishly egocentric and pretentious.

A special case is worth mentioning here. It may happen that one has built up a series of favorable appraisals of alter that have been upheld in subsequent encounters but that another veil is then removed, so to speak. New and different circumstances may cast alter in a different light. A piece of additional information may suggest an unnoticed pattern, or discrepancies between signs given and given off may begin to dawn upon one, or alter may "confess" something previously kept secret. Any of these events and many more like them may lead to an *unmasking* of a concealed identity that so completely changes the growing relationship that one is led to reject it as a source of role-support.

4. And finally, one's initial hunches about alter, the sensed common interests that lead one to re-encounter him, may prove to be well-founded indeed. Sectors of ego's self-structure may mesh well with sectors of alter's self-structure. An agreement, tacit or explicit, may be negotiated to meet periodically for various performances relevant to the role-identities that make up these intermeshing sectors.[20]

In those cases in which early impressions are favorable enough to encourage further encounters, continued exploration tends to set

[20]The analysis of favorable first and second impressions has thoroughly dominated the extensive literature on interpersonal attraction. See, for example, Ted L. Huston, editor, *Foundations of Interpersonal Attraction*, New York: Academic Press, 1974; Bernard I. Murstein, editor, *Theories of Attraction and Love*, New York: Springer Publications, 1971; and Ellen Berscheid and Elaine H. Walster, *Interpersonal Attraction*, Reading, Mass.: Addison-Wesley, 1969.

in motion an important process in relationships, which Simmel recognized as a strain toward "totality."[21]

The persona presented by each, having been warmly received by the other, tends to take on a life of its own in the context of this nascent relationship. But they are only personas, after all, and not the whole and only truth about the parties involved; they are only *subsets* of the respective identity-hierarchies. As a consequence, each person comes to feel a bit uncomfortable with his persona (or character).

First of all, some of the person's other valued role-identities, which alter could support, are not being legitimated in the relationship because they were not included in the initial subset, which is all that alter knows of ego. Second, and perhaps more important, the person fears that alter will discover that ego's persona is not the whole story—that ego has other identities that may not be particularly compatible with those that comprise his persona. And as this persona (or character) has been warmly received by alter, ego is understandably reluctant to have it perhaps embarrassed or discredited by other aspects of his self-structure. He is, in a sense, "passing," the same sense in which we speak of Negroes passing as white. It is not so much that he is passing himself off as something he is not, but that he has passed hinself off as not being some other things that in fact he also is.

People, then, grow uneasy with their personas and experience a strain toward broadening the views of themselves that they allow alters to see. This strain is in part a desire to obtain support for broader ranges of their identities and in part a desire to prevent alters from unmasking their initially unrevealed role-identities. It is, of course, this latter factor that dictates the devious and guarded nature of the process of mutual exploration already discussed.

Tentatively and cautiously, each person attempts to incorporate more and more of his self-structure into the relationship without introducing anything that would spoil it. The greater the number of role-identities that become involved in a relationship, and the more deeply they become involved, the more rewarding and more

[21]Simmel, *op. cit.*, pp. 120–122.

durable the relationship becomes, by reason of being less vulnerable to unmasking. As a result, there is a very strong tendency for the relationship to extend its claims infinitely, to encompass all of each participant's self.

Beyond this internal tendency of a relationship to encompass an increasing number of the participant's role-identities as time passes, there is an external factor that contributes to the broadening. The situation within which any concrete interaction is carried out is never purely relevant to a given identity or subset of identities. As time goes on, the flow of external events calls forth more and more of the total sets of identities of the individuals involved. An overheard remark by a news commentator, a disturbance in a restaurant, a minor accident, reactions to a stranger passing by, these and a thousand other minutiae that crop up while one spends time with others will reveal the parties to each other more broadly, as well as more deeply. No one is so capable of staging the setting of interactions so well, or is in such control of the expressions he gives off, that he is immune to this spill-over of events.[22]

This "strain toward totality" in relationships operates not only to include larger segments of one's self-structure but also to include ever-greater proportions of one's time and other resources. If a particular relationship is a rewarding one, the members may be tempted to exploit it further.[23] If interacting with alter is enjoyable, why not interact more often? If yachting with alter is fun, why not ask him down to the club? In this way, the strain to spend more time with alter gives rise to a strain to include more activities—and thus more role-identities—in the relationship. Conversely, the more identities that become involved in the relationship, the greater the number of activities that alter can legitimately request us to join him in, thereby making further demands upon our time, energy, money, and other resources.

[22]Paul C. Cozby, "Self-Disclosure," *Psychological Bulletin*, 1973, 79: 73–91; Altman and Taylor, *op. cit.*; and Miller, *op. cit.*

[23]L. Rowell Huesmann and George Levinger, "Incremental Exchange Theory: A Formal Model for Progression in Dyadic Social Interaction," in Leonard Berkowitz and Elaine Walster, editors, *Advances in Experimental Social Psychology* (Volume IX), New York: Academic Press, 1976, pp. 191–229.

THE LOGISTICS
OF RELATIONSHIPS

Thus, as Simmel has also argued, the claims of such a relationship tend to be relentless, one-sided, and monopolistic.

> Usually, each claim presses its rights in complete and pitiless indifference to other interests and duties, no matter whether they be in harmony or in utter incompatibility with it. It thus limits the individual's freedom as much as does the large number of claims on him.[24]

His problem as a personality, then, is to limit, adjudicate, and balance all these competing claims upon himself from his various relationships and group memberships in such a fashion that he can still achieve something of the personal ends he entertains.

The logistical problems here are two: first, to juggle the claims of all one's relationships in such a manner that one's personal ends are furthered (or at least not entirely jeopardized) and, second, to manage events pertinent to any given relationship in such a way as to preserve and cultivate it.

The first of these problems involves considerable skill in agenda-construction. In very limited time, one must somehow satisfy the demands of all his relationships, each of which has a tendency to engulf him totally, as we have seen. He must find the time and the resources to keep all his various relationships going, as it were. Though it is quite a feat in itself, it constitutes only the minimum criterion. He must try not only to satisfy his various relationships but also to do so in such a way that his hierarchy of role-identities and his other needs are also satisfied. That is, he must not merely passively comply with the demands made upon him by his relationships but must also optimize the returns from these relationships. These persons who are making demands on him are not miserly creditors and oppressive rulers, after all, but his friends and

[24]Simmel, *op. cit.*, p. 121. *Cf.* William J. Goode, "A Theory of Role Strain," *American Sociological Review*, 1960, 25: 483–496; and Robert K. Merton, "The Role-Set: Problems in Sociological Theory," *British Journal of Sociology*, 1957, 8: 106–120.

his family, people whom he finds rewarding and enjoyable. With only twenty-four hours in a day, how can he optimize his interactions with these people? How can he simultaneously cultivate all these relationships? Time must be found in his agendas to maximize his enjoyment of each of them.[25]

Some of these relationships are less manipulable for purposes of agenda-construction than are others, of course. Work roles, for example, are typically less flexible in their demands than are friendships; as a consequence, friendship activities are usually subordinated to the demands of the work role. One's less flexible relationships set the main outlines of one's agenda, so that the less demanding ones (however rewarding) must be worked into the time left over. As a result, there is a tendency to try to maximize efficiency by getting some of one's other identities legitimated at the same time one is fulfilling these inflexible relationships. Courtship and friendship relations thus tend to blossom in the workplace, when possible, and many identities receive virtually their only exercise within the bounds of demanding family relationships.[26]

This economy of relationships requires us, then, to regulate our personal involvements with sharp eyes toward the ratios of rewards (in role-support and more material aspects) to costs in particular relationships. If a young lad has approximately equivalent romantic interest in two young ladies, one across town and one across the continent, odds are that the hometown girl will prevail, for the cost is lower for equivalent reward.[27]

This differential economy leads to power differentials within a relationship. He who can obtain the same rewards elsewhere for no greater costs is less likely to comply with the demands of the relationship than he who has no alternative sources of reward, at least

[25]Goode, *op. cit.*; and Sam D. Sieber, "Toward a Theory of Role Accumulation," *American Sociological Review*, 1974, 39: 567–578.

[26]Suzanne B. Kurth, "Friendships and Friendly Relations," in McCall *et al.*, *op. cit.*, pp. 136–170.

[27]The strain toward totality that exists in every relationship is hard to comply with at great distance, for it is impossible to include all one's life in letters and rare visits. Frequent face-to-face interaction seems to be a necessary condition for a strong and viable relationship.

within the same price range. This "principle of least interest," first enunciated by Willard Waller,[28] implies that such a power differential entails unequal ability to set the terms of the relationship, to negotiate the common agenda, although this raw opportunism is usually somewhat mitigated by the moral bonds of commitments and ascriptions.

This arranging of relationship-relevant events leads back to the second main logistical problem, which is the management of events in such a way as to preserve and cultivate the relationship. As noted previously, an interpersonal relationship is actually a relationship between two personas, which do not include the entire identity-hierarchies—the entire selves—of the respective individuals but merely biased samples, so that each party is in a sense "passing." One of the problems in maintaining and preserving a relationship, then, is to manage the impingements and possible threats posed by those identities that are perhaps prominent in the individual's hierarchy but are not involved in the relationship and are sometimes even unknown to alter. Unless the relationship is a totally engulfing one, the individual will have an existence outside of and in addition to the relationship. And if he values the relationship for any reason, he must see to it that this outside existence does not have a deleterious influence upon the relationship. In the extreme case, he must prevent alter from discovering the facts about his existence outside the relationship. Deviates, adulterers, criminals, and spies, for instance, must take such preventive measures.[29] But such extreme types are not alone in the practice of duplicity; we all find it necessary and convenient to hide some things from some people, and rare is the youth or spouse who tells everything to his parent or mate.

When the contents of one's other identities are incompatible with one's persona, the danger of this knowledge's coming to alter

[28]Waller, *op. cit.*, pp. 275–277. *Cf.* the discussion of power and authority in relationships in Chapter 6 above.

[29]J. L. Simmons, *Deviants,* Berkeley, Calif.: Glendessary Press, 1969; and John Lofland, *Deviance and Identity,* Englewood Cliffs, N.J.: Prentice-Hall, 1969.

lies at every hand. The person himself may unwittingly impart such knowledge during a direct encounter with alter, or third parties may give him away in various circumstances. Let us treat these two categories of threat separately.

When the person gives himself away, it is through his actions—through signs given or given off, although even in the former case it is usually through a slip or a lapse of attention. Take for example the case of one homosexual informant:

> You know what was really hard? Watching television with my folks. I'd catch myself saying, "There's a good-looking boy."[30]

Similarly, he may give himself away by giving off discrepant signs in the presence of identity-relevant objects, in this instance, for example, by unusual visual attentiveness toward a person of the same sex or a peculiar manner of scanning this person.

One of the most painful and difficult situations to be faced by he who passes is derogation of the content of his concealed role-identity. The cherished alter in the relationship may himself deprecate some particular social role without realizing that the person standing before him, for whom he cares so much, actually holds that role-identity himself. There are then three main possibilities of action open to the person who is passing:

1. He may conform with the general tenor of these remarks himself, thus disparaging, condemning, and ridiculing himself, his role-partners, his memories, and so forth, as the price of maintaining the persona he sees as vital to perpetuating a valued relationship. This maintenance is bought at a high psychological cost indeed. If ego actually agrees with the expressed judgment of alter concerning this social role, he condemns himself. If he still retains a good opinion of himself as a performer of the derogated role, he feels at least partially alienated from the cherished alter.

2. He may "leave the field." That is, he may attempt to ignore this part of the conversation, hoping that the topic will thus be dropped, or he may even try actively to redirect the conversation into areas less relevant to his concealed identities. In extreme cases,

---

[30]Quoted in Simmons, *op. cit.*, p. 82, from which some of the following paragraphs are adapted.

where this sort of redirection is repeatedly denied him, he may break off the encounter altogether. If, for external reasons, breaking it off is impossible, his flight may take the form of psychological withdrawal, in which he continues woodenly to perform the social amenities but is completely alienated from the encounter.

3. He may defend the deprecated social role. His defense may be an abstract one, in which he chides or condemns alter for intolerance and narrow-mindedness. Or it may be a specific defense of the particular role itself, on some sort of logical grounds. Depending on the response of alter to this sort of defense, ego may then come out with a confession (whether defiant or contrite) that he himself holds such a role-identity.

In interviews, many persons have spoken quite bitterly about the results of following this last course of action. Even though his self-revelation may be met with a great show of declared tolerance and acceptance, the person often learns through sad experience that alter will nonetheless usually begin to disengage himself from the relationship or engage in reform attempts, trying to make ego "see the light." In this case, ego is no longer a discreditable person who must manage information but a discredited person who must manage the strained encounters of a disrupted relationship.[31] It seems that the pledge that "you can always tell me everything" should be taken somewhat judiciously in most interpersonal relations.

The second broad category of danger to one's persona comprises the problems of information control posed for us by others with whom we interact.

First of all, of course, the particular alter for whom we are concerned to maintain the persona may himself chance to observe us performing one of our more or less concealed role-identities. It is to guard against this danger that we employ "audience segregation," in which we try to ensure that our performances of incompatible role-identities are witnessed only by disparate audiences, so that no one is confronted inescapably by the incompatibility of

[31]Goffman, *Stigma: Notes on the Management of Spoiled Identity,* Englewood Cliffs, N.J.: Prentice-Hall, 1963, pp. 41–42.

certain portions of our self-structures. This tactic often fails, of course, and Goffman has compiled catalogues of vivid anecdotes detailing the strained encounters attendant upon such failure.[32]

The second danger posed by other persons is that knowledgeable third parties may, deliberately or unwittingly, bring to the attention of alter certain portions of ego's history that discredit the persona that the individual is maintaining for that alter. That is, these third parties may report having heard that ego is a "such-and-such" or that they have actually seen ego (a) performing this concealed role, (b) in role-related establishments, or (c) in the company of persons associated with that role.

The introduction of such embarrassing information by third parties may occur in the presence of both ego and alter, causing an immediate scene, or in the presence of alter alone, in which case he may later confront ego in a dramatic showdown. Or worse yet, alter may for a time keep these revealed facts to himself, so that ego is unaware that alter knows the truth about him; ego then continues to trap himself in his own web of deception and duplicity, depriving himself of any chance of passing off the third party's report as false.

Such, then, are some of the important embarrassments and threats to one's persona that are posed by self and others. As one would suppose, the performer has at his disposal certain limited means to guard against these threats.

To begin with, in countering the threat that he presents to his own persona, the individual must take care to exercise expressive control in every encounter with alter. As emphasized repeatedly in earlier chapters, he must closely monitor and regulate the signs he gives and gives off so that they will be entirely consistent with the persona he is maintaining in the present encounter *and with the persona presented in previous encounters with that same alter.* Such "dramaturgical circumspection" has also been examined in reasonable detail elsewhere.[33]

Second, for every relationship—which means for every persona—he must rewrite his personal history, in such a way as to sup-

[32]*Ibid.* See also Goffman, *Presentation of Self.*

[33]Goffman, *Presentation of Self,* pp. 218–228.

port the persona without misrepresenting the main facts of his life any more than is absolutely necessary. Every interpersonal relationship demands the exchange of biographical sketches, as a result of the strain toward totality, which does not stop at the present and future lives of the participants but demands that their past lives also be incorporated.[34] Although the participants comply with this demand, they also fudge a bit by selectively interpreting and reporting history. As most alters are neither historiographers nor private detectives, the individual has some freedom in this selection—including the freedom deliberately to distort and fabricate.[35]

A third technique, mentioned previously, is audience segregation. With respect to a given persona, ego divides all the people of the world into three main classes, the members of which he associates with and reveals himself to differentially:

1. those who can be trusted actually to help him maintain his persona for alter;

2. those who, if they knew, would probably deliberately give him away to alter (this class includes those of alter's friends and allies who share his particular biases, as well as all those peculiar types Becker has called "moral entrepreneurs");[36]

3. those who could unwittingly give him away, a category that includes two subclasses: (a) those who know him in his concealed role-identities but are unaware that these identities *are* being concealed from alter (these people may then initiate interaction with ego in the forbidden roles in the very presence of alter, thus destroying ego's pretense) and (b) people ego does not know but who may, at some point, report to alter discrediting aspects of ego's history.

[34]Of course, these biographical sketches are very seldom related in one piece but are revealed piecemeal in connection with various events, questions, and anecdotes. The actor must select and reinterpret these revealed bits of personal history so that their cumulative effect is to support his persona.

[35]Samuel Novey, *The Second Look: The Reconstruction of Personal History in Psychiatry and Psychoanalysis,* Baltimore: Johns Hopkins Press, 1968; Goffman, *Stigma,* pp. 62–66; and I. Helling, "Autobiography as Self-Presentation: The Carpenters of Konstanz," in Rom Harré, ed., *Life Sentences: Aspects of the Social Role of Language,* New York: Wiley, 1976.

[36]Becker, *Outsiders,* New York: Free Press, 1963, pp. 135, 147–163.

In audience segregation, ego must, as a minimum, identify members of category (2) and prevent them from learning any embarrassing information. Ideally, persons who may belong to either category (2) or (3) are carefully segregated, perhaps with the knowing assistance of category (1), so that they can observe nothing inconsistent with the persona in question.

With respect to this persona, then, ego leads a double life, one before those who know more than the persona and one before those who do not. But as a person typically must maintain a number of different personas at any given point in his life, he must lead multiple double lives. In this sense, the lives of all of us are saturated with duplicity. In fact, one of our major life tasks is to keep our stories straight for all the various audiences to whom we have told slightly different versions of our lives—slightly different mixtures, that is, of half-truths.

If this formulation seems distasteful, we should remember too that the ability to keep secrets, to deceive, is a distinctively human one. The animals have no secrets. By keeping secrets, we create a second, invisible world alongside the apparent one, adding a whole new dimension to existence.[37] And in a pluralistic world of many competing perspectives, if any one of them is to be honored and maintained for any length of time, other perspectives have to be suppressed temporarily for the sake of the chosen one, although they may have "veto power" over their own suppression. Ethically distasteful or not, some kinds of secrecy and deception are vital parts of human life.

They are so important, in fact, that, to a certain extent, we must help others to deceive us. As Simmel points out, the highly differentiated nature of relationships, involving as they do highly slanted personas,

> . . . require that the friends do not look into those . . . spheres of interest and feeling which, after all, are not included in the relation and which, if touched upon, would make them feel painfully the limits of their mutual understanding.[38]

Relationships are thus hedged about with discretion, which is one kind of tact. The audience must be tactfully considerate if the per-

[37]Simmel, *op. cit.*, p. 330.
[38]*Ibid.*, p. 326.

former is to be able to present himself at all reasonably; it must *trust* the performer to reciprocate this favor by deceiving it only to the extent necessary to maintain the human relationship.

> As a hypothesis regarding future behavior, a hypothesis certain enough to serve as a basis for practical conduct, (trust) is intermediate between knowledge and ignorance about a man. The person who knows completely need not trust; while the person who knows nothing can, on no rational grounds, afford even (trust). Epochs, fields of interest, and individuals differ, characteristically, by the measures of knowledge and ignorance which must mix in order that the single, practical decision based on (trust) arise.[39]

Too many writers have urged upon us the doctrine that, if only we could somehow remove the barriers to complete communication, all mankind's problems would vanish in an orgy of mutual understanding. Instead, we must recognize that, owing to the very peculiar nature of knowledge about persons, relationships necessarily turn on somewhat misguided and misleading premises about the other parties, that social order rests partly upon error, lies, deception, and secrets, as well as upon accurate knowledge.[40]

The maintenance of interpersonal relationships, it should be clear, lies in the elaboration and support of only partial but profitable truths about the parties involved. Needless to say, this task is not always successfully executed, and many relationships die or wither on the vine.

Again, however, this concern to manage events in such a way as to prevent disruption of a well-received persona is merely a minimal criterion for the individual's response to the second problem of logistics. Few personas are so rewarding that we are not tempted to broaden or alter them in attempts to get even more out of relationships. We have already discussed, in a previous section, the many forces that operate to set up a "strain toward totality" in this respect. Personal economy dictates that we try to get as much

[39]*Ibid.,* pp. 318–319. See Harold Garfinkel, "A Conception of and Experiments With 'Trust' as a Condition of Stable Concerted Actions," in O. J. Harvey, editor, *Motivation and Social Interaction,* New York: Ronald, 1963, pp. 187–238; Kim Giffin and Richard Barnes, *Trust of Self and Others,* Columbus: Merrill, 1976; and Millar and Rogers, *op. cit.*

[40]Gustav Ichheiser, *Appearances and Realities: Misunderstanding in Human Relations,* San Francisco: Jossey-Bass, 1970; and Altman and Taylor, *op. cit.*

as possible out of each of our relationships, to include as much of ourselves as is profitable. We must try to cultivate, as well as merely to preserve, our various relationships.

The two criteria are thus not entirely unrelated. We must try to include all those aspects of ourselves that would be reasonably well-received by alter but exclude all those aspects that would threaten the continued existence of the relationship.[41] This stricture presents a rather difficult problem in most cases, for we can only infer from what we know of alter what identities of ours may be deleterious to the relationship. This inference is, of course, a most uncertain one, but we are aided by the fact that very few of our identities would, if known to alter, entirely destroy the relationship. They are, for the most part, identities that are conventionally regarded as deviant in alter's subculture and can therefore be predicted reasonably well. Others of our identities, on the other hand, might not actually destroy the relationship but might color it in an undesirable fashion. It is the exclusion of *these* identities, which are more difficult to determine, that constitutes the real problem of preservation.

CHANGES IN RELATIONSHIPS

Implicit in our discussion thus far has been the assumption that a person's self-structure is a constant and that the problems of preserving and cultivating a relationship consist of deciding which of his given role-identities should be included and which should be excluded. This formulation is, of course, a simplification, for one's self-structure changes in important respects throughout one's life in response to changing patterns of demands, skills, and opportunities, as we shall see in Chapter 8. These changes in the contents of given role-identities and in the hierarchical arrangement of identities naturally have important consequences for the personas and relationships one maintains.

Changes in the content of a role-identity may themselves result

[41]M. M. McCall, *op. cit.*

from many causes. The arrival on the scene of attractive alters may come to dominate one's thinking to such an extent that these new people become vitally incorporated into his imaginations of himself in a particular social role; that is, he may come to form new attachments in the role he shares with the other party in an existing relationship. Other audiences may suggest important new activities or qualities that should pertain to his image of himself in the social role. Whatever the cause of such change in the content of a role-identity, the change itself is often of such nature or magnitude that the other party is no longer willing or able to support ego's role-identity, at least at a competitive cost. As a result, ego becomes less interested in continuing to seek out alter.

Ego's identity-hierarchy may shift in such a fashion that the role-identities shared with the other party are no longer so salient or so highly valued, with the consequence that the rewards obtained from alter are no longer worth the costs involved. Such shifts in hierarchy, it should be noted, usually result from encounters with persons other than alter, in connection with identities not relevant to ego's relationship with alter. These outside encounters may, however, lead ego to cultivate his various identities differentially, so that those shared with alter are no longer so valued as are those shared with certain outsiders. Ego's consequent neglect of alter is thus only an unanticipated consequence of these outside encounters: neither party really wishes or causes the withering of the relationship.

Changes in the costs or rewards of interacting with alter may also affect the relationship. For example, the intervention of physical distance increases the cost of interacting with a given person, and equivalent rewards may be found closer to home and therefore at less cost. Or one party to a relationship may suffer great loss in the resources at his command (he may lose his fortune, fame, position, or beauty), with the result that he is no longer so attractive and rewarding.

But whatever the case, one person often comes to find the relationship less attractive and profitable than he formerly did and begins to hold back a little in the face of its demands. He finds excuses to see alter less often or, at the very least, becomes ambivalent and rather half-hearted in his customary performances for alter. In their encounters, alter thus fails to receive his full measure of role-support and other rewards, which he has been counting on and perhaps sacrificing for, and eventually begins to feel cheated and resentful.

If alter then begins to perceive that it is not external circumstances that are to blame for his lessened rewards, that the failure can rather be attributed to changes in ego (or *perceived* changes, as both parties usually have been acting on more or less false premises about each other anyway), alter too begins to withdraw from the relationship. He too begins to change the content of his role-identity, rearrange his identity-hierarchy, or look tentatively for alternative sources of support for that identity.

The outcome of this progressive withdrawal is variable, however, for the relationship does not lie entirely in the hands of its members. If the ties of ascription, commitment, and investment are not overwhelming, the parties to a progressively less rewarding relationship are allowed simply to give it correspondingly less salience in their respective agendas, in accordance with rational principles of logistics. The two parties thus begin to fade out of each other's lives; they may still consider themselves friends, for example, but they simply seem to see less of each other, ordinarily without much awareness of the fact. The relationship simply *becomes attenuated,* in keeping with the decline in its profitability.

Some relationships, on the other hand, in which the bonds of ascription, commitment, or investment are very strong, are not allowed to become attenuated unchecked, no matter how unrewarding they may be. Husbands and wives, parents and small children, the affianced, life-long business partners, creditors and debtors are not allowed simply to fade out of each other's lives, to stop seeing each other. Beyond some point attenuation is forbidden. These persons are required to interact and exchange with each other at some specified minimal level, no matter how mutually painful or unprofitable it may be for them. The relationship has become an empty round of duties, and we speak of the members as having become *alienated* from it. Unlike relationships that effectively end by fading away, those whose members are alienated from them end only through confrontations and unpleasant scenes in which the members overtly sever the remaining ties, at considerable psychological cost.[42]

As noted earlier, relationships are quite easily formed but are destroyed only with exceeding difficulty. Those who have ever had to look significant others in the eye and tell them that they never want to see them again and to forget all about them know how uncannily difficult it is actually to utter those words. The factors of commitment, attachment, and investment—along with their subjective correlates of faithfulness and gratitude—are strong deterrents to open breaks in interpersonal relationships.

Nonetheless, after longer or shorter periods of progressive deterioration of relationships, such breaks are often made. Typically, an actual break is not made until new attachments and deprivation in the old relationship becomes so vastly important that they outweigh, at least for one party, the existing ties.

Very often the actual break is made not by the offender but by the offended—the party who became alienated only through the signs of alienation given off by the other. The hurt to one's pride is so great that few people can admit to themselves that they have been jilted or that the partners have broken off the relationships. Consequently, the offended one may strike first, as far as the *overt* break is concerned, on the theory that the best ego defense is a good offense.

This sketch of the process of alienation from a relationship is, like those of the other phases of a relationship, necessarily incomplete, but it serves to bring our treatment of the career of a relationship full circle.[43] All relationships begin and end with unfulfilled needs for enactment and support of role-identities.

Not all changes in the self-structures of the participants bring about the eventual death or decay of a relationship, however. Many interpersonal relationships persist for decades, through thick and thin, in the face of considerable changes in the make-ups of the participants. The relationship, defined in terms of the consti-

[42]See the thoughtful analysis in Robert S. Weiss, *Marital Separation,* New York: Basic Books, 1975.

[43]See the analysis of alienation from a relationship in M. M. McCall, *op. cit.*

tuent personas, persists but not unchanged. A lasting interpersonal relationship of any degree of intimacy must change apace with the changing of its members. The contents of the interrelated personas change many times over as the couple progresses, for example, from young lovers, to fiances, to young marrieds, to young parents, to grandparents, and to life companions. The relationship must undergo *metamorphosis* at each major turning point in the personal career of each participant. If it does not or cannot, it will fade away or be destroyed. Relationships are nothing if they are not the projections and expressions of the selves of their members.

In fact, it is primarily within relationships that persons grow and evolve. Most of the new identities that we acquire, as well as the changes in those we already hold, arise from intimate associations with others, who hold these changes up before us and let us try them on before we have to wear them in the public view. Relationships thus contain the seeds of their own destruction; they cause the members to change, and changed members entail altered relationships, perhaps viable and rewarding, perhaps unprofitable and therefore unlikely to survive the rigors of men's logistical problems.

RELATIONSHIPS, INTERACTIONS, AND IDENTITIES

Interpersonal relationships, in summary, are perhaps the major solution to the most human problem of living in terms of one's role-identities.[44] They provide a means for legitimating and enacting these self-conceptions by establishing the nexus of a more or

[44]It is important that this statement not be misconstrued as reflecting any sort of atomistic bias. We do recognize and insist upon the importance of social structures larger than the interpersonal relationship, like families, work associations, political structures, and so on. These larger structures, however, do not directly provide the individual with role-support, intrinsic gratifications, and the like. The latter can be accorded only by men, albeit men in certain social positions in such social structures. Though a social structure is thus certainly greater than the sum of the relationship among its members, it is in these relationships themselves that the individual is most directly sustained, influenced, and developed. This point and nothing more is intended by the statement in the text.

less dependable series of interactions. Entering into relationships is a necessarily hazardous gamble with the empirical world, but social life would be "solitary, poor, nasty, brutish, and short" if millions of human beings did not routinely make such gambles.

The individual develops and grows and lives within a nurturing web of such relationships, as we have seen. Having sketched something of the nature and course of interpersonal ties, we shall turn in the next chapter to the life course of the individual *within* his interpersonal web. And as we do so, we shall see that this human solution has a double edge.

Chapter 8

THE INTERACTIVE
CAREER
OF THE INDIVIDUAL

It should be apparent by now that an interaction—even a simple one like exchanging a greeting on the street or taking a coffee break—is not merely a thing of the moment. It is shaped by the past and influenced by expectations of the future. The lyric poet who stresses the simplicity of the moment is thus likely to lead us astray, because it is shared not only by the participants but also by shadows from the past, which channel the course of today's WHOS, WHATS, WHENS, and WHERES.

We cannot therefore fully understand interactions if we think of them only as isolated occurrences, because in many important ways they are merely the instances of *sequences,* the entire life histories of individuals. We cannot understand the identities and interactions of a particular moment without considering the influences of the relevant life histories. In this chapter, therefore, self-conceptions and encounters will be explored from this life-history perspective. After noting the force of historical and prenatal influences, we shall sketch the development of those human skills and attributes that we have been taking for granted in previous chapters, and then we shall trace the complex interplay between self-images and interaction experiences through the various phases of the life cycle.

Because the interrelationship between one's total life career and particular interactions is a mutual one, it would be misleading to assert either that one's life history shapes one's interactions or that one's interactions make up the life history. Either approach, by itself, leads to a biased view. The two perspectives must be considered together if an adequate picture is to be achieved. *The life history of an individual is a reflexive sequence of interactions in which any given interaction is influenced by the sum of past interactions and in turn influences the sum of future interactions.* And we shall see that this lifetime sequence of interactions simultaneously influences and is influenced by the contents and ordering of the person's role-identities.

BIOLOGICAL AND SOCIAL BEGINNINGS OF THE INDIVIDUAL

We noted in the second chapter that many facts of the individual's life are fairly settled before he tumbles into the empirical world. Even his genetic inheritance is determined in large part by the historical and social forces that led to the particular pairing that produced him, and the social positions occupied by his parents and relatives may cast their shadows over the entire course of his life. The ill-understood but seemingly pervasive effects of prenatal and early postnatal events also exert considerable shaping influence upon the person. He has developed some prototypical attitudes toward social objects and some characteristic behaviors before he even reaches self-awareness.

We have seen that the overwhelming proportion of a person's beliefs, values, likes, and dislikes is learned in wholesale fashion from the surrounding social world. His selections, decisions, and creations are in most cases variations and elaborations of these learned themes, rather than inventions of new themes.

In sum, the individual is born into an already existing empirical world from which he will inherit the outline of his tastes, temperament, and life chances. And one of the earliest things he learns is that he must come to grips with this external world in order to survive and make his way.

We have seen, however, that the individual is not merely the passive recipient of these genetic, natal, and early social influences. Almost from the beginning he *interacts with*, rather than merely responds to, his environment, and he exerts influences upon the very forces that influence him so greatly.[1]

Man enters into the physical world at the moment of conception, and he is immediately and ever after subject to the physical and biological laws of that world. But when does the fledgling individual begin to acquire the characteristics that lead him into the second, symbolic world? Before an individual can be said to possess role-identities, agendas, or attitudes toward social categories, he must first develop the fundamental ability to manipulate symbols themselves. The manipulation of symbols in place of things and the ability to invest them with their own reality (stolen bases and freedom crusades) are necessary prerequisites for entry into man's second, uniquely human world.[2]

Human beings are born with the potential for inhabiting this social world, but this potential is fulfilled somewhat slowly and perhaps reluctantly. At most, the newly born infant can differentiate between discomfort and the absence of discomfort. Even the boundaries between his physical self and the external world are vague and must be learned along with the ability to localize and differentiate nervous sensations. The infant is literally egocentric

[1]Michael Lewis and Leonard A. Rosenblum, editors, *The Effect of the Infant on Its Caregiver*, New York: Wiley, 1973; and H. L. Rheingold, "The Social and Socializing Infant," in David Goslin, editor, *Handbook of Socialization Theory and Research*, New York: Russell Sage Foundation, 1969, pp. 779–790.

[2]John H. Flavell *et al.*, editors, *The Development of Role-Taking and Communication Skills in Children*, New York: Wiley, 1968; for a technical account of the development of symbolic ability, see David McNeill, *The Acquisition of Language: The Study of Developmental Psycholinguistics*, New York: Harper & Row, 1970.

[3]James Mark Baldwin, *Mental Development in the Child and the Race*, New York: Macmillan, 1895, pp. 334–339.

and only slowly learns to recognize and begin to deal with a world external to himself.[3]

This differentiation between self and external world is not simply learned gradually but is forced upon the infant through a series of "shocks"; frustration, which is inevitable, may be a major impetus to learning and developing. The cumulative result of these shocks is that the infant learns that he cannot take the world for granted but must rise from his complete self-immersion to cope with it in some manner. That is, even before anything like a clear pattern of role-identities begins to emerge, the infant is learning that he must deal with reality. This lesson is perhaps the hardest one that the fledgling human must learn.

There has been much speculative writing on the supposed effects of "shocks" like birth, weaning, toilet training, and discipline aimed at enculturation. Without becoming involved with this literature or its internal polemics, we can safely say that severance from the automatic nurture of the womb and the subsequent dependence upon external agents who are always more capricious than was the umbilical cord are certainly traumatic. The neonate "discovers" that he cannot take his comfort and well-being for granted; *he must negotiate with external agents to bring about desired conditions.* And so, in prototype, social life begins—the individual must rely upon interaction with others.

There has grown up a body of literature asserting that the individual never really accepts this necessity; that we all wish to return to the all-embracing womb; that we seek mastery, power, control, security, even the quietus of death as indirect routes back to the prenatal web.[4] We are not so foolish as dogmatically to present and subscribe to any of these notions, nor are we so foolish as to dismiss them entirely. They are provocative, and one senses a bit of truth buried somewhere within them. Perhaps these views represent the metaphysical sense in which we are all "wayfaring strangers, traveling through a world of woe."

[4]Variants of this general point of view have been expressed in an astonishing variety of belief systems, including some schools of Buddhism and early Christianity, German idealism, Russian subjectivism, some implicit tenets of existentialism, the later formulations of Freudianism, and so forth.

Beyond the necessity to negotiate with others for the sake of survival and comfort, the infant is led in another way to interact with others. He is required to take the ways of his society (as interpreted by his family) for his own and to behave in accordance with them. Already, in the first few months of life, the infant begins to receive grooming for the local version of his sex role, for example.[5]

Through bribes and pummeling, but, more important perhaps, through the subtle sanctions of tone of voice, facial expression, and physical handling by the others who inhabit his world, the infant learns which channels through the ocean of theoretically possible life courses are acceptable and unacceptable. The seeds of a full-fledged Bantu warrior or an American middle-class girl are thus planted and nurtured.

The child is channeled by differential sanctions for both his acceptable and his unacceptable behaviors. Much of his activity is a fumbling trial-and-error attempt to cope with the world, and these trials are selectively responded to, shaping his characteristic modes of coping. This statement is true, not only of his concrete acts and spectacular behaviors like sexual explorations, but equally of his subtle and pervasive modes of expression and interaction with others. He thus acquires patterns for winning people over, for accomodating them, and for allaying their wrath, very important tasks for one as powerless as a child. The petulant look, the mischievous smile, the tantrum of the small child are often to be found thirty or forty years later in the adult he has become. Many feel that the biological and social inheritances of the young child effectively determine the main outlines of his subsequent life. "As the twig is bent, so grows the tree." To a considerable extent, this position is no doubt valid, but the society in which the person finds himself always requires a good deal of corrective surgery for the person later, so that these early bents are often removed or perhaps reversed. It is not our intent here to take sides on this important issue but simply to invoke it as a background for our discussion of changes and continuity in the interactive career of the individual.

[5]Eleanor Maccoby, editor, *The Development of Sex Differences*, Palo Alto, Calif.: Stanford University Press, 1966.

THE EMERGENCE
OF ROLE-IDENTITIES[6]

Two main factors in the early history of the child lie behind the eventual emergence of role-identities. The first is that, from the moment of his birth, certain social roles are ascribed to him by his parents and others. Although he is not in the least conscious of these social roles for a considerable time to come, he is cast into a particular sex role, family roles (child, sibling, grandchild, nephew, and so forth), religious role (especially with infant or child baptism), class or caste role, and so on. Parents also try to pass on to their children many of those role-identities that make up their own ideal selves. In these ways, the child becomes the unwitting occupant of the social roles that will later form the basis of his first role-identities.

The second factor in this emergence consists of certain aspects of the child's primary socialization, his gradual acquisition of the basic interactive skills. We shall speak of these as (1) the emerging sense of self and other, (2) role learning and anticipatory socialization, and (3) development of expressive skills.

The Emerging Sense of Self and Other

The first aspect of primary socialization that we shall examine is the child's progressive distinction between self and other, ego and alter. In the beginning he is quite unable to make a distinction between himself and the rest of the world. The sensori-motor stage of the first year and a half involves learning the existence and rough contours of the outside world, largely through frustrations and hard knocks.[7]

As Baldwin argued, the child acquires a sense of the "Not-I" before he begins to become conscious of himself as "I."[8]

---

[6]Chad Gordon, "Development of Evaluated Role Identities," *Annual Review of Sociology*, 1976, 2: 405–433.

[7]John H. Flavell, *The Developmental Psychology of Jean Piaget*, Princeton, N.J.: Van Nostrand, 1963, pp. 85–163.

[8]Baldwin, *op. cit.*, pp. 334–337.

He recognizes his parents in the mirror long before he knows his own image. By ten months he will try to reach and play with the image, but he still does not know that it is his. . . . At eight months the child often cries when strangers appear. The familiar figures of mother and father, brother and sister, are now recognized, and this sense of the identity of another precedes the sense of self-identity. For this reason it is said "The Thou is earlier than the I." One investigator who has worked extensively with babies would date the awareness of the "I" around fifteen months of age.[9]

Allport has distinguished seven aspects of the evolving sense of self: (1) sense of bodily self, (2) sense of continuing self-identity, (3) self-esteem, (4) the extension of self, (5) self-image, (6) self as rational coper, and (7) propriate striving.[10]

The first three are acquired over the course of the first three years of life. The unique stream of proprioceptive sensations allows the child to mark himself off as a quite singular entity, like no other in his experience; hitting his foot with a hammer is very different from hitting a peg. He also comes to distinguish himself from the other persons in his world, partly with the aid of the linguistic categories he is acquiring during this period. As he thus becomes aware of himself as a person, he is very sensitive to any threat to selfhood; if he is not treated as a distinct person, if he is thwarted in his actions, his integrity is threatened. The negativism toward adults and the need for autonomy noted at this age by developmental theorists are perhaps consequences of this fragile new self-esteem.

As these processes continue, the fourth and fifth aspects of selfhood distinguished by Allport are attained in some form between the years of four and six. That is, the child comes to extend his sense of self to include possessions and persons close to him, and—most important for our concerns—he develops a rudimentary *self-image*. He learns that he is a "good boy," that he is sometimes "naughty," and that good boys never hit their little sisters. "By

[9]Gordon W. Allport, *Pattern and Growth in Personality*, New York: Holt, Rinehart & Winston, 1961, pp. 112–113.

[10]*Ibid*., pp. 110–138 (Chapter 6, "The Evolving Sense of Self"). Many of the paragraphs below are based on Allport's treatment of the topic.

the interaction process he comes to know what his parents expect of him, and to compare this expectation with his own behavior.'' This ability to see himself and to see himself as others see him is little developed in childhood but constitutes the foundation on which his role-identities (images of himself in particular social positions) will later form.

These processes are considerably speeded by the child's plunge into the outside world of neighborhood and school during the years from four to twelve, and as a result of this great stimulation he comes to realize himself as a rational agent. The world fascinates him, and he becomes a questioning chatterbox in his attempts to make sense of it.

As he has lost himself, in a sense, in this wider world, his sense of identity becomes more tenuous. During the adolescent years, the search for identity becomes predominant in his strivings.[11] Restlessly and self-consciously, he tries on mask after mask in an attempt to discover just who he shall be. His problem is to hit upon a unique set of social roles with which he can live comfortably for the rest of his life. He tries them on for size, imagining himself in these various social roles and positions, constructing role-identities that are now more, now less important in his thinking about himself. Because he is not yet a fully autonomous and equal citizen, the issue is not so much who he actually *is* but whom he shall *become*. He acquires those long-term plans and purposes that we have called "agendas," and it is this development that Allport describes as the final aspect of selfhood to be attained.

Let us now retrace our steps somewhat, having followed out the thread of evolving self-consciousness. A necessary concomitant of the emerging sense of self-identity and self-image is an increased awareness of other persons and their behavior. He learns how they act and how they expect him to act; he learns how to make some sense of others' behavior and how to act toward them in turn.[12]

[11]Erik H. Erikson, "Identity and the Life Cycle," *Psychological Issues,* 1, No. 1 (1959).

[12]Flavell *et al., op. cit.*; Paul F. Secord and Barbara Hollands Peevers, "The Development and Attribution of Person Concepts," in Theodore Mischel, editor, *Understanding Other Persons*, Oxford: Blackwell, 1974, pp. 117–142;

These developments, of course, are the cognitive processes of interaction discussed in Chapter 6—the imputation of a role to alter and consequent improvisation of one's own role.

Role Learning and Anticipatory Socialization

A key aspect of the development of these cognitive processes is the learning of social roles, such as mother, small boy, brother, teacher, pupil, and so forth. The child learns to act, to feel, and to perceive the world in the manner expected from someone in his position. At the same time, because much of this role-related behavior is toward persons in counterpositions (like mother and teacher), he gradually develops some insight into the make-ups of these counterroles.[13]

At first, the child's conception of roles is amusingly crude. He may deny that a teacher can also be mother or that a storekeeper can be a customer, for these roles belong to widely different spheres of his life.[14] Only very gradually does he come to recognize that one person may perform many roles and may act quite differently at different times. This recognition is, of course, a prerequisite for the ability to imagine *himself* in different roles, for the emergence of role-identities.

Childhood is a time of play in all societies, but this play is not altogether frivolous, nor is it unguided. The playing that children and youths engage in is, among other things, a rehearsal of many of the social roles that the person will later come to perform or at

---

W. J. Livesley and D. J. Bromley, *Person Perception in Childhood and Adolescence,* New York: Wiley, 1973; Eugene A. Weinstein, "The Development of Interpersonal Competence," in Goslin, *op. cit.*, pp. 753–775; and Michael Lewis and Leonard A. Rosenblum, editors, *Friendship and Peer Relations*, New York: Wiley, 1975.

[13]Orville G. Brim, Jr., "Personality Development as Role-Learning," in I. Iscoe and H. W. Stevenson, editors, *Personality Development in Children*, Austin: University of Texas Press, 1960, pp. 127–159; and Paul F. Secord and Carl W. Backman, *Social Psychology* (2nd ed.), New York: McGraw-Hill, 1974, pp. 477–487.

[14]Alfred R. Lindesmith and Anselm L. Strauss, *Social Psychology* (rev. ed.), New York: Holt, Rinehart & Winston, 1956, pp. 394–397.

least will need to know something about. Much of what the child learns through these play activities is *anticipatory socialization* because he is learning something of the shape and content of many roles that he will not be allowed really to perform for many years, if indeed ever. He vicariously and indirectly learns about such social roles as parent, teacher, cowboy, nurse, secret agent, and storekeeper. And on the basis of his crude conceptions he *plays at* performing these and a host of similar roles that are integral parts of his social world and its entertainments.[15]

Such anticipatory socialization leads to the gleaning of notions about all aspects of the role: the performances that seem to portray it, the self-expectations and social expectations that it involves, and the self-conceptions and perspectives on social objects germane to it.

In good part, this indirect role-learning takes place through a host of "role-practice" devices that abound in all social groupings. Toys (like dolls, guns, and cars),[16] "Mother's little helper" tasks, stories and myths, and formal education (including specialized adult socialization programs) are some of the major examples of these role-practice situations. The other persons—and usually the child himself—recognize these activities as experimental and exploratory in nature. Consequently, children and youths are usually allowed far more freedom to make mistakes in their playful rehearsals than are full-fledged performers, and the penalties for error are usually much less severe. The tolerance of wider deviations in the playful performances of fledglings seems to be almost universal. But, at the same time, the social grouping is watchful of its fledglings and does apply corrective measures to these deviations.

Anticipatory socialization, it should be noted, is not confined to the childhood years, although it is perhaps most extensive and intensive then. It continues throughout life, although later phases are characterized by an admixture of full performances and anticipatory rehearsals. In fact, this kind of socialization is one of the

[15]Norman K. Denzin, "Play, Games and Interaction: The Contexts of Childhood Socialization," *Sociological Quarterly*, 1975, 16: 458–478.

[16]Donald W. Ball, "Toward a Sociology of Toys," *Sociological Quarterly*, 1967, 8: 447–455.

fundamental processes that move the person along from phase to phase of the life-trajectory—sometimes in an unwilling movement but always in a more or less inexorable one. It leads the person to school, into marriage and parenthood, along a career line, and into old age. The process grooms the individual for those roles he will come to occupy and provides some glimmering of knowledge for choosing among the alternatives he sees before him.

Anticipatory socialization is a ruthlessly neutral process, however, from the points of view of both society and the individual. It may help prepare the individual for a smooth and happy life, or it may engender such bizarre and unrealistic expectations that the person is doomed, willy-nilly, to a succession of failures. It may lead the person into happy choices or disastrous ones. It may foster the smooth transference of the culture and society from generation to generation, but it may also train a whole generation of individuals to inhabit a world that has already faded into history.

In general terms, the relationship between such role-learning and the later realities of role-performance is variable and problematic. In many cases such training facilitates the transition from phase to phase and prepares the person for the competent and satisfying performance of the roles associated with his social positions. But in many other cases such socialization actually makes performance of the role more difficult than it need have been. And, at the extreme, it may incapacitate the person for the role.[17]

Anticipatory socialization is therefore a mixed blessing, but, like the stereotype, it is a necessary and invaluable process in human conduct, for without its cues and coachings we could not stage our lifetime sequence of performances.[18] Both the social groups and the person have high stakes riding on these eventual performances, which is why the child's playing is not altogether frivolous or unguided.

[17]Ruth Benedict discusses some important special cases of this relationship in her "Continuities and Discontinuities in Cultural Conditioning," *Psychiatry*, 1938, 1: 161–167.

[18]See the fine discussion in Strauss, *Mirrors and Masks*, New York: Free Press, 1959, pp. 89–131.

Development of Expressive Skills

The child's active-expressive processes also develop rapidly during the early years as he acquires language and self-control.[19] Luria has shown in a fascinating series of experiments the role that the child's speech plays in making possible much more complicated physical acts than he was able to perform at lower levels of speech development.[20] At a more social level, speech allows the child to regulate his own moral conduct, shaping his behavior toward what is expected of him in his various social roles. The two-year-old may be heard telling himself: "You be careful. William get hurt. No, I won't get hurt."[21]

As the child gains greater control of his speech, his conversations with himself become less often overt and more often subvocal.[22] At this point the child learns the strategic importance of secrecy and deception and consequently gains greater power in the interaction situation, for he can no longer be "read like a book." Others, too, must now attempt to take his role and devise performances with respect to it. Interactively, the child has begun to come of age. Through altercasting ("I love you, Mama. . . . Mama, can I have a cookie?") and through selective presentation of self ("I'm a big boy now, and I can stay up as late as I want to"), he participates fully in the negotiation of the interactive encounter.

When primary socialization (particularly the development of self-consciousness and of the interactive processes) reacts upon the child's ascribed set of social positions, nascent role-identities

[19]Weinstein, *op. cit.*

[20]Alexander R. Luria, *The Role of Speech in the Regulation of Normal and Abnormal Behavior*, New York: Liveright, 1961.

[21]Louise Bates Ames, "The Sense of Self in Nursery School Children as Manifested by Their Verbal Behavior," *Journal of Genetic Psychology*, 1952, 81: 193–232. See also Denzin, "The Genesis of Self in Early Childhood," *Sociological Quarterly*, 1972, 13: 291–314; and Leonard S. Cottrell, Jr., "Interpersonal Interaction and the Development of the Self," in Goslin, *op. cit.*, pp. 543–570.

[22]For the importance of such internalized speech as the medium of the "inner forum" and all that it entails, see pp. 51–55.

emerge as he begins to form images of self in these various positions.

THE EVOLUTION
OF ROLE-IDENTITIES[23]

Once the child (or any role-learner, for that matter)[24] has learned some of the rudiments of a particular social role, he typically "tries it on for size" by imagining himself as a performer of that role. These first imaginations of self in the role are often purest fantasy, for he is far from ready to give it an actual try. The role of cowboy, for instance, requires many physical attributes and skills that cannot be his for years to come, but rare is the American child, male or female, who never fancied himself a real cowboy.

In these early imaginations, the child often applies to his fantasied performances the high ideal standards for that role that are taught in the official culture to which he has been exposed. To him, the true athlete never smokes, drinks, or violates the spirit of sportsmanship, and the policeman, far from colluding with criminals, is dedicated to the complete eradication of all criminal elements. This process, we must suppose, is the beginning of the idealism that we see in all role-identities, even those of cynical adults.

The child may also modify certain behaviors or characteristics associated with the role when he imaginatively applies it to himself. That is, he may change those aspects of the role that are incongruent with his broader view of himself. For example, he may want to

[23]Gordon, *op. cit.*; and Gordon, "Role and Value Development Across the Life Cycle," in J. W. Jackson, editor, *Role*, London: Cambridge University Press, 1971, pp. 65–105.

[24]The profound importance of adult socialization is underlined in Strauss, *op. cit.*; Howard S. Becker and Strauss, "Careers, Personality and Adult Socialization," *American Journal of Sociology*, 1956, 62: 253–263; Becker, "Personal Change in Adult Life," *Sociometry*, 1964, 27: 40–53; Brim and Stanton Wheeler, editors, *Socialization after Childhood*, New York: Wiley, 1966; John A. Clausen, editor, *Socialization and Society*, Boston: Little, Brown, 1968; and Goslin, *op. cit.*

be a doctor but cannot stand the thought of blood or of cutting someone open, so he tells his family, in all seriousness, "I'm going to be a doctor when I grow up, but I won't hurt anyone." These modifications may remain lifelong facets of his identities and may deeply affect the style of his later performances.

In the beginning, the child typically has only very limited conceptions of the requisite role-behaviors. He usually knows only the most central or dramatic role-behaviors and is quite unaware of the less appealing activities with which every social role is freighted. The little boy sees the engineer as a rugged outdoorsman who directs mammoth machines to build towering bridges across mighty rivers, but he does not recognize the amount of tedious drafting and calculation that goes before. The little girl sees the nurse as helping people to get well but does not also imagine herself removing fecal impactions or emptying bedpans. The extent of such selectivity in role-imaginations is of course variable, depending on the quality and extent of the child's indirect role-learning.

As a result of these factors, role-identities in their early stages are usually amusingly crude and out of touch with reality. They are literally fantastic, for the role-performances can take place only in fantasy, and the contents of the role-identities are quite unrealistic. Only slowly, and often painfully, do the innocent and idealistic role-identities of the young become tempered with somewhat greater realism.

Because a new role-identity is so unrealistic, it is extremely fragile on first exposure to the outside world. Consequently, after a few sad experiences with this sort of thing, the person learns to try to choose as the audience for the first public unveiling of this new identity someone who will be relatively sympathetic. And even to such an audience, the identity is broached gingerly and tentatively; the unveiling usually takes the form of announcing a tentative aspiration to play the particular role. Seldom does the person claim to *be* a "such-and-such" right off. Instead, he tests the feasibility of the identity, admitting only that he might *like to become* a "such-and-such." Even at that, only the consensual aspects of the role-identity are mentioned in this first unveiling, with the person holding back the personal imagery of self in that role until he sees how people are reacting to his mention of the role at all.

If he is ridiculed or rebuked at this point, he is likely to abandon the role identity, although ridicule will lead some people to overcompensate by working fanatically to acquire the roles until they force others to accept them. If the person to whom the role-identity is initially broached is mildly supportive and encouraging at this stage of the game, he becomes a very valuable audience to ego as the first direct source of role-support. Such first audiences often exert incommensurable influence on the further elaboration of the specifics of the role-identity, influences that are never wholly superseded by those of later and perhaps more competent audiences.

If the person's claims to the present or future occupancy of the position are more or less accepted by a number of his previously existing audiences, even if only in a light manner, he will begin to strive to have more of the idiosyncratic aspects of the role-identity directly legitimated. Having secured the position, he quibbles with the others about the exact shape it should take in his particular case. Some of these audiences may be able to affect appreciably the content of the role-identity. For example, the football coach may be able to change greatly the content of Johnny's role-identity as a football player, persuading this self-styled halfback to stop dreaming about broken-field runs and start dreaming about crunching body-blocks, as he tries to teach Johnny to be a lineman.

As the person learns more and more about the role, his imaginations of self in that role come to incorporate a more and more representative range of behaviors and, equally important, some alternative sets of standards for evaluating performances in that role that are held by insiders and by those in associated or counterroles.

The child finds inconsistencies in the world he inhabits, inconsistencies in each of his elders at various times, among different elders, and (when he gets out into the neighborhood, school, church, and so forth) between the subculture he has known at home and the realities of the outside world. The experience of such inconsistencies broadens his prototypical role-identities, but it may also introduce ambiguities and conflicts within them. As a result, his imaginations of himself in that role change quite importantly, even when he has successfully performed that role for long years. Young Turks gradually come to think of themselves as elder statesmen, and changing societal conditions may greatly modify the behaviors or evaluations of a given role during a man's own lifetime, as in the case of blacksmiths, farmers, and the like.

Certain persons in counterroles may figure so prominently in ego's imagery of self in role that they are built into the very content of the role-identity as well as constituting most crucial audiences. This pattern is evident for instance, among long-married couples or between the President of the United States and the Russian premier. The loss of such an alter then greatly changes the role-identity, often to such an extent that ego actually gives up the role; the widow cannot even imagine being remarried.

During one's life, external pressures from various audiences tend (1) to conventionalize and (2) to make more realistic, less lofty, the person's role-identities. Because of constraints and circumstances, he continually must "settle for" situations, relationships, and so forth that are not quite what he had imagined for himself in a particular role. After years of such compromise, the elements he has been forced to settle for tend to become actually the dominant features of his role-identities. Echoes of the loftier and more autistic components continue to be heard at times, influencing his preferences in television programs, occasionally his moods and remarks, and especially the sorts of aspiration and standard he inculcates in his children. Unfulfilled components of role-identities have a way of being visited upon the heads of the succeeding generation.

These factors, then, are some of those that influence the long-term development and change of a particular role-identity. Somewhat similar social influences also produce changes in the whole *set* of identities that a person entertains, and it is to these changes that we now turn.

THE EVOLUTION
OF THE IDENTITY-SET

There are two main aspects to the evolution of the identity-set that we shall discuss: (1) the increasing breadth of a person's identity-set and (2) the shaping of this set into a shifting hierarchical stucture.

As we have seen, the child is born into an initial set of social positions, including sex, race, ethnic, religious, class, and other ascribed positions. As the child begins to grow up, other people, especially the adults responsible for his primary socialization, confer still other social positions upon him, both for the present and as expectations for future attainment. As these conferred positions are transformed into role-identities through the operation of the child's developing self-consciousness, his identity-set becomes ever wider.

The child becomes increasingly exposed to wider influences than those of the family, from school, books, television, and the like, with the result that he learns of new social roles in the world that would gain him approval with some relevant audience (parents, peers, characters in books or on television, and so forth). These roles too become role-identities of his own.

Furthermore, as he learns more about any one role, he automatically learns of its counterroles and of supplementary roles that are associated with it.[25] Budding writers may come to think of becoming editors, and aspiring firemen may become interested in the role of insurance investigator. The young sociology student learns that he should also be interested in becoming a student of statistics.

Still other factors may lead to the acquisition of additional role-identities, of course, but these three are perhaps the most important mechanisms that broaden the individual's set of role-identities.

More complex are the factors that cause the identity-set to develop into an ever-shifting *hierarchy* of role-identities. This hierarchical ordering in terms of prominence initially emerges because

[25]Brim, *op. cit.*

parents and other important childhood audiences reward certain of the child's nascent role-identities with social approval and more or less discourage others. Those that are most rewarded become more prominent in his self-conception, whereas those tentative role-identities that are uniformly discouraged become less important in his thinking about himself.

Cross-cutting the factor of social support or approval is the child's differential success in performing some social roles. Successful performance is of course a very important factor, though not a necessary or sufficient one, in gaining approval for a role-identity. And whatever the reactions of others to his successful performance, it will always gain him some quantity of role-support in at least his own eyes, from himself as audience, for he will know that he *could* bring off the role if he were allowed to do so.

As the child grows up, he acquires new relevant audiences from which to gain approval and role-support—those persons who have special connections with roles he can perform with at least minimal success (the roles of pupil, athlete, friend, and so forth). The first of these outside audiences typically include particular friends, the peer group *per se*, and the teachers at school. At some point and to some extent, the opinions of these new audiences come to outweigh his family's evaluations, at least with respect to certain roles. This change represents a crucial breakthrough in the development of the child, for the self now has outside anchorage points so that it can grow and change in directions not anticipated—or necessarily approved—by the controlling family.

In the beginning, the child's primary audience (the family) weights the importance of the opinions of all his alternative audiences. That is, the parents may not consider the child's teachers or playmates particularly relevant judges of their child. As he grows older, however, and is drawn increasingly into society, these other audiences become more and more important to him, if not to his parents. At this stage, we must take into consideration the evaluation, *by each of his audiences*, of all his alternative audiences.

We must consider, that is, not only the parents' evaluation of teachers and playmates as audiences for their child, but also the teachers' and the playmates' evaluations of the parents and of each other. Each of these evaluations naturally affects the importance that the child attaches to the reactions of a given audience toward his own performances. Some audiences come to be taken more seriously than others, although this ranking is ordinarily somewhat relative to the role-identity in question.[26]

Successful performance of a role gains for the performer a certain amount of role-support from his audience, as we have seen before. Different audiences may, however, confer differing amounts of such support for the very same performance. In any case, a comparatively small quantity of support obtained from a particularly important audience often outweighs a somewhat larger quantity of support from an unimportant audience. In other words, the quantity of role-support gained from a particular audience is *weighted* in terms of the importance of that audience to ego. The importance of the audience is a multiplier of the amount of support it accords ego.

The over-all amount of such support of a role-identity, for all the relevant performances and from all the relevant audiences, constitutes one of the key determinants of the degree of prominence of that identity, as the reader should recall from Chapter 4.

Distinct from this degree of social support of a given role-identity, however, there are also extrinsic and intrinsic rewards and the more personal factors of self-support, commitment, and investment. In the early years of a child's development, his hierarchy of identities is shaped primarily by external agents through the medium of these three categories of social rewards. As he grows older, however, commitment, investment, and self-support of his identities typically assume greater influence in the molding of his ideal self. The ranking of identities in terms of external factors and of internal factors may correspond, but they need not and often do not. When they do not at least roughly correspond, the person is likely to feel discontented with his lot and will be motivated to bring them into closer alignment.

As might be supposed in light of the factors involved in the relative prominence of any role-identity, such identities tend to clump

[26]Assessment of such evaluations of audiences are more fully discussed on p. 261.

together in congruent clusters, all components of any cluster sharing similar degrees of prominence. The basis for this clustering is usually that (1) the same skills or abilities underlie several roles, so that performance of them is likely to achieve similar levels of success, or (2) these roles are commonly associated with one another in the eyes of at least some of a person's audiences, so that the performer of one of the roles is expected to perform all of them. Clustering may also result from the fact that several roles are typically involved in the same type of interaction situation or in a particular career line. This clustering is so prevalent and so important that we may assert that *any role-identity that does not fit with at least one of a person's salient clusters is likely to be sloughed off from the hierarchy.*

As the person drifts through his life course, these clusters themselves tend gradually to change in both prominence and salience as the underlying skills improve and deteriorate, as society makes greater and lesser demands upon certain of his role-identities, and so on.

Some role-identities will gain prominence through practice of skills, maturation, education, or shifts in opportunity structures, all of which serve to increase degree of success in performing them and thus boost their degrees of support and prominence.[27]

Other role-identities decline in prominence. In many cases, the individual simply outgrows them, especially those associated with the first twenty to thirty years of life, with their greater vigor, athletic skill, beauty, occupational horizons, mobility and freedom, and so forth.[28] It is often difficult, however, to know exactly when a person has outgrown them. A man may fancy himself a pretty fair pitcher (though perhaps a bit out of condition) at the same time that younger players consider him to be making a fool of himself with his ineffectual efforts at the annual company-picnic baseball game. Such once-legitimated identities stick around for a long time in an individual's identity-set, eventually (perhaps painfully) to be recognized for what they are—*formerly* legitimate

[27]Gordon *et al.*, "Self-Evaluations of Competence and Worth in Adulthood," in Silvano Arieti, editor, *American Handbook of Psychiatry* (2nd ed.), New York: Basic Books, 1975, pp. 212–229.

[28]*Ibid.*, and Gordon, "Development of Evaluated Role Identities."

role-identities. The star athlete must finally cease thinking of himself as an athlete and must begin regarding himself as a former athlete; the matron must no longer claim to be a debutante but may still think of herself as the ex-belle of high society. These formerly legitimate identities have a somewhat hollow ring about them, but they are nonetheless important as a source of comfort to the aging person and as a means of relating to the people who "knew him when." To a surprising degree, interactions between such persons tend still to be structured in terms of the formerly legitimate identities.

Confinement, migration, mortality, disengagement because of aging, and similar factors may radically alter the kind of people who are available, as role-partners and as audiences, so that quite different role-identities are supported and formerly important ones decline in prominence through want of social support. When one changes his web of face-to-face interactions, he changes himself as well, in the sense that different combinations and contents of role-identities are called forth through interaction.

In the course of his life, then, a person's identity-set becomes progressively broader and more sharply hierarchical, and the elements of this hierarchy change in prominence with the ebb and flow of the life tides in fairly characteristic manner. In the final section of this chapter, we shall sketch more clearly the main directions of these life tides.

INTERACTION THROUGH THE LIFE CYCLE

In every society and epoch there is a model trajectory of successive life phases. These notions that the members of the culture learn are often taken so for granted that they are considered self-evident, and their arbitrariness is never glimpsed. Indeed, as the individual grows up in that social grouping, he internalizes and acts in terms of these conceptions of what each life phase is, so that he makes the conceptions "come true" by dutifully fulfilling them.

The notions of what a child, a girl, or an old man mean are one of the most unthinkingly accepted "givens" in any society. But the culturally defined content of these phases and their relative prestige vary almost endlessly from social group to social group. Within the broad limits of physiology—actually far broader than our own cultural perspective leads us to believe—the life stages are *socially defined*, rather than biologically determined.

The members of various societies, including our own, are so thoroughly enculturated, so buried in the very languages they learn, that they never completely shake off this type of ethnocentrism, and social definitions become their *self-definitions* as they pass through each phase.

We are surprised to read about "an attractive, young thirty-five-year-old girl" in an English novel or the sensuality of a fifty-year-old hero in a German story, to read that Orientals dream and daydream of becoming old, that Romeo and Juliet were "adolescents," that Tamerlane began his conquests in his late forties. Members of other cultures are amazed that we treat children as individuals and pals, that we believe men are "over the hill" at forty, that we glamorize youth.

These social definitions and characterizations of the life phases are models and do not necessarily describe the actual behavior of most members who are in those phases. The model may be unrealistic, so that those in a given phase must bend and compromise the ideal image to some extent. But, realistic description or not, the force of these images can be seen throughout the individual's life, and in fact it is one of the major determinants of the course of that life.

This force is exerted not only upon the behavior of the person; it also tremendously affects the very shape and fabric of the individual by selectively supporting and, at least by default, discouraging various of his identities and (more important perhaps) different aspects of the contents of particular identities. These pressures tend to conventionalize career, marriage, education, creativity, the very self of the person.

The individual is directly and indirectly pressured into "acting his age" by a multitude of small daily influences applied by his fellows. But knowledge of the contents of these social images is not sufficient to explain the individual's self-conceptions and behavior.

This is so because the person's self-conceptions and behavior are not confined to the chronological phase of life he happens to be currently going through. For he has learned something of the images of all the phases; he remembers and he looks ahead, so that his identities and interactions are both reflections of preceding phases and anticipations of subsequent ones. Those phases that are most highly valued in the culture cast a shadow over the occupants of all other phases, and, to the extent that they are capable, persons tend to adopt and carry out modes that are most characteristic of the favored phases. Conversely, the disfavored or despised phases serve as negative models and bases for contemptuous epithets. Myths and mystiques about the various phases may and often do arise, so that those in other phases are not actually emulating or avoiding the conceptions and behaviors that statistically describe a majority of those in a given phase but are acting in terms of a fiction. But as Vaihinger, Bentham, Merton, and others have shown, false conceptions can nevertheless have very real consequences.[29]

Each life phase has its graces and its burdens. Persons often strive to achieve the graces of several phases while minimizing the burdens, and this happy set of circumstances is in fact the essence of "the good life." For example, the ideal career and the ideal womanly role in our culture are often depicted as blithe intermixtures of the prestige, sophistication, and autonomy of the adult, the dash and vigor of youth, and the spontaneity and endless time resources of the child.

Under harsh conditions—social oppression or extreme environment—the phases tend to be truncated; each season is more brief and the entire life trajectory is shortened. Within most social groupings, in fact, the life cycle of the unprivileged classes is foreshortened, and that of the privileged classes is lengthened.

[29]Hans Vaihinger, *The Philosophy of "As If"* (trans. C. K. Ogden), London: Routledge, 1935; Ogden, *Bentham's Theory of Fictions,* Paterson, N.J.: Littlefield Adams, 1959; and Robert K. Merton, *Social Theory and Social Structure* (rev. ed.), New York: Free Press, 1957, pp. 421–436.

This disparity was present among the classes of medieval Europe, and it also holds to some extent for the social classes and majority-minority groupings in contemporary America.

The life phases are not discrete periods. Not only do they flow into one another, but the person also often reaps in later phases what he has sown in preceding ones. As the child begins his interactive career, he is quite dependent upon others for his material and social wants. As a result, he is relatively powerless in his early interactions and relationships. He is seldom able to dictate the terms of interaction directly, to control which roles will be performed by the various actors. Others successfully dictate to him which roles he will perform and which ones they will take on. His only recourse is the tactic of obstruction, to protest and to try to resist this imposition of roles.

As he grows older and acquires such more refined interpersonal tactics as manipulating the assignment of roles by poignantly appealing to certain role-identities of the others, he is able to win for himself a certain measure of independence. Furthermore, his social horizons have broadened, so that he has alternative sources of role-support beyond his family. If he cannot have his way within the purview of the family, he may resort to external sources of support. This possibility, too, increases his independence; the greater the number and significance of alternative audiences, the less dependent he is upon any one of them.

Generally speaking, this trend of increasing independence rises quite steeply until he is a "self-sufficient" young adult who has left the nest to make his way in the wider world. At this zenith, however, most people begin to acquire the impedimenta of families of their own, homes, economic responsibilities, job commitments, and all the rest of the paraphernalia of mature adults.

From this point on, the constraints of these reponsibilities act as sharp drags upon one's independence, and the trend is gradually but ever downward toward the semitotal dependence of senescence (although there is often a temporary upturn when the last of the children has grown up and left home).

This trajectory is largely determined by the fairly typical sequences of roles that most people in our society are expected to pass through during the course of their lives (see Figure 2).[30] The job of society and its manifold agencies is continually to socialize us into these successive roles. The seeds of the corresponding role-identities must be implanted in our minds so that we are led to set up fairly long-term agendas for achieving and legitimating these role-identities.[31]

These long-term agendas, along with their shorter-term counterparts once the roles have been attained, effectively determine the shape and content of the relationships and encounters that predominate at any given point in one's interactive career. The main contours of his interpersonal existence at the moment can be predicted quite nicely once we know his current position in this typical sequence of roles. The identities that guide his social behavior, as well as something of the order of their importance and the tactics for legitimating them, are fairly tightly patterned by the culture for each position in the typical life trajectory (although of course the lives of some persons do not follow this career line).

In the light of these considerations, an inspection of Figure 2 suggests that the role-identity model is perhaps most clearly pertinent to young, increasingly independent persons. These people have not yet been forced to settle down into narrow, stable routines, to compromise and give up many of their previously entertained identities. They have only recently acquired many of their current identities and are not entirely sure of the legitimacy of their claims to them. Furthermore, they still have a good many roles ahead of them from which they must choose.

---

[30]*Cf.* the rather similar trajectory depicted in Gordon, "Role and Value Development across the Life Cycle."

[31]S. L. Pressey and R. G. Kuhlen, *Psychological Development Through the Life-Span*, New York: Harper, 1957; Leonard D. Cain, Jr., "Life Course and Social Structure," in Robert E. L. Faris, editor, *Handbook of Modern Sociology*, Chicago: Rand McNally, 1964, pp. 272–309; Paul B. Baltes and K. Warner Schaie, editors, *Life-Span Developmental Psychology: Personality and Socialization*, New York: Academic Press, 1973; Theodore Lidz, *The Person: His and Her Development Through the Life Cycle*, New York: Basic Books, 1968; and Rose Laub Coser, editor, *Life Cycle and Achievement in America*, New York: Harper Torchbooks, 1969.

Independence	Dependence
	infant
	sibling
	playmate
	pupil
	friend
	enemy
	athlete
	religious role
	worker
	colleague
	sex role
	adult citizen
	spouse
	parent
	in-law
	grandparent
	aged role (disengaged)

Independence	Dependence

Figure 2.   Typical Sequence of Social Roles in American Society

Settled, middle-aged people, on the other hand, have few roles left ahead of them in life, and most of these remaining future roles are not particularly exciting compared to those still facing the young. Furthermore, many of these remaining future roles—like grandparent or the aged role (in its primary form of retirement from work)—are not achieved through the actions of ego himself but are conferred on him by the actions of others, such as his children and his employer.

Consequently, it is perhaps not difficult to understand why many middle-aged people are somewhat prone to "make fools of themselves" by trying to reactivate glamorous roles they have more or less used up or passed by—sex role, athlete, alternative occupational roles, and the like.

But whatever one's position in the life cycle, his role-identities exert a very great influence upon the structuring of his daily life, and we wish now to examine in detail the manner in which they do so.

Chapter 9

THE LOGISTICS
OF
IDENTITY

One of the fundamental discoveries of biology and animal ecology is that every living organism inhabits a "niche," or opportunity structure, which more or less routinely provides it with a modicum of necessities and comforts.[1] This niche is typically an accommodation that falls short of the most ideal conditions yet is considerably above the organism's minimal tolerance levels. That is, the empirical niche within which an organism lives its daily life is considerably better than a random combination of conditions but rather less than perfect.

The development and maintenance of such a niche are a necessary condition for survival itself. But the niche exacts its price too; the characteristics of the live organism are results of the modifications that the niche conditions work upon the organism's potential.[2] In some respects the conditions of the niche bring out the "best" in the organism. The field cat rises to the occasion of a stark environment and becomes exceedingly swift and canny. But in other respects the organism must lose in maintaining an adaptive adjustment with its niche. The fur that might have been sleek

[1]George L. Clarke, *Elements of Ecology,* New York: Wiley, 1954, pp. 465–469; and Eugene P. Odum, *Ecology,* New York: Holt, Rinehart & Winston, 1963, pp. 25–28.

[2]Bruce Wallace and Adrian M. Srb, *Adaptation* (2nd ed.), Englewood Cliffs, N.J.: Prentice-Hall, 1964, pp. 93–99.

becomes frayed and patched by the exigencies of food-getting and defense. The shrub is stunted by the wind, its bark becomes protectively gnarled, and its flowering season is brief.

A large number and variety of studies have demonstrated that humans also live their daily lives essentially within the confines of ecological niches.[3] For any living organism, such a niche consists of more than merely physical conditions; it consists also of a web of accommodative relationships with members of the same and other species.

And so it is with human beings; as we daily inhabit the intersection of our physical and our symbolic worlds, we do so within the web of a few locales and a small number of other people. In considering WHO comes together with whom to engage in WHAT social acts WHEN and WHERE, one of the things that catches the observer's eye is a rather remarkable short-term stability of patterning in these respects. Most people's rounds of everyday activity are remarkably routine and regularized. During one's life these locales and associates may, of course, shift quite radically, but they usually display a grossly predictable stability over stretches measured in months.[4]

Out of all the people in one's locale, one interacts over and over again with but a handful and not at all with the vast bulk of them. Furthermore, the distribution of activities over this limited set of alters is also highly patterned. One does ''such-and-such'' with Jason but ''this-and-that'' with Ed; one does a lot of things—but never drinks or plays chess—with Harry. There is a good deal of difference between what one does with each of his various alters respectively, but there is very little variation over moderate stretches of time in what one does with any given one of these alters.[5]

[3]Clarke, *op. cit.*; Amos H. Hawley, *Human Ecology*, New York: Ronald, 1950; and Otis Dudley Duncan, ''Social Organization and the Ecosystem,'' in Robert E. L. Faris, editor, *Handbook of Modern Sociology*, Chicago: Rand McNally, 1964, pp. 36–82.

[4]Alexander Szalai, editor, *The Use of Time*, The Hague: Mouton, 1973; and F. Stuart Chapin, Jr., *Human Activity Patterns in the City: Things People Do in Time and in Space*, New York: Wiley, 1974.

[5]Jeremy Boissevain and J. Clyde Mitchell, editors, *Network Analysis: Studies in Human Interaction*, The Hague: Mouton, 1973; and Boissevain, *Friends of Friends: Networks, Manipulators, and Coalitions*, Oxford: Blackwell, 1974.

It is this patterning of one's interaction time-budget that constitutes the focal concern of this book. WHO comes together to engage in WHAT social acts WHEN and WHERE? This question has been our touchstone throughout our various considerations of how and why men interact with others. We have endeavored to construct a framework within which we might begin to *explain* the contours and changes of a person's interaction time-budget.[6]

Given a particular individual located in space and in time (including his point in the life cycle), a great many conceivable interactions are automatically ruled out for him, as we have seen in Chapter 2. Personal, cultural, and (especially) social factors, as well as intrinsic limitations on the four ws, greatly limit his opportunity structure and dictate the broad outlines of his interaction time-budget.

Most pointedly in Chapters 2 and 7, we have recognized that much of the stable patterning of an individual's interaction time-budget results from the demands of his formal positions in various social structures: for the adult, his work and family organizations in particular. The demands of the professor's position dictate, for example, that he spend more time with his research assistant than with the registrar; that he lecture his students and seek advice from his colleagues but seldom that he seek advice from his students and lecture his colleagues.

Although these considerations of social position and social role are perhaps the most visible determinants in the allocation of one's limited interactional resources, they still fail to account for much of this patterning that is of great human interest. The formal demands of social position do not explain why it is that the professor seeks out one colleague for a coffee break (or why he takes a coffee break at all) but is too busy when another calls; why he takes time to joke with one secretary (if he does at all) but not with another; why he prepares diligently for some of his courses (if any) but neglects others.

The demands of formal positions do not account for the distribution of the more sociable, relatively voluntary, and unprescribed aspects of a person's interactions or for his violations and

[6]See pp. 269–271 for some suggested lines of research in the empirical explanation of observed interaction time-budgets.

abrogations of those demands. Or, as Homans puts it, knowledge of formal positions does not account for the subinstitutional or elementary social behavior that has been noted by every modern student of concrete social structures.[7]

Nor, in fact, do such institutional factors explain why the person takes on or acquiesces in the demands of a particular formal position in the first place. Although the bonds of employment, family, church, residence, and so on are typically very strong, they are never so strong that the individual is prevented from renouncing the demands of these positions (or at least heavily compromising them) and seeking out new alters and activities.

It has seemed reasonable to us, then, to drive the explanations of interactive patterning back to broader and more personal factors like role-identities and their hierarchies. From this perspective, the individual is viewed as acquiescing in the formal demands of social positions to the degree (1) that they are tolerable in view of his conceptions of himself, in general and in a specific position, and (2) that they are necessary for obtaining role-support and a context for enacting those of his role-identities that are directly relevant to those institutional positions. Formal demands, like any other interaction proposal, must be weighed and interactively negotiated in terms of the three cost-reward calculi.[8]

Even when these demands are complied with, the specifics of his actual role-performance are constructed in such a way as to express and enact his role-*identity* rather than his social role.[9] And simultaneously, within the remaining degrees of freedom, he attempts to work into his performances other, less directly relevant role-identities. Quite often, in an institutional context, this "working in" involves some "misuse of office" but nevertheless continues

[7]George C. Homans, *Social Behavior* (rev. ed.), New York: Harcourt, 1974, pp. 1–6, 356–373.

[8]Barney Glaser, editor, *Organizational Careers: A Sourcebook for Theory,* Chicago: Aldine, 1968; John Van Maanen, ed., *Organizational Careers: Some New Perspectives,* New York: Wiley, 1977; William J. Goode, "A Theory of Role Strain," *American Sociological Review,* 1960, 25: 483–496; and Carl W. Backman and Paul F. Secord, "The Self and Role Selection," in Chad Gordon and Kenneth J. Gergen, editors, *The Self in Social Interaction* (Volume I), New York: Wiley, 1968, pp. 289–296.

[9]Phillip W. Blumstein, "Identity Bargaining and Self-Conception," *Social Forces,* 1975, 53: 476–485.

to occur, for the individual acts in terms of his values and attachments, as well as of his ascriptions and commitments.[10] The freedoms allowed us by our positions are variable, but even children and slaves possess a good deal of freedom to allocate their resources, and, conversely, no dictator is so absolute and no wanderer is so footloose that he can act solely in terms of personal whim.

To understand in any detail WHAT a person is likely to do, therefore, we must look to his self-conceptions, to the contents of his role-identities, for it is through them that the demands of social structures are filtered. To predict what he is *most* likely to do, in the long or the short run, we must look, respectively, to the prominence or salience hierarchies of those role-identities. To predict WHO may do WHAT with him, we must know these role-identity hierarchies not only for ego but also for relevant alters; these hierarchies constitute the existing opportunity structure for him. This structure becomes operative only when it is perceived (and misperceived) by ego. Persons furnish opportunities only with respect to ego's role-identities, in that they are perceived as possible role-partners, possible sources of gratification. But interaction is costly as well as rewarding, of course, so that many of these interaction opportunities are discarded as unprofitable in the light of available alternatives. Nevertheless, the individual still retains a vast number of interaction possibilities from which to choose. In the final analysis, then, predicting and explaining WHO comes together to engage in WHAT social acts WHEN and WHERE comes down to facing ego's problem of logistics and allocation: Given finite time, energy, and resources, which of these innumerable interaction possibilities constitute, on balance, the most profitable lines of investment for the persons involved?

THE LOGISTICAL PROBLEM

A fundamental aspect of human behavior is that the pursuit of any given course of action simultaneously renders a large number

[10]Suzanne B. Kurth, ''Friendship and Friendly Relations,'' in George J. McCall *et al., Social Relationships,* Chicago: Aldine, 1970, pp. 136–170; and Erv-

of alternative courses of action impossible. This is so not only for a particular moment but also for an ongoing trend of a particular interaction or of a relationship.[11] Try as we may, it is impossible to "freeze" a given phase of an interaction or a relationship and remain within it. By taking one route we must miss those things that might have happened along the other routes; one can only be a newlywed once and for a little while; if we go to the seashore we must forgo the mountains; the first flush of a friendly association is soon and forever transmuted into something different. The logistical problem of choice and allocation lends a haunting quality to human life because, in the act of "choosing," we veto a host of other choices and in time discover that we have been imprisoned by our own prior decisions, if only because of the investments we have made.

The basic life task facing the individual is therefore, given only a finite store of time and other resources, to juggle the multitudinous commitments and demands of his positions and relationships and the demands following from his role-identity hierarchies in such a way as to negotiate a "safe" and "meaningful" passage through life. Furthermore, he cannot linger in negotiating such a passage, for in lingering he exhausts one of his scarcest resources—time.[12]

The individual must negotiate this passage within the contours of his niche, his opportunity structure. Like all other living organisms, the individual attempts to create and adapt his life situation to provide fairly routinely for his needs and desires, but, unlike those of other species, these needs include the legitimation and enactment of his role-identities.

Like other organisms, man not only shapes but *is shaped by* his opportunity structure. As we have seen, the life situation exerts persistent pressure upon the individual to make his identities more conventional and more realistic. It selectively supports, blocks,

ing Goffman, "The Underlife of a Public Institution: A Study of Ways of Making Out in a Mental Hospital," in Goffman, *Asylums*, Garden City, N.Y.: Doubleday, 1961, pp. 171–320.

[11]Sasha R. Weitman, "Intimacies: Notes Toward a Theory of Social Inclusion and Exclusion," *Archives Européennes de Sociologie*, 1970, 11: 348–367.

[12]Murray A. Geisler, editor, *Logistics*, New York: American Elsevier, 1975.

and neglects the legitimation and enactment of particular identities, and as a result the person himself in time changes. Like that of the field cat, man's niche brings out some of the "best" in him, but it also exacts a price.

The multitude of daily influences that constrain the individual to accommodate to his life situation tend—but only tend—to lead and push him toward adopting a more comfortable life style. As the individual expresses himself in a variety of situations, as he attempts to enact his identities, the differential encouragements and discouragements of others, as well as the differential opportunities he sees, tend to impel him into those circumstances in which he can "do better" for himself. But this process seldom reaches its theoretical limit, the complete adjustment of the person and his niche. For the individual may be unable or unwilling to succumb to such a process, and the boundaries we discussed in the second chapter may prevent him from doing so even when he acquiesces. As a result most people settle, and are settled, into social and ecological niches that sustain them but still leave something to be desired.

Although man's *opportunities* are thus limited, as by the laws of physics and physiology, his *aspirations* are not. There is only enough time for us to raise one or two families; we can come to know in depth only a few score people in our lifetimes; we shall be able to finish reading only a few hundred more books. This and others of the many nuances of the logistical problem are well expressed in a letter written by one of Aldous Huxley's characters:

> Midsummer Day, Helen. But you're too young, I expect, to think much about the significance of special days. You've only been in the world for about seven thousand days altogether; and one has got to have lived through at least ten thousand before one begins to realize that there aren't an indefinite number of them and that you can't do exactly what you want with them. I've been here more than thirteen thousand days, and the end's visible, the boundless possibilities have narrowed down. One must cut according to one's cloth; and one's cloth is not only exiguous; it's also of one special kind—

and generally of poor quality at that. When one's young, one thinks one can tailor one's time into all sorts of splendid and fantastic garments—shakoes and chasubles and Ph.D gowns; Nijinsky's tights and Rimbaud's slateblue trousers and Garibaldi's red shirt. But by the time you've lived ten thousand days, you begin to realize that you'll be lucky if you succeed in cutting one decent workaday suit out of the time at your disposal. It's a depressing realization; and Midsummer is one of the days that brings it home. The longest day. One of the sixty or seventy longest days of one's five-and-twenty thousand. And what have I done with this longest day—longest of so few, of so uniform, of so shoddy? The catalogue of my occupations would be humiliatingly absurd and pointless. The only creditable, and in any profound sense of the word, reasonable thing I've done is to think a little about you, Helen, and write this letter . . .[13]

Here is perhaps the most intractable component of man's logistical problem: An individual's intrinsic resources—his time and energies—are insufficient to allow him to be and do all the things he dreams of being and doing. He must therefore differentially *allocate* these limited resources among his various aspirations. This requirement is further underlined by the fact that the committed pursuit of some of his role-identities entails the forgoing and, occasionally, the actual repudiation of others of his identities.

The problem is complicated by the fact that human beings are not socially equal but are ascribed and committed to a set of relative positions in the society, so that social opportunities for legitimating and enacting role-identities are limited, scarce, and differentially available. (This differential availability is perhaps the nub of that grab bag of ills, injustices, and moralistic prejudices that constitute "social problems.") As a consequence, some of an individual's role-identities are differentially favored by the opportunities open to him because of his particular set of positions in the society. Those that are more conventional and realistic in light of his societal positions are reasonably likely to attain some enactment and legitimation, whereas his more exotic identities are likely to be denied such opportunities.

[13]Aldous Huxley, *Eyeless in Gaza,* New York: Harper, 1936, pp. 254–255.

These conditions combine, then, to produce a modicum of discontent as well as a certain amount of fulfillment *vis-à-vis* one's niche. In this sense we are all amenable to the seductions of more favorable opportunities, more pleasant niches, although the alternatives must be perceived as offering great enough improvement over our present conditions to override the costs of renouncing our present commitments, attachments, and investments.

This admixture of fulfillments and discontents engenders a very common ambivalence toward the daily round. Wherever one goes —to restaurants, to offices, to houses, to markets—one overhears conversations expressing hopes and wishes to escape the current routine. But it is ironic that, when separation from the daily round does occur—temporarily, through "time off," or more permanently, because of personal upheaval or disaster—the individual experiences an acute sense of hollowness and of being adrift. This discomfort at separation from daily routine often comes as a surprise to the individual, and only then does he realize that he has so well adapted himself to his niche that his life seems meaningful largely in terms of it. The sailor returns to the sea, the officer signs up for another hitch, and the housewife welcomes the end of the family vacation because the sea, the army, and the home are not merely work places—they have become ways of life.

This common and recurrent ambivalence that people feel toward their life circumstances leads them to imagine or perceive others as living lives that are more rewarding and meaningful. At the other pole, however, we also have the very frequent experience of thinking, "I'd hate to be in that fix" and "I wouldn't want to be in his shoes," when we hear of a particular life situation. And between these two extremes we almost daily wonder "what it would be like" to occupy some fancied niche.

Each of these reactions is but a special case of a ubiquitous human process; the speculative appraisal of the ratio of possible rewards to possible costs that might accrue if we were to follow a particular course. This appraisal is carried out by hypothetically placing ourselves in that situation, which is made possible, as we have seen, by the human ability to manipulate the symbols that stand for the social objects (including the self) involved in the course we are contemplating. In this fashion, we imagine how it might be to accept an office job in Portland, Oregon; to be married to Joan; to have hamburger steak for supper.

The fact that we calculate costs and rewards in terms of our own anticipated responses is what engenders such a peculiar *subjectivity* in such calculations. "Why does he do it?" is one of the most frequent of human questions. *From our perspectives* we cannot understand why others make the logistical choices they do: skip classes to waste their time drinking coffee, lavish their money on frivolities, spend so much time primping and preening, leave a devoted spouse and lovely children to run off with a "no-good." We are continually asking the motivations of others—continually seeking some explanation for behavior that seems logistically so unreasonable.

But *from the other's perspective*—from the point of view of his role-identities, and his perception of opportunities—his behavior is usually eminently reasonable. If his sex role-identity is highly valued and he is currently gambling on its support from a particular alter and the opportunity for a coffee date arises, while the role-identities of scholar and eventual breadwinner are far less prominent, then the choice of coffee date over class is a clear one. If music gives us the sense of contentment we crave, it is sensible to buy a hi-fi phonograph rather than smart clothes or medical insurance. If one's spouse altercasts one into roles one is unwilling and unable to perform, so that the marriage has become an empty round of duties, it is not altogether unreasonable to seek an outside relationship with a kindred spirit. And as an extreme case, if the life situation is perceived as so threatening that any utterance or movement is likely to result in terrible retribution, it is quite logical to sit perfectly still for a long, long period of time, as the catatonic does.

These considerations leave us with two fundamentally important generalizations. First, *cost-reward calculations are subjective*. Second, *one's interpretation of another's behavioral choices is always, to some extent, egocentric*, that is, made from the perspective of *his own* subjective calculi.

Taken together, these two principles yield the ramification we have considered previously: that, literally, people can understand one another only to the extent that they can take one another's roles, see through behaviors to others' role-identities.[14] Several empirical researches have demonstrated that, as divergence in attitudes, beliefs, and values increases, so do intolerance and rejection.[15] If perspectives are widely divergent, all but the most superficial interactions are likely to be precluded. This point further suggests that misunderstandings and conflict over definitions of situations may always be a potential concomitant of human diversity.

Another major ramification of the subjectivity of the cost-reward calculus is that the effective opportunity structure is phenomenological; that is, it exists for the individual only so far as he has knowledge of it. All the factors that limit and bias our social perceptions, discussed in Chapter 5, therefore also limit the individual's opportunity structure.

A further important implication of the fact that cost-reward calculations are subjective is that the *actual* opportunities potentially available to an individual may differ markedly from his *perceived* opportunities; they may be either greater or smaller. Basically such disparity involves "errors" in calculating costs and rewards.

	Overestimation	Underestimation
Rewards	"Total reward"	"No reward opportunity"
Costs	"Total cost"	"No cost"

Figure 3.   Limiting Cases of Erroneous Cost-Reward Appraisals

The simplest case and one of the most frequent, as we have seen, is the error of omission in which the person does not perceive a reward opportunity that actually "exists." One of the functions of experience and one of the aims of education and counseling is, of course, to increase the individual's awareness of the opportunities potentially open to him.

[14]See pp. 126–132.

[15]Milton Rokeach, *The Open and Closed Mind,* New York: Basic Books, 1960; and J. L. Simmons, "Tolerance of Divergent Attitudes," *Social Forces,* 1965, 43: 347–352.

The converse error of omission, in which the individual wrongly perceives *no cost* to himself, is also interesting and not infrequent. This error is perhaps made most frequently in planning short-term agendas. The individual frequently assumes that he has greater amounts of free time and energy than he actually has, not fully realizing that the pursuit of any opportunity entails the loss of other opportunities and that time and energy spent diminish the time and energy available for subsequent opportunities during any short-term period. We have all had the experience of having entire days "stolen" from us through acceding to "trivial" commitments and opportunities.

The other two limiting special cases of error in cost-reward calculations—when the person anticipates that either the reward or the cost will be "total"—occur less frequently, yet they have some importance for understanding certain phenomena.

Judgments of "total" cost or reward are usually relevant to only a single role-identity or cluster of them. If the identity or cluster is highly valued, such judgments can obviously have profound effects upon one's self. For example, Becker has demonstrated the effectiveness of the stereotyped anticipation of total cost when one engages in deviant behavior as one of the most important mechanisms of social control.[16] Large proportions of the population internalize the judgments that using drugs, being arrested, or losing one's virginity before marriage will automatically result in irrevocable ruin and stigma—total cost. Interviews with people who have made such "trespasses" reveal an almost uniform astonishment that subsequent life goes on much as it had before; one continues to read the paper, brush one's teeth, and have occasional headaches. Few courses of action in fact entail total cost to the person.

Lack of knowledge, a high valuation of an identity, and a strong need for its legitimation and fulfillment sometimes combine to produce the opposite judgment—anticipation of a virtually total or complete *reward.* "As soon as we get married," "after I receive my degree," "if only we get a chance to go to the Coast," we

[16]Howard S. Becker, "Marihuana Use and Social Control," *Social Problems,* 1955, 3: 35–44.

dream, our lives will be transformed into qualitatively better and richer ones.

> Bearded, with tawny faces, as they sat on the quay, looking listlessly at nothing with their travelled eyes, I questioned them:
>
> "We have adventured," they said.
>
> "Tell me of your travels, O mariners, of that you have sought and found, of high perils undergone and great salvage and of those fortunate islands which lie in a quiet sea, azure beyond my dreaming."
>
> "We have found nothing. There is nothing saved," they said.
>
> "But tell me, O mariners, for I have travelled a little. I have looked for the woman I might have loved, and the friend we hear of, and the country where I am not. Tell me of your discoveries."
>
> One of them answered:
>
> "We tell you the truth. We are old, withered mariners, and long and far have we wandered in the seas of no discovery. We have been to the end of the last ocean, but there was nothing, not even the things of which you speak. We have adventured, but we have not found anything, and here we are again in the port of our nativity, and there is only one thing we expect. Is it not so, comrades?"
>
> Each raised a hand of asseveration; and they said:
>
> "We tell you the truth: there are no fortunate islands."
>
> And they fell into their old silence.[17]

The point in Dowson's allegory is sharply drawn: that some islands may certainly be more fortunate than others, but that nowhere exists the niche that is perfect. However exceptional the marriage, someone must carry out the garbage; becoming a professional involves more a *shift* in freedoms and obligations than a qualitative change; and the Coast may prove to be more similar to than different from the place one is fleeing.

Innocence is perhaps the most general factor that heightens the likelihood of such extreme errors in cost-reward appraisals. It follows that the young, as a social category, are more prone to such

[17]Ernest Dowson, "The Fortunate Islands," in his *Decorations: In Verse and Prose,* London: Smithers, 1899, pp. 43–44, reprinted in Richard G. Hubler, editor, *The World's Shortest Stories,* New York: Duell, Sloan & Pearce, 1961, p. 127.

miscalculations than the older members of a society and that accuracy of appraisal should increase as a simple function of those factors that increase the amount and breadth of experience.

But innocence is not confined to youth. Our store of experience does accumulate as we live, but mainly with respect to our niches, and, if external conditions change rapidly or if we move out from the niches we have come to know and be accommodated to, we discover that we are again novices. This factor is what makes traveling an adventure, and it is also what lends a strong flavor of desperation to collective-behavior phenomena like crowds and social movements.[18]

In fact, if a society is undergoing rather rapid social change it may well occur that the young, as a social category, are more in tune with actual empirical conditions than are the old, for adaptation by the older age groups is impeded by the necessity for unlearning their appraisal habits as well as for developing new, more appropriate ones.

The types of erroneous cost-reward appraisal we have been discussing are the limiting extremes of such miscalculations. Similar over- and underestimation of costs, rewards, or both color the bulk of our subjective calculations, though in less dramatic degree.

Perhaps the most common type of *underestimating costs* is that in which we fail to foresee all that a given course of action entails. It is almost a maxim that courses of action chosen as means to ends have a way of becoming ends in themselves. We discover—often to our disillusionment—that marriage involves much more than playing house; that a career entails many duties and commitments not apparent to the outsider or trainee; that parenthood entails far more than cuddling and displaying cute babies; that moving to another region necessarily involves a plethora of annoyances and inconveniences. Seldom does it prove to be true that there are no strings attached. Perhaps the most frequent source of this type of underestimation of cost is that we perceive, beforehand and from the outside, only the more dramatic and spectacular aspects of the

[18]Ralph H. Turner and Lewis Killian, *Collective Behavior* (2nd ed.), Englewood Cliffs, N.J.: Prentice-Hall, 1972.

course of action and that we fail to see the large extent to which the course, if chosen, will comprise small routine tasks. We shall return to this point in a later section of this chapter.

We are perhaps led most often to *overestimate rewards* because of the need to legitimate and fulfill highly valued identities or clusters of identities. The press of this need may, and often does, lead us to unrealism in gauging the relative rewards of a course of action. This point is well expressed by the almost universal adage that love is blind. The overestimation of reward is also often a result of the innocent beforehand appraisals discussed above, although the two kinds of error may vary independently, even in this case; for example, one may accurately gauge the rewards of professional success but underestimate the costs, or, conversely, one may accurately estimate the costs of moving to another region but overestimate the rewards.

This simultaneous underestimation of costs and overestimation of rewards is extremely common, leading us to perceive greater profits in a line of action than we are actually likely to receive. This facet of the idealism endemic in role-identities is a great motivating force, and its consequences for the patterning of the four ws are more apparent than those of somewhat similar errors. Overestimation of costs, for example, and underestimation of rewards, serve largely as artificial restrictions upon the individual's perceived opportunity structure. The individual fails to perceive as profitable certain courses of action that in fact would pay off rather nicely. The institutional and cultural inculcation of these errors with respect to certain spheres is, as we have seen, one of the most potent means of social control, leading individuals themselves to reject certain actions as not worth the candle.

Finally, one other special case of errors in anticipating costs and rewards must be noted here because it occurs so frequently in daily life: the case in which the costs or rewards are not so much greater or less than anticipated but are *different in content*. This problem is a further source of surprise in human encounters. If the costs and rewards are different from those expected but are commensurate, the individual is likely to call it a fair enough bargain and not to experience lasting disillusionment. And this outcome is, in fact, perhaps the most common of all.

Given this perceived opportunity structure, with all its faults and biases, the individual must do his best to cope with the logistical problem by allocating his limited resources among alternative opportunities in the manner that seems, on balance, most profitable. The success of this decision-making can be no greater than the accuracy with which he perceives his opportunity structure, and it may be a good deal less, for he must not only appraise potential profit but must also determine the optimal *timing* of his various investments. He must, that is, plan or schedule his various enterprises in what we have called "an agenda of performances."

AGENDAS

Some of these agendas are quite long-term, even to the extent of covering the outlines of one's remaining lifetime. Career and family agendas, in particular, often span decades. One plans to become a supervisor or to write the definitive book in some field before one dies; one plans to marry as soon as Dick gets out of the army and to have three children, spaced not more than two years apart. Nested within these relatively long-term agendas are various shorter-term agendas, covering particular weeks or perhaps only an afternoon or a lunch hour.[19]

As with so many of the concepts and processes discussed in this book, agendas need not be *deliberate* plans, and frequently they are not. In interviews, people often struggle to verbalize and express their own agendas and plans for the future, yet a cursory glance at an informant's life history reveals the unmistakable signs of a pattern of choices and predispositions carried out. Often the agendas are so taken for granted or so habitual that the person is

[19]George A. Miller, Eugene Galanter, and Karl H. Pribram, *Plans and the Structure of Behavior,* New York: Holt, Rinehart & Winston, 1960.

not even aware of them; those who say that they have no plans or goals nevertheless display striking sets of priorities and regularities in their behavior.

Long-term agendas, in particular, are often so abstract and perhaps so ineffable that their influence upon daily living is only indirect, although pervasive. The goal of raising happy, healthy children, for example, serves only as an overarching guideline; it does not directly specify what one should do with Billy today. Because long-term agendas can only be carried out through a whole series of shorter-term agendas, constituting poorly specified sets of steps toward achievement of overarching goals, it is most useful to focus upon short-term agendas in dealing with logistics of behavior. These short-term agendas are ''where we live,'' so to speak.[20]

The principal determinant of these agendas is the salience hierarchy of one's role-identities, as discussed in Chapter 4. The juxtaposition of one's prominence hierarchy and calculi of current needs with his over-all perceived opportunity structure gives rise in complex fashion to an ordering of role-identities in terms of salience. In constructing one's agendas, priority is given to the more salient or preferred identities, and the others are worked in as time and resources permit. The relationship between short- and long-term agendas lies in the nature of the perceived opportunity structures. If a short-run opportunity to further a long-term agenda should be encountered, the role-identity corresponding to the latter will (other things being equal) become more salient in the short run and may find a place in one's short-term plans. More generally, one's agendas tend to give preference to those identities and relationships to which one is more strongly attached and that are currently salient in view of perceived opportunities for one's various social enterprises.

As discussed in earlier chapters, agenda-construction is, in one sense, greatly simplified by the existence of interpersonal relationships. Such relationships serve as endurable, dependably recurring sources of the rewards one seeks, at a cost that is reliably estab-

[20]Martin Wenglinsky, ''Errands,'' in Arnold Birenbaum and Edward Sagarin, editors, *People in Places: The Sociology of the Familiar*, New York: Praeger, 1973, pp. 83–100.

lished. Furthermore, they make possible the use of short-term "credit" through the phenomenon of trading in futures. Many of the contingencies of agenda-construction can thus be eliminated by planning to go back to these predictable sources whenever rewards or opportunities of certain types are needed or desired.

On the other hand, the existence of such relationships can also complicate agenda-construction, for relationships have a way of making demands upon a person. That is, they impose certain constraints upon his freedom to allocate his time and resources at will. Not only must he spare the time to fulfill his obligations to a relationship when he may have very little to spare at all, but also he can seldom draw upon the relationship whenever he simply feels like doing so. Ordinarily, he must wait to interact with the other party until it is more or less mutually convenient to do so. His agenda, then, is not altogether a personal matter but must be *interactively* determined.

Some of the individual's relationships and opportunities are less flexible than are others in this respect, and, when a highly valued role-identity is tied up with one of these, it does much to limit his freedom in planning for the legitimation and fulfillment of the rest of his identities. The demands of certain less flexible positions and relationships, like those of work and family, tend to structure the days and the lives of most persons the world over.

The individual thus has commitments, as well as preferences and attachments, and these commitments are the other major determinant of agendas. The binding force of commitments is not only a moral one, or the fear of retribution. The individual accepts his commitments also because they are directly and indirectly intertwined with his preferences and attachments. The honoring of relevant commitments is thus a basic strategy in the process of negotiated exchange.

The individual usually has a good measure of freedom in determining how to meet his commitments, and he chooses, among the alternatives, those that are also likely to legitimate and fulfill his highly valued identities and attachments. At work and with his family, the individual is likely to concentrate upon those aspects of his performances that are most germane to his more salient identities. Through this kind of selection among alternative ways of meeting our commitments and through differential concentration on certain aspects of these commitments, we bring to life the bare outlines of our social roles and positions by performing them in our own personal styles. These approaches are the main strategies in the handling of discrepancies between commitments and preferences.

In their agendas, people generally favor those commitments that are relevant to the higher ranking identities of their role-hierarchies, and they tend to neglect, hedge, or fulfill only perfunctorily those that are not.

Another consideration affecting short-term agendas is that the individual gives preference to alters and situations facilitating *multiply relevant* performances, that he may thus enact or gain support for more than one of his most salient identities. This preference is a major strategy for handling the limitations imposed upon man by his biological nature; it is the most efficient use of one's limited resources.

Agendas must also be arranged in such a way that the individual can maintain "information control," through audience segregation and control of the situation itself. Most adults in modern societies perform numerous, somewhat compartmentalized roles within the course of a day, and the recurrent maintenance of these separate performances and the transitions among them call for complex agendas. They demand, among other things, wristwatches, appointment books, and fine memories.

Finally, the person must plan his short-term agendas in such a way as to continue gradual progress with regard to his overarching long-term agendas. A woman must watch her eating from day to day if she wishes to lose weight; the athlete must work out regularly; the successful student must set aside daily blocks of time for his studies.

CHANGES IN AGENDA

But agenda decisions are based only upon estimates and expectations and the latter are subject to bias, error, and innocence and to all the vicissitudes of the empirical world. Agendas, particularly long-term agendas, are constructed on the basis of such inadequate knowledge that from an objective point of view they appear to be little better than guesses made in the dark. Most people marry the first persons they have serious affairs with; most of us choose careers on the basis of fragmentary knowledge and legends about three or four fields; and our places of residence are often chosen by weighing information gleaned from advertisements, hearsay, and travelogues. In most cases individuals become so involved with the pursuit of these long-term agendas, that the latter become the frames of reference for the lives they live, and the fact that they were arrived at hastily and in the dark recedes into unimportance.

Such long-term agendas are the overarching frames of reference that structure much of the individual's short-term agendas. A shift in long-term plans therefore usually produces a major reshuffling of the individual's daily routine as well.

Long-term agendas are far less subject to hasty revision than are short-term ones, but when they are revised it is usually because of "life crises." Gross failures, like family breakdowns, flunking out, "blacklisting"; "accidents" like being crippled, severe illness, imprisonment; or the effects of large social events like depressions and major wars—such occurrences may jeopardize or destroy lifetime agendas and necessitate major revisions of plans, goals, and corresponding daily activities. There usually also occurs a reshuffling of role-identity hierarchies as a result of such life crises.

Even with the most careful planning we are all subject, in the actuarial sense, to the possibility of such crises.

A far more important consequence of the imperfect knowledge of human beings arises as the person attempts to realize long-term agendas through the concrete details of short-term agendas. *The relationship between long-term and short-term agendas is problematic.* It does not necessarily follow that dating Jackie will lead to a satisfying married life; a promotion does not always follow from conscientious work; a cross-country vacation may not prove relaxing or invigorating; investment in bonds may provide no secure retirement at all if inflation continues.

Perhaps the most common factor leading to systematic changes in the logistics of daily behavior is the revision of short-term agendas in order more adequately to realize long-term agendas. Movement toward fulfillment of these long-term plans tends to go in fits and starts, rather than in straightforward progression. Digressions and even complete reversals are not at all infrequent. We learn to make daily logistical decisions as we go along rather than before we start, and our revisions call for continual reshuffling of short-term agendas.

Another source of instability and flux in the logistics of daily activities is the interplay between the role-identity hierarchy and the ebb and flow of external events. Some role-identities are more sensitive to the rise of opportunities than others. The rejuggling of agendas in midstream is very often caused by the appearance of unanticipated opportunities to legitimate and fulfill highly valued identities, particularly if these needs are not altogether met routinely in the daily round and one's established relationships.

Upon occasion, we are all willing to abrogate other interactions and compromise our commitments to pursue interaction opportunities relevant to particularly valued role-identities or identities that are particularly in need of legitimation. If these interaction opportunities strongly contradict our commitments—if the rankings of our identities on personal factors differ too much from their rankings on social factors[21]—we are likely to compromise our commitments to make the most of the unexpected opportunities. This sort of "pre-empting" of the individual's more mundane logistical agendas through the appearance of such opportunities is an important facet of human existence and not infrequently turns the course of a person's life.

Just what kinds of event have this ability to pre-empt planned agendas is, of course, an invaluable clue to the personal value ranking of the individual's role-identities, as distinct from the ranking we infer from his positions and "public" behavior. But such pre-emption is not necessarily, perhaps not usually, the result of duplicity on the individual's part. He is often unable to verbalize what kinds of situation can demand "prime time" from him,

[21]*Cf.* p. 218.

and, if he is aware of such pre-emptions at all, he is frequently surprised by them himself.

And more generally, there are a number of human pursuits—love, friendship, even hobbies—in which we are often a little surprised by our willingness to "drop everything else" to interact with particular alters in ways extremely fulfilling to us. People often say that they themselves do not understand why it seems so important for them to be with particular someones or why they feel so attached in love, friendship or hero worship to given alters. What we are too busy to do and what commands our "prime time" are not simple functions of our commitments alone, although such logistical decisions are often explained verbally in terms of these commitments. Explanation of behavior in terms of commitments is often only plausible at best, and one is often convinced that the real reasons are different. These seemingly irrational attachments or pursuits are currently often explained in terms of the constructs of psychoanalytic theory, but it must be remembered that this framework can itself serve as a rationalization.

During periods when the individual is highly involved, the time stretching between these "prime" encounters seems a series of unimportant interludes. These pre-emptive opportunities may become the focal point for structuring the individual's agendas, with the result that subjective time is measured from prime encounter to prime encounter. At the extreme, the person may have the subjective feeling of "coming alive" only within these prime encounters.

Such periods often carry us to high levels of emotional intensity, and we often organize our memories of our pasts around them. But by their very nature, they are temporary. They usually have one of two outcomes: Either they do not survive the passage of time and the flux of events, or they lead to corresponding commitments, and the encounters become routinized as an intrinsic aspect of the fabric of the person's daily life.

These pre-emptive, prime opportunities effect changes in our short-term agendas not only directly, as we have been discussing, but also indirectly. That is, *other people's* pre-emptive opportunities affect our agendas as do our own, for these agendas have been interactively negotiated and required social coordination. If the other person is tied up with something that "just happened to come up," he may not appear at the appointed time and place; indeed, we may be unable to locate him for a day or two. Our own agendas are then thrown into considerable confusion, and we must muddle through until we can make alternative arrangements with that person.

In a multitude of ways, then, agendas are vulnerable and very much open to *ad hoc* changes. Nonetheless, our daily rounds and the larger contours of our lives are largely planned rather than accidental. For all their fragility, agendas can be said to be the chief *proximate* cause of the patterning of observed interaction time-budgets, and their own derivation from the perceived opportunity structure, the salience hierarchy, and the shape and content of the ideal self is, therefore, a prime subject of social psychological study.

THE REALIZATION OF IDENTITY IN DAILY INTERACTIONS

The realities of daily life are not altogether conducive or friendly to the desires of any animal but especially not to those of man, the dreaming animal. Through his dreaming, his symbolic ability, man creates for himself a whole class of particularly vulnerable desires, the wish to live his life in keeping with his idealized conceptions of himself.

We have seen throughout this book that this desire is a very difficult one to fulfill. Ranged against our dramatic role-identities are our personal limitations, our mundane routines, and the jolts of external events. The make-ups of our role-identity hierarchies are not the only factors that shape our daily interactions. The characteristics of the situations, our cost-reward calculations, the vagaries of bargaining and persuasive rhetoric, the degrees to which our hierarchies mesh with those of the alters with whom we are thrown together, and many other factors all help to determine the courses of actual encounters and to lend color and pathos to human interactions.

As a consequence, we have argued, the most frequent pattern of interaction is that of *accommodation,* in which each actor accepts only imperfect fulfillment of his views of himself in return for performing mildly inconvenient or slightly distasteful services. Every interaction, let alone every human relationship, involves a certain amount of "carrying out the garbage," and every actor must perform a share of uninteresting, effort-consuming, perhaps mildly distasteful tasks if he wants to reap the benefits of acceptance as a full-fledged participant in interactions and relationships.

The empirical world is thus something of an uncertain market place for the fulfillment of man's second, symbolic nature. The same symbolic ability that gives rise to his role-identities and the resulting problems also allows him to imagine other worlds more friendly to the realization of his self-conceptions, so that he becomes discontented with the unfavorable realities of the empirical world. Given this "gift" for dramatization and idealization, it would seem that any existent niche must appear mundane and bleak indeed. Man would seem condemned to have his personal dramas routinized and trivialized by events of the empirical world.

Yet, paradoxically enough, this symbolic ability turns out to be man's major defense against the compromising of his dramatic conceptions by drab reality. The link between our idealistic role-identities and the mundane details of our daily lives is forged by the *creative interpretation of these details* as enactments of aspects of our role-identities. On our way to work we attempt to converse with the cleverness of favorite fictional characters; we hold our cigarettes pensively as befits Thinking Men; our casual flirtations with waitresses may be touched by a Tristan-and-Isolde theme; after the movie we pour ourselves drinks with the loose-handed aloofness of the Western hero; we scramble breakfast eggs with the pixie petulance of Young Wives; we put our toy thermoses in our toy lunch boxes and walk groaning toward the door just like Daddy.

We manage to achieve modicums of fulfillment by investing the routines and trivia of our daily lives with dramatic connotations.

This often overlooked facet of our ability to manipulate symbols is one of the most important, for it is largely through employing it that we are able to live our lives in this intersection of the physical and the ideal worlds.

It must also be noted that this ability is a mixed blessing, however. Lighting a cigarette can be transformed into a dramatic moment, but, by the same process, the miscarrying of such a gesture can engender feelings of abject shame.[22] This possibility is the lesson of the dramaturgical theorists. A brief exchange of verbal symbols can lead to hours or months of either glowing happiness or abject misery. Men kill or give up their own lives for the sake of pieces of cloth floating in the wind, and the human race may yet perish because of certain differences in defining abstract social objects.

This interpretive dramatization of concrete daily activities is the means by which we breathe life into the role-blueprints that, having been learned and internalized from the culture, have become the structural skeletons of our role-identities.

The creative superimposition of identities upon events is, furthermore, not confined to the current flow of activities. It lies at the heart of daydreaming, dreams, and autistic thinking more generally. Recollected past events and anticipated future ones are raised to the level of allegories, through investment with symbolic relevance to our role-identities. In addition to the freedom to choose the situations that stimulate us, noted by Mead, we thus have considerable measures of freedom in interpreting the meanings of situations and encounters for our identities. We are only partly bound by physical events and only tenuously bound to the present. Our symbolic proclivities allow us to people the empirical world with characters, events, and objects that no positivist could hope to detect.

THE WHY

What is the meaning of it all, of the repetitive patterning of one's human life? Probably most people accept their lives and

[22]Erving Goffman, *The Presentation of Self in Everyday Life,* Garden City, N.J.: Doubleday Anchor, 1957.

their "meanings" as given and reflect upon them only rarely, in moments of personal disorder. Most people, throughout most of history, have reflected the cultures they grew up in, in the important sense that they have taken the culturally defined patterns and meanings of life for granted, even though they may have balked and quibbled about specifics.

Those who have become disengaged from the culturally derived "answers," on the other hand, have usually taken one of two paths: dedication to alternative belief systems represented by social movements, religions, or ideologies, or profound disillusionment with life, in its specifics and in general. Some of the most moving passages in literature and the history of ideas are expressive of one or the other of these alternative stances: the dedication of Socrates, St. Augustine, Marx, Einstein, on the one hand, and the poetic despair of Ecclesiastes, Donne, and Shakespeare, on the other.

Shakespeare tells us that life is a tale told by an idiot, full of sound and fury signifying nothing; Voltaire says that we must cultivate our gardens; Socrates and Freud tell us to know ourselves; the Parsonians enjoin us to fulfill our role-expectations; and Cicero counsels us to seize the day.

We have explored in this book the WHO, WHAT, WHEN, and WHERE of social man, but we can go no further with our tentative answers to the question, WHY? From here, beyond the role-identity model, the reader must become his own explorer.

EPILOGUE:
A RESEARCH
PERSPECTIVE

Research perspectives in social psychology are currently very much in transition, amid widespread commentary and critical stock-taking.[1]

Until fairly recently, social psychological research was, for the most part, a very tidy enterprise of rigorously controlled laboratory experimentation undertaken in a search for invariant laws of behavior.[2] Such laws were seen as universal functional relationships between operationally defined variables; if the social psychologist performed a specified operational procedure of manipulation, then by performing another specified operational procedure of measurement he could expect to observe a numerically specified outcome. Social psychological theory was seen as a rigorously deductive systematization of independently discovered and verified laws. The central criterion was seen as *prediction*; laws should enable prediction of concrete outcomes, and theories should en-

[1]See, *e.g.*, Lloyd H. Strickland, Frances E. Aboud, and Kenneth J. Gergen, editors, *Social Psychology in Transition*, New York: Plenum Press, 1976; Nigel Armistead, editor, *Reconstructing Social Psychology*, Baltimore: Penguin Books, 1974; Alan C. Elms, "The Crisis of Confidence in Social Psychology," *The American Psychologist*, 1975, 30: 967–976; and Joachim Israel and Henri Tajfel, editors, *The Context of Social Psychology: A Critical Assessment*, New York: Academic Press, 1972.

[2]Rom Harré and Paul F. Secord, *The Explanation of Social Behaviour*, Oxford: Blackwell, 1972.

252

able prediction of laws. Accordingly, great emphasis was placed on the *testing of hypotheses* (i.e., predictions), a task for which laboratory experiments are well suited.

In recent years a great many social psychologists have come to abandon (and, often, to repudiate) that tidy enterprise and to construct an alternative research perspective.

Beyond doubt the most significant impetus to this intellectual outmigration has been the failure of the traditional enterprise in its own terms. Despite the prodigious and coordinated efforts of many excellent researchers, the discovery of any social psychological laws came to seem unattainable; the frustrating instability and divergence of experimental results had become agonizing.[3] Most disheartening of all, there had emerged considerable evidence that much of this failure may stem from inherent difficulties in the method of laboratory experimentation on which the traditional enterprise is founded.[4] Reactive effects, demand characteristics, experimenter bias, reliance on deception, and lack of external validity have emerged as serious difficulties in laboratory experimentation.

To some degree, this movement away from the traditional enterprise has also received external impetus from the post-positivist revolution in the philosophy of science. In particular, Kuhn's demonstration that in the normal work of scientists theories are not tested but rather *used* has been widely influential.[5] Some social psychologists have also become acquainted with the philosophers' rejection of the concept of theory as deductive systematization of laws in favor of a view of theory as a picture or a model of generative processes.[6] Indeed, the positivistic conception of law itself has been substantially rejected by philosophers of science.

[3]Strickland *et al., op. cit.*

[4]Harré and Secord, *op. cit.*

[5]Thomas S. Kuhn, *The Structure of Scientific Revolutions* (2nd ed.), Chicago: University of Chicago Press, 1970.

[6]*E.g.*, Peter Achinstein, *Concepts of Science*, Baltimore: Johns Hopkins Press, 1968; and Rom Harré, *The Principles of Scientific Thinking*, Chicago: University of Chicago Press, 1970.

But technical factors have by no means been the sole sources of disenchantment with the traditional enterprise. Of at least equal importance has been the somewhat forced acceptance of an "anthropomorphic model of man"—i.e., the idea that for scientific purposes people must be treated as if they were human beings.[7] The traditional enterprise treated people quite mechanically, as passive and reliable responders to external stimuli that might be manipulated by the experimenter. As noted previously, social psychologists gradually came to notice that laboratory subjects are not entirely able (even when willing) to perform in that manner. The motives, interpretations, and self-concepts of people render them poor subjects for highly constrained experimental situations in which information and social interaction are severely restricted.

Once again, external impetus from the philosophy of science has been somewhat influential in reinforcing this movement. The distinctions between a science of movements and a science of actions have been more clearly drawn, as have the respective roles of reasons and causes in explaining human behavior.[8] Analysis of agency as a mode of causation has led to a view that human beings must be viewed as agents acting according to plans and rules, on the basis of meanings, and that it is unscientific to treat them as anything else.[9]

Given the greater credence in the anthropomorphic model of man and disenchantment with laboratory experimentation, the emerging enterprise of social psychological research has been centering on people in naturalistic field settings and on observational rather than experimental methods.[10] Laboratory studies are more often required to document their "mundane realism," and experimental methodology has been forced to adapt to field settings.[11]

[7]Harré and Secord, *op. cit.*

[8]See, *e.g.*, Alvin I. Goldman, *A Theory of Human Action,* Englewood Cliffs, N.J.: Prentice-Hall, 1970.

[9]*Ibid.*; Harré and Secord, *op. cit.*

[10]See, *e.g.*, William J. McGuire, "The Yin and Yang of Progress in Social Psychology: Seven Koan," *Journal of Personality and Social Psychology,* 1973, 26: 446–456; and Edwin P. Willems and Harold L. Rausch, editors, *Naturalistic Viewpoints in Psychological Research,* New York: Holt, 1969.

[11]Leonard Bickman and Thomas Henchy, editors, *Beyond the Laboratory: Field Research in Social Psychology,* New York: McGraw-Hill, 1972; Paul G.

With the decline in experimental testing of hypotheses, there has emerged an emphasis on constructing causal models to descriptively analyze complex interrelationships among observed variables.[12] Operationalism has been displaced by sophisticated techniques of measurement and validation.[13] The search for and testing of laws of behavior and deductive theories increasingly give way to a search for explanatory ideas and models—interpretive schemata.[14] The social psychologist's ability to predict is no longer as criterial as his ability to understand and explain.

It is against this background that we seek to consider how the ideas set forth in the preceding chapters have been—and may be—employed in social psychological research, both quantitative and qualitative.

QUANTITATIVE RESEARCH

For present purposes, quantitative research will be construed as any research that employs at least some standardized procedures of data collection and at least some statistical procedure of data analysis. Although in this type of research some concepts or variables may be manipulated or inferred rather than measured, measurement is a central concern. We begin, then, by considering how some of the distinctive concepts of this book may be measured.

Measurement of Concepts

The measures discussed in this section are, let us emphasize, only some suggested procedures and do not in any sense exhaust

Swingle, editor, *Social Psychology in Natural Settings,* Chicago: Aldine, 1973; and Thomas D. Cook and Donald T. Campbell, ''The Design and Conduct of Quasi-Experiments and True Experiments in Field Settings,'' in Marvin D. Dunnette, editor, *Handbook of Industrial and Organizational Psychology,* Chicago: Rand McNally, 1976, pp. 223–326.

[12]McGuire, *op. cit.*; Cook and Campbell, *op. cit.*; and David Heise, *Causal Analysis,* New York: Wiley, 1976.

[13]See, *e.g.*, Chapters 1–5 in Herbert L. Costner, editor, *Sociological Methodology 1973-1974,* San Francisco: Jossey-Bass, 1974.

[14]Harré and Secord, *op. cit.*

the potentially fruitful alternatives. Furthermore, the differential validity and precision of these alternative measures have not been conclusively established, with few exceptions, so that at present choosing among them is largely a matter of personal preference and the practical constraints of one's concrete study.

The Four Ws

The question of WHO comes together to engage in WHAT social acts WHEN and WHERE has been our empirical touchstone throughout this book, for the four ws are dependent variables that are relatively easy to measure. Easy, that is, in the sense that the very direct and clear-cut indicators are potentially available. In the actualities of practical research, however, such data are relatively expensive and difficult to obtain with adequate validity.

The most directly valid method for obtaining such data is, of course, simply to watch someone continuously and record with whom he does what, when, and where. This method has been profitably exploited by workers in "psychological ecology,"[15] but they have found it feasible only with respect to children; and even then certain questions must be raised about the effects of the ever-present adult observer, taking notes, on the child's behavior. Of course, with today's sophisticated technology for electronic and visual eavesdropping and surveillance, it should be possible to maintain continuous observation without the reactive effects of a visible observer.[16]

A less direct data source is to be found in the various time-budget studies initiated by rural sociologists and others around 1920 and developed most thoroughly by Sorokin and Berger in 1939.[17] After a prolonged lapse, time-budget studies have under-

[15]See, e.g., Roger G. Barker and Herbert F. Wright, *Midwest and Its Children,* New York: Harper, 1955; Barker, editor, *The Stream of Behavior,* New York: Appleton-Century-Crofts, 1963; and Barker, *Ecological Psychology,* Stanford, Calif.: Stanford University Press, 1968.

[16]See Ralph K. Schwitzgebel, "Development of an Electronic Rehabilitation System for Parolees," *Law and Computer Technology,* 1969, 2: 9–12.

[17]Pitirim A. Sorokin and Clarence Q. Berger, *Time-Budgets of Human Behavior,* Cambridge: Harvard University Press, 1939, contains a review of earlier research.

gone a revival in a larger context.[18] In these studies, individuals are asked to keep records of how much time they spend in various sorts of activity and social contexts, and statistical comparisons are made among certain aggregates in terms of such allocations of time.[19]

We have adapted and modified this technique to obtain more purely *interaction time-budgets* for individuals, sets of descriptive data on the four ws that constitute the basic facts to be explained in this theoretical framework. That is, we have asked individuals to record each of their focused human encounters over a specified period of time, recording WHO was present, WHAT transpired, WHERE it happened, and WHEN it began and ended.[20] This task turns out to be rather difficult for the respondents to execute with any reasonable degree of detail and completeness, particularly for stretches of time longer than a single day. Therefore, our most extensive explorations have employed specially skilled respondents (for example, psychiatric nurses) who have daily practice in keeping such records (in the form of ward notes). In these cases, we have been able to obtain excellent data for periods of up to two weeks, which we judge on other grounds to be about the practical optimum for our purposes.

From these time-budgets, or interaction logs, the WHO, WHEN, and WHERE can be directly assessed with high degrees of precision and reliability.[21] Assessment of the WHAT, on the other hand, presents somewhat peculiar difficulties, in that it is much more open to differential interpretation and selective reporting by the respondents. Furthermore, our interest in the WHAT of interaction lies primarily in its relevance to the content of role-identities and

[18]F. Stuart Chapin, Jr., *Human Activity Patterns in the City: Things People Do in Time and in Space,* New York: Wiley, 1974; and the multinational study report in Alexander Szalai, editor, *The Use of Time,* The Hague: Mouton, 1973.

[19]See, for example, the research instruments published in Chapin, *op. cit.*

[20]Very similar procedures have now been frequently employed in social network research. See the discussions in, *e.g.,* Jeremy Boissevain and J. Clyde Mitchell, editors, *Network Analysis: Studies in Human Interaction,* The Hague: Mouton, 1973.

[21]Of course, more abstract classifications of WHOs and WHEREs can present greater difficulties. For relevant procedures, see Chapin, *op. cit.,* and Boissevain and Mitchell, *op. cit.*

the interactive roles that emerge through the processes of negotiated exchange. Therefore, a special and idiosyncratic set of categories must be devised for each respondent in terms of which we can code or content-analyze the descriptions of his various encounters.[22]

Role-Identity Sets

Turning now from *explicanda* to *explicans*, the first concept we must consider is the role-identity.[23] In measuring an individual's role-identities, the initial step is simply to identify each of them, to discover his identity-*set*. We have typically begun by administering the Twenty Statements Test of Self-Attitudes (TST), an unstructured instrument designed to measure a person's self-conception.[24] This test usually reveals a number of his more salient identities, but it is not at all comprehensive in this respect.[25]

Consequently, our use of the TST has been primarily as a jumping-off point for a semistructured interview in which the individual is probed systematically in an attempt to identify all his important role-identities. As an aid to comprehensiveness, we typically employ a set list of broad *categories* of social roles, each of which is successively explored for those members that are relevant to the respondent. These categories include: racial and ethnic; sexual; family; occupational; religious; recreational (including hobbies); "social" (leader, joiner, hostess etc.); "philosophical" (human being, thinker, etc.); and "deviant" (marijuana user, alcoholic etc.) roles, though not necessarily in that order.[26] An attempt is made to focus only on those identities that are still current in the person's thinking about himself, but this criterion is meant explicitly to *include* important identities that the person is not yet able to perform directly (the identity of wife for an unmarried woman to whom this identity is still important).

[22]*Cf.* the various activity codes in Chapin, *op. cit.*

[23]*Cf.* pp. 65–68.

[24]Manford H. Kuhn and Thomas S. McPartland, "An Empirical Investigation of Self-Attitudes," *American Sociological Review*, 1954, 19: 68–76.

[25]Chad Gordon, "Self-Conceptions Methodologies," *Journal of Nervous and Mental Disease*, 1969, 148: 328–364.

[26]*Ibid.* Gordon presents a more differentiated set of categories that has been used with some success.

When the scale of a study does not permit interviewing of this intensive type, structured questionnaires may be used in which respondents are asked to select from among a comprehensive list of social roles all of those which occur in his thinking about himself. Such instruments have proved successful in comparing identity-sets across persons,[27] and represent a substantial improvement over unstructured instruments such as the TST. Nevertheless, even with frequent written probes and accompanying open-ended response categories, structured questionnaires are less likely than interviews to bring out that unusual role-identity or two that occupy an important place in virtually every respondent's thinking.

Role-Identity Contents

The researcher most often is interested not only in naming a person's various role-identities but also in determining the *contents* of at least some of those identities—i.e., what the person thinks about himself as an occupant of those social roles. At times we have left this determination of content to a separate interview, but very often it is profitably and quite naturally combined with the attempt merely to identify the person's identity-set.

Whether thus combined or separated, the semistructured interview to determine the contents of the role-identities asks of the person about each of his identities in turn, "How do you like to think of yourself as being and acting as an _____?" Suitable alternative phrases are employed occasionally to avert monotony, and a good number of probes is ordinarily required to specify adequately the detailed imagery of self. Particular attention is paid to concrete activities, style and manner, appearance, level of aspiration, reference groups and significant others, recurrent themes, and unusually vivid daydreams or semiplans. Specification of the associated intrinsic and extrinsic gratifications[28] is also of particular importance for subsequent measurement of the prominence and salience hierarchies.

Currently, the interview technique of heuristic elicitation (developed by cognitive anthropologists in the field of descriptive

[27]See, *e.g.,* Suzanne B. Kurth, "Determinants of Verbal Self-Disclosure," unpublished Ph.D. dissertation, University of Illinois at Chicago Circle, 1971.

[28]*Cf.* pp. 75–79, 146–151.

semantics) is being explored as a potentially more powerful means of determining the semantic contents of self-in-a-role and of person-in-a-role.[29]

A somewhat related approach has been taken by several scholars at Indiana University, focusing on the generic semantic content of person-in-a-role. Subjects are asked to rate the generic occupants of specified roles and counter-roles on a large number of test items, and discriminant functions are statistically extracted to characterize the respective generic identities. Subjects may also be asked to rate themselves as occupant of the specified role, and the discrepancies between their own profiles and the generic discriminant function are taken to reflect the more idiosyncratic aspects of role-identity.[30]

Prominence Hierarchy

These role-identities are not, of course, equally important but are ranged in two hierarchies, the first of which is the prominence hierarchy, or ideal self.[31] This hierarchy may be measured either analytically or globally.

ANALYTIC MEASUREMENT.[32]   Analytically, each role-identity may be scored in terms of each of six determinants; the complex average of such scores serves as the over-all prominence score in terms of which the role-identities may be ordered. These determinants cannot practically be measured directly, but the respondent can be asked to *rate* each role-identity on, say, a 10-point scale for each

[29]George J. McCall, Joe R. Harding, and Dorothy Clement, unpublished manuscript. More generally, see, *e.g.*, Paul Kay, "Some Theoretical Implications of Ethnographic Semantics," *Current Directions in Anthropology*, 1970, 3 (3, pt. 2): 19–35.

[30]See, *e.g.*, Peter J. Burke and Judy C. Tully, "The Measurement of Role/Identity," *Social Forces*, 1977, 55: 881–899; and Burke, "The Self: Measurement Requirements from an Interactionist Perspective," paper presented at annual meeting, American Sociological Association, Chicago, 1977.

[31]*Cf.* pp. 74–77.

[32]See, *e.g.*, David S. Robbins, "The Logistics of Role-Identity Elaboration," unpublished M.A. thesis, University of Missouri-St. Louis, 1975.

determining factor. The six relevant factors, with their corresponding questions, might be as follows:

1. Average past degree of *self-support*: "How well do I do at being the sort of _____ I like to think of myself as being?"
2. Average past degree of *social support*: "How well do others, on the average, think I do at being the sort of _____ I like to think of myself as being?"

[Still more analytically, we may ask the respondent to rate how important each of his relevant audiences regards the opinion of each of his other relevant audiences, including himself. From this operation, we can obtain for each audience the average rated importance of its opinion (I^i). We can then further ask the respondent to rate the degree (s^i) to which each distinct audience supports his role-identity. For each audience (a^i), the weighted degree of support ($I^i \times s^i$) can thus be calculated. The average of such weighted supports constitutes the over-all average past degree of social support of that identity, corresponding to the result of the simpler operation described.]

3. Average past degree of *intrinsic gratifications* associated with the role-identity. "How much do I enjoy doing the things I do as a _____?"
4. Average past degree of *extrinsic gratifications* associated with the role-identity. "Aside from sheer enjoyment, how much do I get out of doing the things I do as a _____?"
5. Average past degree of *commitment*. "How deeply have I staked myself on being the sort of _____ I like to think of myself as being?"
6. Average past degree of *investment*. "How much time, energy, and resources have I put into being the sort of _____ I like to think of myself as being?"

Having rated his various role-identities according to these six factors, the person has not yet specified their over-all prominence, for the factors are seldom of equal weight. Relative weights must be empirically determined, perhaps by having the respondent estimate them or perhaps by a careful series of experiments.

GLOBAL MEASUREMENT.[33]   Although such analytic measurement of the prominence hierarchy is important to this theoretical framework, a less arduous approximation is quite satisfactory for most research purposes. That is, we may simply have the individual rate (or rank-order) his various role-identities directly with respect to over-all prominence, on the basis of the question, "Disregarding how you 'ought' to feel, how important is it *to you personally* to be a _____?"

Salience Hierarchy

Role-identities may also be ordered in terms of less stable determinants, yielding a hierarchy of their salience as sources of performance in given situations. In view of the more transitory nature of this hierarchy, we have sometimes referred to it as the "situational self."[34]

The first and most stable factor in this hierarchical ordering is the degree of prominence of a role-identity, as already discussed. The remaining factors are essentially those of "utility," as economic theorists employ this term.

Practically speaking, at least three of these utility factors— current need for support (self and social) of a given role-identity, current need or desire for the intrinsic gratifications associated with the performance of that identity, and current need or desire for the corresponding extrinsic gratifications—are probably best measured relatively and indirectly. That is, one is well advised simply to *rank* role-identities according to each of these three factors rather than to attempt to measure them absolutely even in terms of a rating scale. Furthermore, it is probably better for the researcher himself to carry out this ranking operation in terms of his knowledge of average past levels (determined in assessing prominence) and of recent levels of "inputs," for asking the respondent to do the ranking often appears itself to *alter* the salience hierarchy as he becomes artificially aware of unfulfilled needs and desires. Ranking by the observer is undoubtedly less sensitive and precise than the respondent could achieve, but it ordinarily serves to

[33]See, *e.g.*, Kurth, *op. cit.*
[34]*Cf.* pp. 79–83.

distinguish validly those identities in considerable need from those in negligible need.

The fifth determinant, the perceived opportunity structure, can profitably be entrusted to the respondent as far as standing opportunities in the form of relationships or institutions are concerned. He can be asked to rank-order the opportunities he perceives *profitably* to acquire each of the three categories of reward associated with a given role-identity; that is, he can generate three rank-orders of opportunities with respect to a given role-identity, one each for support, intrinsic rewards, and extrinsic rewards. For less predictable, more situational opportunities, the researcher has little recourse except to *infer* the type and level of opportunity the situation presents to the particular person in question.

As with the prominence hierarchy, the question of relative weights of factors must be considered, here in two forms rather than in only one. First, the weights attached to the three types of reward must be established, so that the three rank-orders of opportunities constructed by the respondent can be combined into a single perceived opportunity structure. Second, the relative weights of the prominence, need, and opportunity-structure factors must be established, so that a single over-all salience score can be assigned to the given role-identity.

As this discussion makes rather painfully evident, the measurement of the salience hierarchy is a much more difficult and less certain operation than those entertained previously. A rather intimate degree of familiarity with the subject's life situation and recent past is required in order for the researcher to make the necessary inferences.

In many studies, of course, reliance on such intensive knowledge about individual subjects is simply out of the question; in such cases, data on salience must be obtained more directly from the subjects themselves. One approach is to ask subjects to directly rate identities as to prominence, current "utility," and perceived opportunity for enactment, with the investigator subsequently combining the several ratings into a crude index of salience.[35] A second approach is to administer the TST, interpreting the order

[35]Robbins, *op. cit.*

of appearance of role-identities as reflecting the order of salience of those identities. It has been demonstrated, however, that such an interpretation may be quite misleading;[36] and in any case, there is no assurance that the identities of interest will appear at all on the TST.

If the researcher's interest lies in relating the shifting salience hierarchy to variations in the four ws, the salience interpretation of TST responses might prove more useful when administered in the manner described by Mahoney.[37] In this procedure, subjects are given a packet of ten TST forms and a list of randomly assigned times (over a period of several days) at which subjects are to self-administer a TST and to describe the social situation prevailing at that moment. With the subject caught up in the currents of personal agendas and real-life situations, his TST responses are rather more likely to reflect situational shifts of the self than are such responses in a testing session. Any observed shifts in the TST pattern might be interestingly related to interaction time-budgets obtained over the same time period.

Opportunity Structures

Interaction-opportunity structures are, in a sense, routinely mapped in the course of network analysis studies.[38] Persons, places, and times known and accessible to an individual largely define his opportunities to enact various role-identities; certain combinations of WHO, WHERE, and WHEN differentially favor particular performances. Interaction time-budget data on an individual, if fairly recent and reasonably extensive, will suffice for the broad-brush depiction of such an opportunity structure. What we would seek to superimpose on the results of a network analysis, to permit much finer analysis, is an assessment of the contents, prominence, and salience of the role-identities of each person in the individual's social network.

[36]Gordon, *op. cit.*

[37]E. R. Mahoney, "The Processual Characteristics of Self-Conception," *Sociological Quarterly,* 1973, 14: 517–533.

[38]See, for example, Boissevain and Mitchell, *op. cit.*

Agendas

Agendas, or schedules of performance, are more easily measured the shorter the span of the agenda. One has only to ask a person's plans for the remainder of the day, and he can give a reasonably detailed answer. In many cases, a glance at an appointment
book will do, and, to the extent that others are intimately involved, they too can tell us much of the person's agenda. But with
longer-term agendas the person himself may have only an inchoate
awareness of their contours and may be little more informative
than the existing institutional calendars, which schedule for him
the swimming season at the municipal pool and the final exams in
Engineering 105.

In such cases, rather detailed probing in a semistructured interview is required to obtain any concrete sense of the person's plans
for the coming year or so. When the time span is even greater,
agendas tend to be phrased in terms of overarching goals and expectations. Most of our research, fortunately enough, deals with
time spans of one or several weeks, so that the relevant agendas can
be had for the asking if one is willing to prod just a bit.

Role-Performance and Persona

As mentioned in our discussion of interaction time-budgets,
assessment of the WHAT of interaction requires special content
analysis. To determine what role-identities were staged in a given
performance, we can only examine the performance and compare
it with the detailed contents of the person's various role-identities.
All those identities whose contents are at least partially reflected in
the performance are said themselves to be involved; thus, almost
every concrete performance is a *multiply relevant* performance,
relevant to more than one role-identity. (There are some circumstances, like the initial encounter between unacquainted individuals, in which we wish to refer to this set of role-identities
underlying the actor's performance as constituting his persona
with respect to alter.)[39]

The advent of videotaping has, of course, considerably en-

[39]*Cf.* pp. 84–85, 179–184.

hanced the ease and adequacy of assessing role-identities performed (or persona presented) in a concrete interaction episode. In
one study, for example, scoring from videotape records achieved
excellent intercoder reliability.[40]

Role-Support

The determination of the degree of role-support earned through
a given performance is based upon a very similar procedure. The
degree of *self-support* of a given identity obtained from a single
performance can be determined only by detailed comparison of
the contents of the identity and of the actor's performance respectively and by rating this comparison on a scale from complete con-
gruity to complete contradiction. Measurement of *social support*
of the identity involves much the same procedure, except that the
contents of the role-identity must be compared with the picture of
the actor *implied by* alter's reactions and performance. To make
this procedure still more difficult, we must remember that these
content analyses and ratings are more or less "objective" measures, whereas the actor himself ordinarily makes such ratings
through the screen of defenses mentioned in Chapter 4. Nonetheless, such observer ratings usually provide bases for valid *comparisons* (of different performances, alters' reactions, and so
forth), even though they are somewhat deficient for absolute
measurement.[41]

Again, with the advent of videotaping, a whole family of self-
confrontation techniques has emerged.[42] We suggest that it might
prove instructive to have subjects rate earned role-support
(especially self-support) from videotapes of their own performances. Comparisons with observer ratings of the same tapes

[40]Kurth, *op. cit.*

[41]*Cf.* the discussion of congruency by validation and congruency by implication in Paul F. Secord and Carl W. Backman, *Social Psychology* (2nd ed.), New
York: McGraw-Hill, 1974, pp. 528–553. See also Phillip W. Blumstein, "An Experiment in Identity Bargaining," unpublished Ph.D. dissertation, Vanderbilt
University, 1970.

[42]*E.g.,* Robert H. Geertsma and James B. Mackie, editors, *Studies in Self-
Cognition: Techniques of Videotape Self-Observation in the Behavioral Sciences,*
Baltimore: Williams & Wilkins, 1969.

might cast some light on the effects of the screen of defenses, as well as allow for some cross-validation of ratings.

The measures described in this section do not cover all the concepts developed in this book, nor do they exhaust the many alternative means of measuring those concepts that have been treated in this epilogue. They should, however, suggest to the reader some of the ways in which the theoretical concepts of this book can be turned into researchable ideas. It is seldom necessary, as we have seen, to measure any of these variable quantities absolutely. It usually suffices to achieve merely relative comparisons on such variables, for our propositions most often specify only that a *difference* in one variable is related to a *difference* in another variable. Given such relative measurement, a good many powerful research designs and statistical techniques are at our disposal.

Finally, we should also reiterate that quantitative research does not always seek to measure all pertinent variables and concepts. As we shall see shortly, key variables are sometimes experimentally *manipulated* or even simply *inferred* rather than measured, even in quite rigorous studies.

Nomothetic Studies

Quantitative research in social psychology typically examines a number of persons within a single study, aggregating the data from all persons for statistical analysis. Comparability and standardization of data are prime considerations within such nomothetic studies. If, for example, one wished to examine the prominence of the role-identity of student in such a study, one's data collection procedures must be such that each person's student identity is evidenced and that prominence is assessed in comparable fashion across all persons. There may be no interest in assessing the remainder of any person's identity-set or prominence hierarchy, since only a single feature is being compared across persons.

In many such studies, less intensive and perhaps cruder measures from among those discussed above may be quite appropriate (and much less expensive). Indeed, in some research designs, variables may reasonably be manipulated or inferred rather than measured at all.

One such area of significant research activity has been the study of *identity bargaining,* typically conducted in laboratory settings. Many of the ideas concerning the negotiation of identities developed in Chapter 6 have been used to guide and direct research on social interaction, and many others could be similarly employed.

In some of the existing studies, relevant identities have been *measured.* Kurth, for example, obtained measures of role-identity sets, prominence hierarchies, and role-performance (or personas) in her study of negotiated self-disclosure.[43] Blumstein measured the prominence of three "identities" (or dimensions of self-conception) in his study of identity bargaining.[44]

Identities have also been *manipulated* in such research, through the effects of rigged outcomes,[45] altercasting by research confederates,[46] or assignment of identities to be role-played.[47] (Of course, social support and opportunity structures have been similarly manipulated in many of these same studies.)

Finally, identities have sometimes been merely *inferred,* as in Alexander's many "situated-identity analyses" of paradigmatic research situations.[48] The plausibility of identity inference from mere knowledge of alternative action possibilities has been demonstrated most dramatically in Heise's Subject-Verb-Object research.[49]

Such studies have already importantly illuminated the multiplex processes of face-to-face social interaction. This book suggests

[43]Kurth, *op. cit.*

[44]Blumstein, *op. cit.*; and Blumstein, "Identity Bargaining and Self-Conception," *Social Forces,* 1975, 53: 476–485.

[45]*E.g.,* Bert R. Brown, "Face-Saving Following Experimentally Induced Embarrassment," *Journal of Experimental Social Psychology,* 1970, 6: 225–271.

[46]Blumstein, *op. cit.*

[47]Eugene A. Weinstein, Mary Glenn Wiley, and William DeVaughn, "Role and Interpersonal Style as Components of Social Interaction," *Social Forces,* 1966, 45: 210–216; and Harré and Secord, *op. cit.*

[48]*E.g.,* C. Norman Alexander and G. W. Knight, "Situated Identities and Social Psychological Experimentation," *Sociometry,* 1971, 34: 65–82.

[49]Heise, "Social Action as the Control of Affect," *Behavioral Science,* 1977, 22: 163–177.

that further study of identity bargaining could additionally do much to clarify, for example, the labeling theory of deviance or the problem of sustaining the task-focus of social acts.

Beyond the analysis of single episodes of face-to-face interaction, illumination of time-budgets and social networks is an important concern of this book: WHO come together for WHAT social acts WHEN and WHERE?

We suggest that many of the results of time-budget research could fruitfully be viewed through the lens of the role-identity model of social interaction. To take one example, a major focus of time-budget research has been the discrepancies between actual and desired time allocations among activities as an important negative social indicator of quality of life.[50] Since activities link fairly cleanly to role-identities, actual allocation to activities could be recoded as allocation to identities. The proportion of time allocated to various identities could then be compared with the prominence (or, better, the salience) of those identities as a more interpretable indicator of discontent.

Similarly, many of the results of social network analysis might be importantly illuminated by some of the ideas developed in this book. In the analysis of personal networks,[51] for example, we might anticipate that observed patterns of clustering of linkages would correspond closely to the individual's various personas (clustering of role-identities) and that multiplexity of linkages would be readily interpretable in terms of the careers of relationships (as developed in Chapter 7).

Finally, we note that developmental and life-cycle studies have been shown, through Gordon's review articles,[52] to attain a new dimension of coherence within the framework of the acquisition, development, and relinquishment of role-identities (see Chapter 8). We are especially interested in studies of sets of adults all hav-

---

[50]Chapin, *op. cit.*; and Richard Hobson and Stuart H. Mann, "A Social Indicator Based on Time Allocation," *Social Indicators Research*, 1975, 1: 439–457.

[51]*E.g.*, Boissevain, *Friends of Friends: Networks, Manipulators and Coalitions*, Oxford: Blackwell, 1974.

[52]*E.g.*, Gordon, "Development of Evaluated Role-Identities," *Annual Review of Sociology*, 1976, 2: 405–433; and Gordon, "Role and Value Develop-

ing to incorporate into their self-structures the same new role-identity (e.g., that of soldier or prisoner) or all having to relinquish the same former role-identity (e.g., that of worker or spouse). Studies of life-crises, such as imprisonment or retirement, have frequently been concerned with effects on the self but have seldom employed a sufficiently differentiated conceptualization of self and social interaction.

Idiographic Studies

Although the great majority of social psychological studies aggregate data from a number of persons, some influential research has focused on intensive analysis of the distinctive dynamics of individuals.[53] In certain closely related fields, the methodology of single-subject research has been quite thoroughly developed,[54] as has the study of individual lives.[55] Since the construction of individual lives is a major theme of this book, we take some special interest in idiographic research of that type.

Part of the appeal of such intensive analysis of individual functioning lies in the necessity of employing all of our concepts and ideas together, rather than selecting only one or a few as in most nomothetic research. Furthermore, intensive study permits the use of the more detailed and precise measures suggested for these concepts. Finally, there is a distinctive satisfaction involved in really fine-grained analysis of ongoing life-process.

The study of lives has traditionally dealt with long-term dynamics of the individual and with relatively enduring changes in social behavior. It would be interesting indeed to obtain the relevant

ment Across the Life Cycle," in J. W. Jackson, editor, *Role*, London: Cambridge University Press, 1971, pp. 65–105.

[53]M. Brewster Smith, Jerome S. Bruner, and Robert W. White, *Opinions and Personality*, New York: Wiley, 1956; and Milton Rokeach, *The Three Christs of Ypsilanti*, New York: Knopf, 1964, are representative examples.

[54]See, *e.g.*, John M. Gottman, "*N*-of-One and *N*-of-Two Research in Psychotherapy," *Psychological Bulletin*, 1973, 82: 87–101; and D. H. Barlow and M. Hersen, "Single-Case Experimental Designs," *Archives of General Psychiatry*, 1973, 29: 319–325.

[55]*E.g.*, Robert W. White, editor, *The Study of Lives*, New York: Atherton, 1963.

data to view these changes in terms of the relatively slow flux of the contents and prominence of role-identities and of long-range agendas.

Most of our own idiographic studies have dealt, however, with much shorter segments of lives and have centered on the short-term dynamics of the salience hierarchy, or situational self, in relation to interaction time-budgets. On the basis of a thorough mapping of the identity-set, identity contents, prominence hierarchy, interaction-opportunity structure, and needs for various rewards, the initial salience hierarchy of an individual can be quite adequately estimated. If very accurate interaction time-budget data are continually obtained thereafter, such data permit calculation of short-term changes in the salience hierarchy. The researcher then has two parallel time-series, one pertaining to salience and one pertaining to the four ws. From knowledge of the salience hierarchy at time t, predictions can be made concerning the four ws at time $t + 1$: then from interaction time-budget data on $t + 1$, the salience hierarchy can be re-estimated to make predictions about interaction at $t + 2$, and so on.

It is sometimes useful to intervene in these time-series by experimentally creating certain presumed changes in the person's salience hierarchy and analyzing the effects of these changes on his interactive roles, agendas, personas, or interactive time-budget. These experimental alterations of salience may be attempted through positive or negative manipulation of needs for rewards, opportunity structures, or the contents of his role-identities.

Of course, idiographic studies need not be restricted to the study of individual persons but might with equal justification study the distinctive dynamics of particular interpersonal relationships (see Chapter 7).

QUALITATIVE RESEARCH

Not all social psychological research has employed standardized data collection procedures and statistical analysis. Qualitative studies of identities and interactions, based on participant observation methodology,[56] have proved particularly influential throughout the past several decades, especially among sociological social psychologists. In the newer research perspective—with its emphasis on naturalistic field studies and on understanding as a criterion—studies of this type are much more frequently and deliberately called for.[57]

Analytic descriptions of bounded or situated social interactions are importantly sought. Lofland's recent book[58] cogently explicates the distinctive utility of this type of research and also represents an unusually complete manual for undertaking studies of situations and (especially) strategies for dealing with situations. Harré and Secord[59] develop a somewhat more sophisticated explication of why such studies are particularly necessary and also articulate a general framework for analyzing social episodes.

The frameworks of both Lofland and Harré and Secord heavily emphasize the importance of meanings, plans, dramaturgy, identities, and personas. Accordingly, the role-identity model of self and interaction developed in this book is well suited for use as an interpretive schema in developing analytic descriptions of interactions through qualitative research.

One of the clearest examples is the participant observation analysis by Roebuck and Frese of an after-hours club as "a regular place for irregular people."[60] From the wide variety of deviant actors involved as patrons or employees of the club, Roebuck and Frese systematically obtained data on identity-sets, identity contents, and prominence hierarchies (through both global and analytic procedures). Extensive observational data were gathered on subsettings and interaction patterns within the club. On the basis of these several kinds of data, but without statistical analysis, the

[56]The general methodology is reviewed in, *e.g.*, George J. McCall and J. L. Simmons, *Issues in Participant Observation: A Text and Reader,* Reading, Mass.: Addison-Wesley, 1969.

[57]See, *e.g.*, Harré and Secord, *op. cit.*

[58]John Lofland, *Doing Social Life: The Qualitative Study of Human Interaction in Natural Settings,* New York: Wiley, 1976.

[59]Harré and Secord, *op. cit.*

[60]Julian B. Roebuck and Wolfgang Frese, *The Rendevous: A Case Study of an After-Hours Club,* New York: Free Press, 1976.

investigators were able to answer their own questions, "Who goes there? When? To do What with Whom? Where in the Setting?"[61]

A quite similar example is an observational study of a public school as interaction opportunity structure, being conducted by Clement, Harding, and others.[62] The focus here is on age, sex, and racial identities as these are manifested and developed in a desegregating school system.

Of course, close determination of identities, role-support, or the four WS, as in these examples, affords more powerful analysis within the framework of our ideas. But the utility of such ideas as an interpretive schema may still prove considerable even when data collection is not tightly or explicitly linked to these distinctive concepts. An excellent example of this more interpretive use of the role-identity model is the qualitative analysis of the professional socialization of nurses by Oleson and Whittaker.[63]

In conclusion, we note again that the lines of quantitative and qualitative research briefly mentioned in this epilogue are but a few of the many fruitful possibilities that could be explored within the theoretical framework propounded in the rest of the book. It is our fervent hope that others will continue to see sufficient promise in this framework to join us in empirical research that may refine, extend, buttress, and modify the role-identity model and its theoretical relationship to the question of WHO comes together to engage in WHAT social acts WHEN and WHERE.

[61]Many of the qualitative studies of identities and interactions focus on some type of deviants or deviance. For a general review of the approach, see George J. McCall, *Observing the Law: Field Methods in the Study of Crime and the Criminal Justice System,* New York: Free Press, 1978.

[62]Clement and Harding, "Progress Report to National Institute of Education," unpublished manuscript.

[63]Virginia L. Oleson and Elvi W. Whittaker, *The Silent Dialogue: A Study in the Social Psychology of Professional Socialization,* San Francisco: Jossey-Bass, 1968.

Index